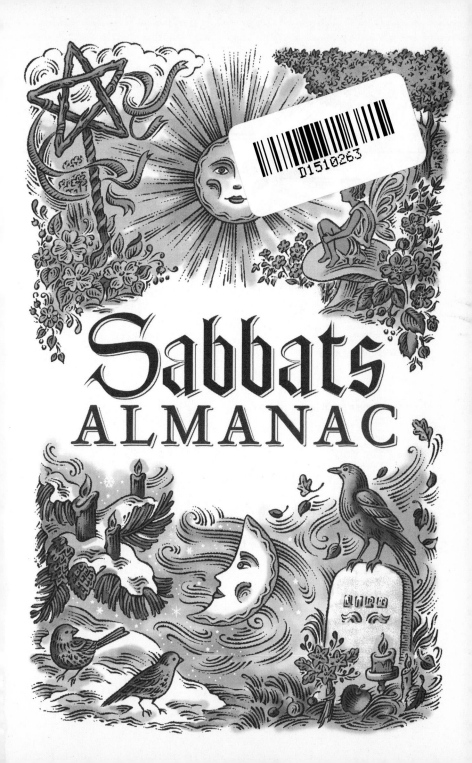

Sabbats
ALMANAC

Llewellyn's Sabbats Almanac:
Samhain 2012 to Mabon 2013

© 2012 Llewellyn Worldwide Ltd.
Llewellyn is a registered trademark of Llewellyn Worldwide Ltd.

Cover art © Carolyn Vibbert/Susan and Co.
Cover design by Ellen Lawson
Editing by Ed Day
Interior Art: © Carolyn Vibbert/Susan and Co., excluding illustrations on pages 37, 72, 74, 109, 111, 145, 147, 182, 184, 217, 249, 250, and 290, which are © Wen Hsu

You can order annuals and books from *New Worlds*, Llewellyn's catalog. To request a free copy call toll free: 1-877-NEW WRLD, or order online by visiting our Web site at http://subscriptions.llewellyn.com

ISBN: 978-0-7387-1499-8

Llewellyn Worldwide Ltd.
2143 Wooddale Drive
Woodbury, MN 55125-2989
www.llewellyn.com

Printed in the United States of America

2012

JANUARY
S	M	T	W	T	F	S
1	2	3	4	5	6	7
8	9	10	11	12	13	14
15	16	17	18	19	20	21
22	23	24	25	26	27	28
29	30	31				

FEBRUARY
S	M	T	W	T	F	S
			1	2	3	4
5	6	7	8	9	10	11
12	13	14	15	16	17	18
19	20	21	22	23	24	25
26	27	28	29			

MARCH
S	M	T	W	T	F	S
				1	2	3
4	5	6	7	8	9	10
11	12	13	14	15	16	17
18	19	20	21	22	23	24
25	26	27	28	29	30	31

APRIL
S	M	T	W	T	F	S
1	2	3	4	5	6	7
8	9	10	11	12	13	14
15	16	17	18	19	20	21
22	23	24	25	26	27	28
29	30					

MAY
S	M	T	W	T	F	S
		1	2	3	4	5
6	7	8	9	10	11	12
13	14	15	16	17	18	19
20	21	22	23	24	25	26
27	28	29	30	31		

JUNE
S	M	T	W	T	F	S
					1	2
3	4	5	6	7	8	9
10	11	12	13	14	15	16
17	18	19	20	21	22	23
24	25	26	27	28	29	30

JULY
S	M	T	W	T	F	S
1	2	3	4	5	6	7
8	9	10	11	12	13	14
15	16	17	18	19	20	21
22	23	24	25	26	27	28
29	30	31				

AUGUST
S	M	T	W	T	F	S
			1	2	3	4
5	6	7	8	9	10	11
12	13	14	15	16	17	18
19	20	21	22	23	24	25
26	27	28	29	30	31	

SEPTEMBER
S	M	T	W	T	F	S
						1
2	3	4	5	6	7	8
9	10	11	12	13	14	15
16	17	18	19	20	21	22
23	24	25	26	27	28	29
30						

OCTOBER
S	M	T	W	T	F	S
	1	2	3	4	5	6
7	8	9	10	11	12	13
14	15	16	17	18	19	20
21	22	23	24	25	26	27
28	29	30	31			

NOVEMBER
S	M	T	W	T	F	S
				1	2	3
4	5	6	7	8	9	10
11	12	13	14	15	16	17
18	19	20	21	22	23	24
25	26	27	28	29	30	

DECEMBER
S	M	T	W	T	F	S
						1
2	3	4	5	6	7	8
9	10	11	12	13	14	15
16	17	18	19	20	21	22
23	24	25	26	27	28	29
30	31					

2013

JANUARY
S	M	T	W	T	F	S
		1	2	3	4	5
6	7	8	9	10	11	12
13	14	15	16	17	18	19
20	21	22	23	24	25	26
27	28	29	30	31		

FEBRUARY
S	M	T	W	T	F	S
					1	2
3	4	5	6	7	8	9
10	11	12	13	14	15	16
17	18	19	20	21	22	23
24	25	26	27	28		

MARCH
S	M	T	W	T	F	S
					1	2
3	4	5	6	7	8	9
10	11	12	13	14	15	16
17	18	19	20	21	22	23
24	25	26	27	28	29	30
31						

APRIL
S	M	T	W	T	F	S
	1	2	3	4	5	6
7	8	9	10	11	12	13
14	15	16	17	18	19	20
21	22	23	24	25	26	27
28	29	30				

MAY
S	M	T	W	T	F	S
			1	2	3	4
5	6	7	8	9	10	11
12	13	14	15	16	17	18
19	20	21	22	23	24	25
26	27	28	29	30	31	

JUNE
S	M	T	W	T	F	S
						1
2	3	4	5	6	7	8
9	10	11	12	13	14	15
16	17	18	19	20	21	22
23	24	25	26	27	28	29
30						

JULY
S	M	T	W	T	F	S
	1	2	3	4	5	6
7	8	9	10	11	12	13
14	15	16	17	18	19	20
21	22	23	24	25	26	27
28	29	30	31			

AUGUST
S	M	T	W	T	F	S
				1	2	3
4	5	6	7	8	9	10
11	12	13	14	15	16	17
18	19	20	21	22	23	24
25	26	27	28	29	30	31

SEPTEMBER
S	M	T	W	T	F	S
1	2	3	4	5	6	7
8	9	10	11	12	13	14
15	16	17	18	19	20	21
22	23	24	25	26	27	28
29	30					

OCTOBER
S	M	T	W	T	F	S
		1	2	3	4	5
6	7	8	9	10	11	12
13	14	15	16	17	18	19
20	21	22	23	24	25	26
27	28	29	30	31		

NOVEMBER
S	M	T	W	T	F	S
					1	2
3	4	5	6	7	8	9
10	11	12	13	14	15	16
17	18	19	20	21	22	23
24	25	26	27	28	29	30

DECEMBER
S	M	T	W	T	F	S
1	2	3	4	5	6	7
8	9	10	11	12	13	14
15	16	17	18	19	20	21
22	23	24	25	26	27	28
29	30	31				

Contents

Lammas

Mabon

Introduction

NEARLY EVERYONE HAS A favorite sabbat. There are numerous ways to observe any tradition. This annual edition of the *Sabbats Almanac* provides a wealth of lore, celebrations, creative projects, and recipes to enhance your holiday.

For this edition, a mix of up-and-coming writers—**Dallas Jennifer Cobb, Melanie Marquis, Suzanne Ress,** and **Natalie Zaman**—join more established writers—**Deborah Blake, Raven Digitalis, Ellen Dugan,** and **Janina Renée**—in sharing their ideas and wisdom. These include a variety of paths such as Garden Witchery or Green Witchery as well as the authors' personal approaches to each sabbat. Each chapter closes with an extended ritual, which may be adapted for both solitary practitioners and covens.

In addition to these insights and rituals, specialists in astrology, history, cooking, crafts, and family impart their expertise throughout.

Daniel Pharr gives an overview of planetary influences most relevant for each sabbat season and provides details and a short ritual for selected events, including New and Full Moons, retrograde motion, planetary positions, and more.

Susan Pesznecker explores the realm of old-world Pagans, with a focus on customs such as ritual bread baking for Lammas and lesser-known facets of well-known symbols like the pumpkin and the maypole.

Kristin Madden conjures up a feast for each festival that includes an appetizer, entrée, dessert, and beverage.

Linda Raedisch offers instructions on craft projects that can also be incorporated into your practice.

Sandra Kynes focuses on activities the entire family can share to commemorate each sabbat.

About the Authors

Deborah Blake is the author of *Circle, Coven & Grove: A Year of Magickal Practice; Everyday Witch A to Z: An Amusing, Inspiring & Informative Guide to the Wonderful World of Witchcraft; The Goddess is in the Details: Wisdom for the Everyday Witch; Everyday Witch A to Z Spellbook*; and *Witchcraft on a Shoestring*. Her award-winning short story, "Dead and (Mostly) Gone" is included in the *Pagan Anthology of Short Fiction: 13 Prize Winning Tales* (Llewellyn, 2008). When not writing, Deborah runs the Artisans' Guild, a cooperative shop she founded with a friend, and works as a jewelry-maker, tarot reader, ordained minister, and an intuitive energy healer. She lives in a 100-year-old farmhouse in rural upstate New York with five cats who supervise all her activities, both magickal and mundane.

Life is what you make it, and **Dallas Jennifer Cobb** has made a magical life in a waterfront village on the shores of great Lake Ontario. Forever scheming novel ways to pay the bills, she practices manifestation magic and wildlands witchcraft. She currently teaches Pilates, works in a library, and writes to finance long hours spent following her heart's desire—time with family, in nature, and on the water. Contact her at jennifer.cobb@live.com.

Raven Digitalis (Missoula, MT) is the author of *Empathy, Planetary Spells & Rituals, Shadow Magick Compendium*, and *Goth Craft*. He is a Neopagan Priest and cofounder of the "Eastern Hellenistic" magickal system and training coven Opus Aima Obscuræ, and is a radio and club deejay of Gothic and industrial music. Also trained in Georgian witchcraft and Buddhist philosophy, Raven has been a Witch since 1999, a Priest since 2003, and an empath all of his life. Raven holds a degree in anthropology from the University of Montana and is also an animal rights activist, black-and-white photographic artist, Tarot reader, and is the co-owner of Twigs & Brews Herbs, specializing in bath salts, herbal blends, essential oils, soaps, candles, and incenses. He has appeared on the cover of *new Witch* magazine (now *Witches & Pagans*), is a regular contributor to *Dragon's Blood* and *The Ninth Gate* magazines, and has been featured on MTV News and CBS PsychicRadio. For more, visit www.ravendigitalis.com.

Ellen Dugan, the "Garden Witch," is an award-winning author and psychic-clairvoyant. A practicing Witch for more than twenty-five years, she is the author of ten Llewellyn books: *Garden Witchery, Elements of Witchcraft, Cottage Witchery, Autumn Equinox, The Enchanted Cat, Herb Magic for Beginners, Natural Witchery, How to Enchant a Man* and her latest books, *A Garden Witch's Herbal* and *Book of Witchery*. Ellen wholeheartedly encourages folks to personalize their spellcraft—to go outside and to get their hands dirty to discover the wonder and magick of the natural world. Ellen and her family live in Missouri. For further information, visit her website at www.ellendugan.com.

Sandra Kynes describes herself as an explorer of Celtic history, myth, and magic. Her curiosity has taken her to live in New York City, Europe, England, and New England. Spiritually her inquisitiveness has led her to investigate the roots of her beliefs and to study ancient texts such as the Mabinogion. One thing she discovered about herself is that she tends to see the world a little differently than most people. She likes finding connections between things and creating new ways and methods for exploring the world, which has been the inspiration for most of her books. A lifelong interest in archaeology was deepened during the time she lived in England. Tracking down remnants of stone circles and other ancient sites is a passion she pursues on return visits to the British Isles. In addition to seven books, Sandra's writing has been published in numerous Llewellyn

Magical Almanacs, Spell-A-Day, and *Witches' Calendars.* Additional writing appears on her website, Celtic Soul, at www.kynes.net.

Kristin Madden is an author and mother, as well as an environmental chemist and wildlife rehabilitator. She is the director of Ardantane's School of Shamanic Studies. A Druid and tutor in the Order of Bards, Ovates, and Druids, Kristin is also a member of the Druid College of Healing and is on the board of Silver Moon Health Services. She has been a freelance writer and editor since 1995. Her work has appeared in *Whole Life Times, PARABOLA,* and many other publications. Kristin is the author of five books including *Mabon: Celebrating the Autumn Equinox* and *The Book of Shamanic Healing.* Kristin was raised in a shamanic home and has had ongoing experience with Eastern and Western mystic paths since 1972. Over more than a decade, she has offered a variety of shamanic and general metaphysical workshops across the United States. Kristin is active in both pagan parenting and pagan home-schooling communities locally and globally. She also served on a master's degree thesis committee for a program on the use of visual imagery and parapsychology in therapy with ADD/ADHD children.

Melanie Marquis is a lifelong practitioner of magick, the founder of United Witches global coven, and the author of *The Witch's Bag of Tricks* (Llewellyn, 2011). An eclectic folk witch, mother, tarot reader, environmentalist, and folk artist, she enjoys a busy life enriched with personalized magick and practical spirituality. Visit her online at www.melaniemarquis.com or www.unitedwitches.org.

Susan Pesznecker, a.k.a. Moonwriter, is a writer, college English teacher, nurse, and hearth Pagan living in northwestern Oregon. She holds a master's degree in nonfiction writing and loves to read, watch the stars, camp with her wonder poodle, and work in her own biodynamic garden. Sue is Dean of Students and teaches nature studies and herbology in the online Grey School of Wizardry (greyschool.com). She's the author of *Gargoyles* (New Page, 2007), *Crafting Magick with Pen and Ink* (Llewellyn, 2009), and *The*

Magickal Retreat: Making Time for Solitude, Intention & Rejuvenation (Llewellyn, 2012). She also regularly contributes to many of the Llewellyn annuals and to Australia's *Spellcraft* magazine. Visit Sue on her Facebook page: http://www.facebook.com/susan.pesznecker.

Born and raised in the desert Southwest, **Daniel Pharr** knew his path was a Pagan one after being introduced to the ancient ways of the goddess almost twenty years ago. He has studied extensively with several nationally recognized Pagan institutions and learned the arts of healing (including Reiki, reflexology, therapeutic touch, and massage), tarot, astrology, intuitive counseling, and herbalism. As a healer and psychic, he believes his experience in these areas have brought him in touch with the lunar energies he writes of in this book. It is the knowledge and use of these energies which make him successful, and his private practice extends to corporations and organizations as well as individuals. Pharr is also a scuba instructor, a martial arts teacher with a Black Belt in Kenpo Karate, and a certified firewalker instructor. www.dannypharr.com.

Linda Raedisch hails from the leafy kettle holes of New Jersey's Watchung Mountains. She is the author of *Night of the Witches: Folklore, Traditions and Recipes for Celebrating Walpurgis Night* (Llewellyn, 2011) and a frequent contributor to Llewellyn's annuals. Linda attended college Out West where she continually flip-flopped between a fine arts and a creative writing major. Back in her natural setting, she enjoys combining her twin passions in new and interesting ways.

Janina Renée is a scholar of folklore, psychology, medical anthropology, the material culture of magic, ritual studies, history, and literature. Her books include *Tarot Spells, Tarot Your Everyday Guide* (winner of the 2001 Coalition of Visionary Resources award for best Self Help book), *Tarot for a New Generation* (2002 COVR winner, best General Interest Title), and *By Candlelight: Rites for Celebration, Blessing, and Prayer* (2005 COVR runner-up, Spirituality). Since Janina was brought into the Craft in 1973, she has been exploring new ways that the old ways can contribute to the art of living, and enrich our larger culture. Janina continues to work on multiple books, with ongoing research projects exploring the ways folk magic and medicinal techniques can apply to modern problems, including the modulation of Asperger's Syndrome and other neurosensory processing problems.

Suzanne Ress has been practicing Wicca for about twelve years as leader of a small coven, but she has been aware of having a special connection to nature and animal spirits since she was a young child. She has been writing creatively most of her life—short stories, novels, and nonfiction articles for a variety of publications—and finds it to be an important outlet for her considerable creative powers. Other outlets she regularly makes use of are metalsmithing, mosaic works, painting, and all kinds of dance. She is also a professional aromatic herb grower and beekeeper. Although she is American of Welsh ancestry by birth, she has lived in northern Italy for nearly twenty years. She recently discovered that the small mountain in the pre-alpine hills she and her family and animals inhabit was once the site of an ancient Insubrian Celtic sacred place. Not surprisingly, the top of the mountain has remained a fulcrum of sacredness throughout the millennia, transforming from Celtic "Dunn" to Roman fortress, to its current form—Catholic chapel, and this grounding in blessedness makes Suzanne's everyday life especially magical.

When she's not chasing free-range hens, **Natalie Zaman** is trying to figure out the universe. Her work has appeared in *FATE, Sage Woman, newWitch*, and she currently writes a recurring feature called "The Wandering Witch" for *Witches and Pagans*. Natalie has also published work for children, and co-publishes, edits, and writes for broomstix.com, a project for Pagan children and their families. Her YA novel *Sirenz Back in Fashion*, a follow up to her debut, *Sirenz*, was published by Flux in 2012.

Samhain

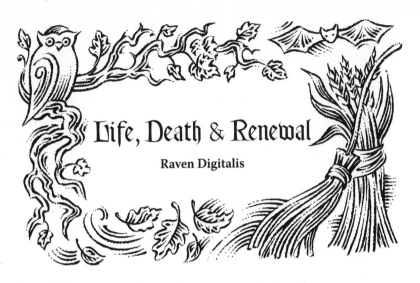

Life, Death & Renewal

Raven Digitalis

WHEN JOE AVERAGE IS asked to think about witchcraft celebrations, he's likely to think of Halloween. It's undeniably the most renowned holiday associated with witchcraft and the supernatural, and its festive-but-spooky symbolism tells people that there's more to the holiday than meets the eye. Halloween is, even to the masses, a boisterous and celebratory day of everything that goes bump in the night! Psychologically, I find this seasonal celebration to be a healthy way for the public to look into the dreadful shadows and turn it into festive fun, even if most people in the Western world don't observe the holiday with the reverence or depth that we do.

November 1 marks the beginning of the Celtic year. This is the time to celebrate renewal, generation, and all those who have walked the path of life before us. The inevitability of death is something to celebrate rather than fear or push into the recesses of our minds.

This is an ideal time to renew or create vows and shed the negative past and embrace the positive future—this is your life, your magick, and your time to fully utilize it. This is a fantastic time of year to deepen your volunteer work, whether that's at a local Pagan gathering or at a nonprofit organization. Consider volunteering at a food bank, an animal shelter, a retirement home, a hospital, an environmental protection agency, or a humanitarian organization, to name a few. The purpose of volunteer work—which we in my spiritual tradition actually *require* for advancement in training—is to cultivate humility, generosity, and community support. It's time for us Witches, Wiccans, Pagans, heathens, occultists and otherwise mystically inclined people to integrate our love and compassion into our greater communities. Samhain is an ideal time to begin or strengthen such devoted acts of compassion to fellow humans, animal allies, and our sustainable Earth.

Samhain (pronounced "Saw-Wane" or "Sow-in") is an ancient Gaelic name for this particular Celtic harvest festival. Samhain is also called Hallowe'en, Sav'n, Samhuinn, Hallowmas, All Hallows, Winternight, Ancestor Night, Last Harvest, Blood Harvest, Feast of the Dead, and other names that refer to the ancient Celtic holiday. Gerald Gardner adopted Samhain and other harvest festivals and solar celebrations in the late 1940s when he created Wicca, hence our carrying on of such celebrations presently in the Neopagan movement.

It's good to carry on the tradition of carving jack-o'-lanterns, which used to be left out to scare away evil spirits. Apple bobbing was, in Western history, a form of divination used for issues of the heart. Extravagant costumes were originally used to both scare away and blend in with malicious spirits because, as it is said, the "veil between the worlds is at its thinnest during this time of year." Many ancient Halloween traditions are carried over to this time in popular culture, even if most people don't understand their histories. (This reminds me of the time my grandpa, rest his soul, was spouting off about his confusion regarding the prevalence of rabbits and eggs during Easter—I didn't feel quite right explaining the rich fertility symbolism of ancient Pagan cultures!)

On October 31, the Sun is in Scorpio, the astrological sign of emotional depth and personal shadow. In Wicca, this is when the ever-changing Goddess is in her Crone aspect—she who bestows wisdom and deepened consciousness. The dualistic God aspects of

Wicca, which were greatly expounded upon in the poetic work of Robert Graves, finds the Oak King slumbering, but beginning to gain strength in the Earth's womb, while the Holly King is strong and fully resurrected as the Lord of Shadows. The Oak King can be seen in the Celtic Horned Gods, the Green Man, solar deities, and others. The Holly King can be seen entities such as Jack Frost, Santa Claus, and the Grim Reaper. When observing Samhain, it's wise to consider these placements of masculine and feminine vibration, regardless of which archetype one personally identifies with.

Being the final of the three Wiccan harvest festivals of the year, Samhain is neither autumn nor winter, much as Beltane (May Day) is neither spring nor summer. In a sense, Samhain can be seen as the "seasonal dusk" while Beltane is the "seasonal dawn." To clearly glimpse the meaning of a sabbat, I believe that a person should meditate on its polar opposite on the Wheel of the Year. Beltane celebrates light, fertility, life, joy, extroversion, and warm, frisky unity. Samhain, on the other hand, observes the antithesis: darkness, sterility (in the form of the coming frost), death, sorrow, introversion, and cold solemnitude. The more fearful among us may interpret these things as evil or frightening, but they're really anything but. Samhain and its associated celebrations and symbolisms are observations of the darker half of the year, as well as of darker side of the self, rather than a celebration of scary things that we try to avoid. Death is celebrated, yes, but this is a celebration of *life* in disguise!

At this time, we celebrate the necessity of death as another stage of personal development. This is an opportunity to come to terms with the mysterious inevitability of crossing over, which both helps us find closure with the deaths of our loved ones and prepares us for our own passing. Of course, a certain amount of trust in the universe is necessary to celebrate dying as an aspect of living, but inner conflict is integral to Samhain for this is also a season of paradox. We celebrate and embrace community, in part, because our minds are naturally drawing inward at this time; we must seek the remedy of community support to avoid an overabundance of introspection. Introversion and solitude are encouraged by many covens at this time because we need it sometimes. If we choose to disregard the deeper levels of our mind—including all those things that we normally don't wish to acknowledge—we're ultimately only living half the Wheel.

Personally, I'm naturally more attuned to the darker portions of the year. I'm into Gothic culture, art, and literature, and have no problem admitting my pull to darkness. At the same time, it's important for people like me to remember that neither the darkness nor light is more important than the other. Balanced spiritual living should include a reverence for both sacred light and darkness.

Late October and early November also mark a number of non-Celtic ancestral celebrations, perhaps the most notable of which is *Dia de los Muertos*: the Day of the Dead. This traditional Mexican celebration takes place on November 2 (sometimes additionally on November 1). When Mexico became Christianized, this ancestral festival shifted from its original monthlong observation in the Aztec calendar, to a particular date aligned with All Saints' Day, which was already aligned with older Celtic festivals.

The Day of the Dead is a time when families, following tradition, invite their loved ones to join them in a meal. The graves of loved ones are visited. Gorgeous parades celebrating the glory of life and its inevitable accompaniment of death, accompany this holiday. Intricate sugar skulls and cakes are left as offerings for the departed. Witches and other spiritual people can incorporate many of these things into their own Samhain practices. My own spiritual community has the honor of distributing handmade sugar skulls during the annual Dia de los Muertos parade in our hometown of Missoula, Montana. This time of year is an ideal time for community building, interpersonal support, and family bonding.

The name of my personal spiritual system is *Opus Aima Obscuræ*, which translates to "Work of the Great Dark Mother." OAO was formed by Estha McNevin and myself, offering a platform for community involvement and clerical training in a modern occult system.

OAO observes a wide variety of cross-cultural spiritual and magickal celebrations, including Dia de los Muertos, alongside Samhain.

While Beltane is the ejaculatory force of the season, Samhain is the energetic low, bringing us humans close to the underworld and the ghosts of those past. Because issues inevitably come up for everyone, everywhere, one of OAO's services is offering a "call out" for people to send us items and spells they wish for us to burn in our Samhain banishing fire, if they are unable to attend our ceremony or conduct their own fire ritual. People send poppets, cigarette packs, ex-lovers' clothing, bank statements, old bills, journals filled with negative writings, and other items worthy of casting to flame. The announcement for this service is sent out via email and Facebook.

At the same time, I encourage readers to practice their own Samhain rites (such as the one to follow) and banish their own items whenever possible.

Though the immense beauty of nature surrounds us at all times, autumn tends to be particularly venerated among Neopagans. This is the time we can smell fallen leaves around us, feel the biting chill of the wind, and come to the realization that it's getting darker earlier in the day. Because we Witches and esoteric folk tend to be some of the most emotionally sensitive people on the planet (from my experience, anyway), we may also feel our emotions shift with the season quite heavily around this time. We may feel more seasonal depression and have a responsibility to respond to this lull with mindfulness and crafty action. As it gets darker, we in turn receive the opportunity to view the shadows of our minds more clearly. This shadow self—our unconscious self and deeper mind—is the terrain of repressed thoughts, emotions, habits, and traumas of the past. Shadow isn't a bad thing by any means; on the positive side, facing the shadow gives a person a unique opportunity to grow, evolve, and further know oneself. Self-awareness is the cornerstone of any occult or spiritual path.

A highly potent method of working with one's own shadow during this time of year is to construct a poppet. Poppets are dolls that represent certain attributes of the magician. In the case of Samhain poppets, the dolls should represent everything that a person wishes to banish from their life forever. It's time for you to move beyond guilt, beyond sorrow, beyond fear. We must learn from our mistakes, not dwell on them. Dedicate November 1 as the beginning of your life's next step—enter the New Year with gusto!

To construct your own poppet, which will be used in the Samhain ritual on page 43, simply cut the shape of a person out of fabric. Use whatever fabric vibrates with you; I am fond of using old T-shirts. Stitch it up the sides and leave a part of it open to stuff with items. The doll can be anywhere from three inches to three feet high. It's important that the doll be a good size for your use, which includes stuffing it with fallen leaves, herbs, banishing spells, and written petitions identifying what you aim to release! The following items are "all purpose" banishing herbs and components, so feel free to use any combination or just focus on a few ingredients that are especially pertinent to your work. You could also simply add these elements to bolster your favorite spells. Remember, there is no wrong way to make your banishing poppet; it should simply represent everything that you wish to rid yourself of forever. (Many of these herbs are poisonous and should not be handled with bare hands, and their smoke should not be inhaled. Please consult herbal books before using anything I recommend.)

Banishing herbs include basil, asafoetida, black pepper, peppercorns, chili peppers, agrimony, nightshade, patchouli, cypress, datura, poplar, alder, belladonna, bistort, comfrey, boneset, elm, hemlock, poke root, eucalyptus, henbane, cedar, elecampane, ivy, kava-kava, mullein, poplar, skullcap, slippery elm, valerian, basil, garlic, onion, hydrangea, nettles, poplar, cloves, galbanum, olive leaves, bay laurel, mandrake, and choice others.*

Other nonherbal items for banishing include sulfur, salt, ash (any sort), Four Thieves vinegar (a hoodoo concoction), black sand or black salt (also called Witch's sand/salt), snakeskin (for shedding the past), dead bugs (for death energy), and dust from a windowsill or corner of the house (as well as any dried up, fallen plant detritus).

One year, a student of mine had sealed his poppet but later recalled things he wished to add. He decided to take a black drawstring bag and write out his additional banishing messages, placed them inside the bag with herbs and various spellcrafting components, and tied the bag around the poppet's neck to represent additional baggage. He also chose to sever the head of the doll (leaving it hanging by a string) to represent forgetfulness and disconnection and tied a cigarette to its hand to banish that particular attachment.

You, too, can get extremely creative! Make that poppet ugly, make it vile and gross ... it must represent that which you demand to rid yourself of! Keep in mind that even though a person's shadow side isn't entirely bad, and is a key to a magician's self-awareness, the *Samhain poppet* in particular represents undesirable aspects of your conscious and unconscious mind. If you wish to banish anger issues, try putting some hot sauce (fire in a bottle) or some rust (ruled by the aggressive planet Mars) into your poppet. If you feel overwrought with depressive tendencies, try adding weeping willow (even the tree's name is sad) and tissues that contain your tears. Add some dragon's blood for a boost. For banishing a bad habit, add catnip, rue, or eucalyptus. Throw in some rowan berries to help pull your energy back to yourself if it was fractured in the past. The poppet is an effigy of your hindrances; your Chronzon (as Thelema might term it). Stomp on the doll. Spit at it. Throw it around and tell it who's boss. Get creative and have fun with it!

*For herb and plant recommendations, you may wish to reference magickal herbal books such as those by Scott Cunningham and Paul Beyerl. Remember to add your own hair, fingernail clippings, and a drop of your own blood to the poppet to help bind it to your person. When you burn the doll in the ritual starting on page 43, the link will be severed and your shadow commanded.

Cosmic Sway

Daniel Pharr

SAMHAIN WAS FIRST CONSIDERED a high holiday by the Celts and Druids, who believed darkness came before light. The Celtic culture was lunar based and their high holidays occurred on New and Full Moons. Instead of sophisticated astronomical calculations, the Celts simply counted the lunar cycles of their year, starting with Samhain, and made appropriate adjustments to New and Full Moons without concern. They knew that the late autumn rise of Pleiades would bring the new year in the next lunar cycle.

The traditional date for Samhain is October 31, but the celestial calculation puts Samhain on November 6. The Celts would have likely moved the holiday to the Scorpio New Moon on November 13 to symbolize the start of the new year. The last harvest day would have been under the light of the Taurus Full Moon on October 29.

The energies of the Taurus Full Moon on October 29 will feel strong and permanent, providing a powerful influence in most matters. This is a time for doers, not thinkers. Decision-making will be difficult and the fear of change may be intense. Deeds should run to the practical, whether it's a magical act of release or a physical act rooted in common sense, take the bull by the horns, jump in, and act. This Full Moon begins the waning portion of the lunar cycle and is therefore better suited for finishing than for starting. The Taurus Full Moon is in the Fourth House, ruling the Seventh House, in opposition to Saturn, and is all about relationships of all kinds, from personal to planetary. These interpersonal energies may well bring on internal doubts leading to indecision and uneasiness. This is a good time for hands-on work. Instead of "working" on relationships, grab hold of the aspects and values in life that are enduring. Approach relationships from a place of strong compassion, with hugs rather than words.

Relationships: Time for Positive Action

Saturn will be stepping in with a lesson in self-worth through its opposition with the Moon. The value placed on the self is reflected in life's relationships. Strong supportive relationships indicate a strong self-worth. By approaching relationships with compassionate strength and strong compassion, others see self-confidence and inner-strength. Mercury in Sagittarius will bring out the inner philosopher and create an opportunity for strong spiritual debate. However, Mercury is also retrograde and will hinder all forms of communication. If the question right now is "Relationships," the answer is "Actions, not words." The Moon is trine Pluto and this enhances leadership. People prefer to follow actions. Deeds and actions are noticed and may well beget a position of leadership or send a powerful message. Mars in Sagittarius enhances leadership qualities but Venus in Libra asks that these qualities and deeds be focused in relationships.

Burning of the Roots Ritual

Burning of the Roots is a simple ritual, for an individual or a group, and since this time is about relationships and deeds, this ritual is perfect. Begin by gathering the community around a fire, casting a circle as practice dictates, and smudging the participants. Each participant will have brought roots from their garden or any garden into the circle. Taking turns spontaneously, each participant takes a root in hand, visualizes an action, emotion, condition, aspect, or malady from their life over the past year, which is not wanted in the new year, and visualizes the root taking on that negative, unwanted energy. Step forward toward the fire and name it aloud, such as, "I burn the root of harshness," or "I burn the root of jealousy," or "I burn the root of procrastination," or any other quality that the participant wants to leave behind in the waning year. Then place the root on the burning fire and watch as the fire burns that malady in effigy. Continue this process until everyone has burned all the roots they desire to burn. Make a pact with each other to support the group in the things that have been let go. For example, if you should witness one of the participants about to eat a piece of candy after having burned the root of consuming sugar, interject by saying, "Excuse me, but I believe you burned that root." This ritual should be performed on the last waning Moon of the year, and October 29 is just right.

Solar Samhain

October 31, the solar Samhain, arrives under a waning Gemini Moon. Strength of values and concern about relationships are still prominent. The Venus trine to this Gemini Moon will bring a sense of balance and harmony to relationships, and the Gemini Moon in the Tenth House will bring recognition for efforts and achievements, which, together, should silence any internal arguments between the head and heart caused by the lunar opposition of Mercury. In order to fully shine on this day, select activities that will allow passions and creativity to run free and the thirst for knowledge and philosophical conversations to be quenched.

Samhain, as calculated midway between the Autumnal Equinox and the Winter Solstice, occurs on November 6. The Moon will be waning in Leo. A strong sense of security is provided from family and family gatherings. Sharing wisdom is of primary concern and is motivated by the Leo Moon. Venus in Libra and in the Sixth House bring peace and harmony to relationships, while the Moon trine Mars and sextile Jupiter bring out optimism and self-confidence. All of this energy is combined with the power of the Scorpio Sun.

Dine with the Dead

This Samhain evening is a good time for Dining with the Dead, a simple but formal ritual dinner eaten while honoring the both recent and ancient dead. Set a place for each person attending, plus an extra place for those who have passed. Serve foods that were important to the deceased or are remembered with the deceased. Cast a circle in the customary manner, around the table and attendees. Call the dead to the room. "Tonight we dine with the dead and we ask the dead to dine with us." Each person, in order around the table, beginning in the east, calls someone deceased to the table, "I, Daniel Pharr, do hereby summon and request that my father, James Pharr, join us for dinner." Take a moment to experience the presence of the person summoned before the next person seated at the table calls their guest. Continue until everyone has done so. Next, everyone takes a small portion of the dish associated with the first person summoned, and the summoner tells a story, a truth, or an anecdote, about the deceased person. If anyone else has a story about that person, they should also share it before moving to the next summoner, deceased guest, and dish. At the end of the evening's ritual, thank and release the summoned guests and take down your circle as you would any other.

Scorpio New Moon

The Scorpio New Moon on November 13 would have been the Celts' choice for Samhain this year. As the end of last year and the beginning of the new year, celebrating with a bale fire would certainly be appropriate. This Scorpio New Moon in the Ninth House enhances the ability to vision the future in a global manner. The Moon conjunct with the North Node improves intuition. Mercury in Sagittarius and the Sun in the Ninth House, give global visioning an adventuresome and spiritual energy. Sit by the fire tonight, let Mars in the Tenth House stimulate the influence of the other celestial connections, and experience the coming year in both mind and body.

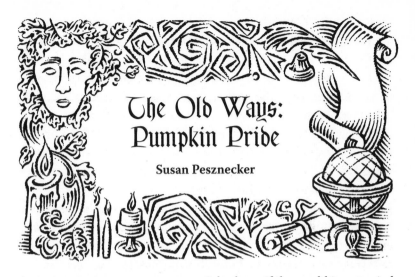

The Old Ways: Pumpkin Pride

Susan Pesznecker

AUTUMN COMES AND SUDDENLY it looks as if the world is occupied by pumpkins. Driving around the neighborhood, pumpkin vines and their giant fruit suddenly emerge from summer hiding places beneath fading shrubs and gardens. Grocery stores set up pumpkin corrals outside their entryways, enticing children with mountains of future jack-o'-lanterns. Pumpkin patches offer the chance to select the perfect pumpkin while enjoying corn mazes, hayrides, hot cider, and pumpkin-flinging trebuchets. And the farmers' market, only weeks ago heaped with fresh berries and tomatoes, is now piled with rainbow arrays of pumpkins, squashes, and gourds—kissing cousins from a big family.

And speaking of family, the family Cucurbitaceae is host to pumpkins, gourds, and a number of hard squashes, like the Hubbard, the golden butternut, and the gorgeous red turban. The "winter squashes," including pumpkin, have dense, tough, inedible skin that resists moisture loss and external damage, accounting for their long storage ability. Winter squashes contain large seeds, most of which are edible and can be pressed to yield oil. Gourds are a special type of Cucurbitaceae with a skin that dries and hardens. Gourds have long been used by aboriginal people to create ceremonial vessels, rattles, serving utensils, and storage containers; modern craftspeople use gourds to craft birdhouses and other fanciful items.

The pumpkin is a fruit, and the word "pumpkin" comes from the Greek word *pepon*, "large melon." No one is certain where the plant originated, but they're believed to be native to North America. The size range of pumpkins is impressively variable: small decorative versions may weigh only a pound, while prizewinners regularly top half a ton. In 2010, the world pumpkin record was reset by a New York specimen weighing 1,810.5 lbs!

Pumpkins gain their orange color from high levels of beta carotene, making them rich in vitamin A and delicious in a number of foods and baked goods. Pumpkin seeds—known in Hispanic culture as *pepitas*—are roasted for eating or cooking. The seeds can be pressed to make pumpkin oil. Some also enjoy the thick pumpkin leaves as a steamed or sautéed vegetable.

Probably the most well-known version of the pumpkin is the traditional jack-o'-lantern, a carved, hollowed-out pumpkin with candles inserted to make the fruit into a glowing, flickering, decorative source of light. The practice may date back to the Celts, who used to carve various types of vegetable lanterns for practical use. Legend suggests the turnip was the first vegetable lantern, carved with fantastic faces designed to frighten away evil spirits. Rutabagas, large beets, and other sturdy root vegetables were used as well, and thick cabbage stems were carved into "kail-runt torches." Carving small vegetables was difficult, but they had the advantage of providing portable light. Nevertheless, it's not hard to imagine the pleasure with which the larger, easier-to-carve pumpkin supplanted small, tough, harder-to-carve veggies.

We've all watched jack-o'-lanterns flicker in the dark. Legend says they're named for the flickering ghostly light known as "will-o'-the-wisp" that lingers over peat bogs. Other tales link the name to "man with lantern" or "night watchman." In ancient times, any sturdy source of light was valued for practical use and for protection.

Life then was more difficult and fraught with peril: to go out at night could mean being lost, eaten, or—worse—ensnared by malevolent entities, and vegetable lanterns provided a way to carve a little bit of safe space out of the darkness. The small lanterns also protected candles from wind and rain and helped them burn more slowly.

One of the diciest times of year for ancient peoples was the period of All Hallow's Eve or Samhain—the ancient Celts' term for the crossquarter sabbat people today call Halloween. Samhain is a time when the veils between life and death are thin and spirits wander freely between the worlds. It's a time of liminal space, and it's often regarded by magickal folk as the turning point of the year—the new year, so to speak. In times past, Samhain was greeted with both excitement and anxiety. The idea of the year's fresh turning was a good one, but there was fear, too, for or no one wanted to be swept away into "other space" by a wandering apparition. Eventually, lit jack-o'-lanterns were left out on doorsteps on All Hallow's Eve to protect homes from wandering spirits, again using frightening, carved faces for added effect.

A traditional story about jack-o'-lanterns tells of Stingy Jack, an evil miser who liked to trick others and decided to outwit the devil. At one point, he tricked the devil into climbing an apple tree, holding him there by encircling the tree with crosses, while forcing the devil to relinquish claims on Jack's soul forever. When Stingy Jack finally died, he was refused by St. Peter at heaven's gates and so was forced to head, instead, for hell. The devil greeted him there, but reminding him of their earlier pact for safeguarding Jack's soul, would not admit him. Stingy Jack was thus doomed to wander forever in the dark spaces between heaven and hell. He had no light, so the devil tossed him a hellish ember; Jack installed this in a carved turnip and from that time wandered aimlessly with his turnip lantern held before him.

The pumpkin was a harvest symbol long before it became associated with Halloween. Pumpkins ripen in autumn, reaching their peak as temperature drops and winter's sleeping "death" begins to steal over the world. Pumpkins themselves look like glowing lamps, their brilliant orange, gold, and white colors vivid against barren fields. It's no surprise that we've come to regard them as potent signs of the harvest, vibrant splashes of life against a stark background.

Samhain today continues to be regarded as both sacred and malevolent, and pumpkins have been swept along in the fray. The jack-o'-lantern often makes an appearance in Halloween tales and films. In "The Legend of Sleepy Hollow," a headless horseman terrorizes the community, pumpkin head tucked under one arm. The film *Halloween III* poses a terrifying scenario with pumpkin head Halloween masks melting the wearers' heads, killing them and releasing hordes of beetles, roaches, and other vermin. But of course, it's not all bad news: after all, Harry Potter's favorite drink is pumpkin juice.

Magickally, pumpkins are associated with prosperity and protection. They're also something of an aphrodisiac. Researchers testing the power of scent on male sexual desire found that the smell of pumpkin pie was at the top of the list. Luckily for matchmakers everywhere, pumpkin pie is easy to make. Pumpkin puree, eggs, milk, and spices—cinnamon, ginger, and cloves—are stirred smooth, poured into a pie shell, and baked. Early American settlers used a simpler approach: they hollowed out small pumpkins, filled them with eggs, milk, sugar, and spices, and baked them until done. Today, cooks simmer soups and stews inside whole pumpkins.

Whether you prefer to bake pies, carve jack-o'-lanterns, or simply walk through a field of ripe pumpkins, enjoy embracing the season through this rich magickal tradition.

For Further Reading:

Goldwert, Lindsay. "Pumpkin Pie Smell Stimulates Arousal in Men; Scent is Sexy Aphrodisiac, Says Study." *New York Daily News.* 24 Nov. 2010. Web. 12 Oct. 2011. <http://articles.nydailynews.com/2010-11-24/entertainment/27082315_1_pumpkin-pie-scent-traditional-thanksgiving-dessert>

Feasts and Treats

Kristin Madden

WHILE PUMPKINS ARE SEASONAL for months in many areas during the autumn, popular culture has firmly solidified their place as symbols of the Samhain-Halloween season. Pumpkins, along with the blessings that may be found in darkness, are at the heart of our recipes for this sabbat. Each brings a tasty and interesting twist to the traditional themes of the holiday.

Kaddo Bourani

Pumpkins are an iconic symbol, but do you want to serve the same old pie and roasted seeds? This Afghan dish will bring a unique and delicious celebration of pumpkin to your Samhain feast.

Prep Time: 15 minutes
Cooking time: 3 hours
Serves: 2–4

1 sugar/pie pumpkin, about 3 pounds
⅛ cup vegetable oil
1 cup sugar

Yogurt Sauce
1 cup plain yogurt

1 garlic clove, minced
½ teaspoon dried mint
¼ teaspoon salt

Tomato Meat Sauce
¼ cup vegetable oil
1 onion, diced
1½ pounds ground beef
1 large tomato, seeded and chopped
2 garlic cloves, roasted and mashed
1½ teaspoons salt
1 teaspoon (each) pepper, coriander, and tumeric
2 tablespoons tomato paste
1⅓ cups water

Remove rind from pumpkin. Cut in half. Remove seeds and strings. Cut each half into 4 pieces. Coat pumpkin with oil and sugar. Bake in covered baking dish at 300 degrees F for 3 hours. Baste with pan juices at 2 hours.

Combine yogurt sauce ingredients and refrigerate.

Sauté onions in oil until golden brown. Add beef and cook for 5 minutes. Add remaining ingredients except tomato paste and water. Cook 5 minutes. Add tomato paste and water. Bring to a boil; then simmer for 15 minutes.

Place 2 to 4 warm pumpkin pieces on plate. Top with yogurt, then add the meat sauce and serve.

Zucchini Bread

This is a richer version of the usual zucchini bread, honoring the dark half of the year and reminding us that there is joy and sweetness, even among the shadows. It will warm body and soul, especially when served with a pumpkin spice latté.

Prep Time: 15 minutes
Cooking Time: 60 minutes
Quantity: 2 loaves

2 cups flour
½ tablespoon (each) cinnamon, mace, nutmeg
1 teaspoon salt
2 teaspoons baking soda
½ teaspoon baking powder
3 eggs
2 cups brown sugar
1 cup olive oil
1½ teaspoons vanilla extract
2 cups zucchini, peeled and grated
1 cup raisins

Sift together flour, spices, salt, baking soda, and baking powder. Mix eggs, sugar, oil, and vanilla in a separate bowl. Next, add zucchini and then the egg mixture to the flour mix. Add raisins.

Spoon into two well-greased and floured bread pans. Bake for 60 minutes at 350 degrees F.

Pumpkin Spice Latté

Here is a special Samhain coffee to help you stay awake and alert for all the festivities. This is another beautiful celebration of the most popular fruit of the season: the pumpkin. It is a perfect complement to that dark zucchini bread.

Prep Time: 20 minutes
Cook Time: 5–10 minutes
Serves: 2

1 tablespoon canned pumpkin
1 cup cream
½ teaspoon (each) mace, cinnamon, nutmeg
½–1 cup brewed coffee

Heat pumpkin, cream, and ¼ teaspoon of each spice on medium heat in a saucepan. Blend on high for 20 to 30 seconds. Gradually add coffee. Pour into mugs and dust with remaining spices.

Pumpkin Mousse in Mini-Pumpkins

Spice up your Samhain feast with this fun alternative to pumpkin pie. Pumpkin mousse is light and rich. Kids and adults alike will love this fabulous holiday dessert. Served in mini-pumpkins.

Prep Time: 20 minutes
Cooking Time: 15 minutes
Chill Time: overnight
Serves 6–8

1 package unflavored gelatin
½ cup milk
3 large eggs
2 cups heavy cream (divided)
¾ cup honey
1 teaspoon cinnamon
¼ teaspoon (each) cloves, mace, nutmeg, and ginger
1½ cups pumpkin purée
2 teaspoons vanilla extract
6–8 cooking pumpkins, 3–4 inches in diameter

The night before, prepare the mousse filling. In a small bowl, sprinkle unflavored gelatin over ½ cup milk and set aside. Separate eggs, placing whites and yolks in two medium bowls.

In a large saucepan, combine 1 cup heavy cream, honey, and spices over medium heat until honey dissolves. Add milk and gelatin mixture. Stir until dissolved. Add egg yolks, whisking constantly. Cook until nearly boiling. Add canned pumpkin puree. Stir 2 minutes until smooth. Remove from heat. Whisk in 1 teaspoon vanilla.

Beat egg whites until stiff peaks form. Fold into pumpkin mixture. Pour into a cold bowl and refrigerate mousse overnight.

About two hours before serving, wash and scoop out seeds and string from the small pumpkins. Bake for 15 to 20 minutes at 250 degrees F. Allow to cool completely. While the pumpkins cool, Whip the remaining 1 cup cream and 1 teaspoon vanilla extract.

Spoon chilled mousse into pumpkins. Top with whipped cream.

Crafty Crafts

Linda Raedisch

THANKS TO THE EARLY influences of Robert Graves, Margaret Murray, and Gerald Gardner, Wicca bears a decidedly English stamp. But not all Witches live in England. The Craft has moved out into the world, picking up such accoutrements as spirit catchers, smudge sticks, and chakra work. Some of the Crafty Crafts in this book do indeed pay homage to the snowdrops and standing stones of the British Isles, while others will take us to the Baltic Lands, Japan, Siberia, and, yes, New Jersey.

I am principally a paper artist, but where there's a Witch, there's fire. For each sabbat you will find a craft involving fire, whether it's sunshine, the glowing tip of an incense stick, a candle flame or the tiny fairy light inside a bulb. At the beginning of each Crafty Craft section, you will find thematic musings, general festooning, and on-the-fly ideas, as well as a healthy dose of folklore. Read on to find step-by-step instructions for more complex crafts—though you'll notice I've snuck in a few folkloric morsels, too!

Beyond Black and Orange

When celebrating Samhain and her more secular daughter, Halloween, it's too easy to fall back on the old color scheme of orange and black. The orange, of course, is for the pumpkins, but have you ever wondered why black is the color of mourning in Western tradition? Mourning is not just the period of keenest grief but also the time when survivors are most likely to be harmed by contact with a dead family member who has not yet loosened his or her grip upon this world. To dress in black is to make oneself invisible to the dead. Therefore, for the layperson, black is entirely appropriate for Halloween. But the Wiccan, who reaches out to the spirits, should consider wearing another color, especially at Samhain. Children, on the other hand, perhaps should be dressed in black, since their liminal status places them closer to the threshold between the worlds (Where do you think they get all that imagination?) and therefore makes them more vulnerable to the influence of the dead.

Is there life after orange? Expand your palette to include some of the other wonderful colors around at this season. Chrysanthemums are just making their debut, while dahlias are often at their peak, displaying all their lovely hues of deep burgundy, crimson, butter yellow, russet, purple, and white. If your zinnias, nasturtiums, cock's combs, and cosmos are still hanging on, invite them to the party, too. Weaving fall flowers in among the ghosts and witches on your front lawn will add a deeper, more vibrant sense of reverence to the season.

Marigolds are an intrinsic part of the Mexican and Mexican-American Day of the Dead celebration. On the night of November 2, the graveyards glow not just with the light of votive candles but with thousands of these golden flowers. Marigolds frame the *ofrendas*, household altars where sugar skulls, fruit, and toys are set out for returning spirits both large and small. The name "marigold" identifies the flower with the Virgin Mary, but the Aztec marigold, *Tagetes erecta*, has always been sacred in Mexico. Then as now, it was the flower of the dead, just as yellow, for the Aztecs, was the color of the dead. *Tagetes* is a New World genus, converted to Catholicism only after the arrival of Cortez. (American marigolds share a name, but not a genus, with the Old World pot marigold or *calendula*.) In Tibet, where Buddhists hold saffron to be the most sacred color of all, marigolds are grown specifically as temple offerings.

Season of the Wisp

Okay, so you've carved your jack-o'-lantern (or your turnips, if you're that sort of person), shaken things up with a few loud bouquets and prepared your offerings for those who are even now slipping out from behind the veil. One question remains: What are you going to wear? Some Pagans regard this, the Celtic New Year and Feast of the Dead, as a solemn occasion, one to be marked reverently in their usual ritual garb. But I know plenty of Witches who are just nuts about Halloween, so it's safe to assume that some of you are going to need costumes.

Halloween in many parts of the United States can be anywhere between 25 and 75 degrees Fahrenheit. One just never knows, which is why I like a costume in which the headdress carries the day. For the following get-up, a gauzy white dress is best, but if you have to throw on a winter coat, it won't spoil the effect. What is it? A will-o'-the-wisp!

Our friend Will used to be quite famous. Back in Ireland, *Sean na gealaige*, "Jack of the bright light," was happy to share the stage with his little brother, *Liam na lasoige*, "William with the little flame." It was after the Irish emigrated to North America and discovered how much easier it was to carve the New World pumpkin than the hard, knobby turnip that jack-o'-lantern started to steal the spotlight.

The will-o'-the-wisp, to my mind, is a more primitive expression of the rootless, wandering spirit. Instead of a lantern, he carries a mere burning wisp of straw, not to light his own way, but to lure travelers from the path at night. He draws them into the tangle of the woods, leads them stumbling over the tussocks and thence into the bog where he makes his watery home. I grew up with New Jersey's Great Swamp, a wonderful wilderness of wetlands, quite literally in my backyard, so Will is a creature close to my heart. People do get lost in the Swamp from time to time, though they are usually found the next day. Wetlands are mesmerizing to the human psyche. Are they water? Are they land? Unsuitable for either farming or building, they exist on the periphery of daily business.

Bogs especially are portals to the underworld, or perhaps to a brighter world, where the blue sky is always reflected on the black face of the water. The bog at night is a spooky place. Both the Scandinavians and the Slavic Wends believed that the little bobbing lights seen above the sedge were the spirits of unbaptized babies. In Nordic folklore, they are the souls of children born in secret and killed by their mothers, their tiny bodies disposed of in the black earth of the bog. Such spirits were understandably outraged, not to mention lonely. The Finnish *Liekkio* was confined to the forest and had a somewhat less dangerous reputation than the Nordic *utnaburdin* who were relentless in their search for someone to baptize them. This search usually ended with the hapless traveler joining the *utnaburdin* in death beneath the black water.

To transform yourself into a will-o'-the-wisp, for one night only, start by making yourself a crown of braided rushes, straw, or other dry plant material. For comfort's sake, attach the crown to a band of brown felt so you won't be prickled. To help yourself blend in with your woodsy surroundings, you'll also need a set of twig horns. Birch or oak works nicely. (If you are making this costume for a little girl—a Wilhelmina-o'-the-wisp—I suggest you coat the twigs in silver glitter so she can compete with all those twinkling fairy princesses out there.) Attach two short, sturdy rolls of felt to the crown to serve as "holsters" for the twig horns. This way, you can easily transport your headdress, sliding the twigs in at the last minute. If the twigs break, they can be easily replaced.

Tack a generous length of cheesecloth to the back of the crown so it flows down like a veil: this is the mist rising up from the water. Dress in white, for the will-o'-the-wisp is an innocent, but add a pair of long, black gloves as a token of the mire in which he resides. A single battery-powered Christmas candle with a bit of straw wrapped around it can serve as the "little flame."

Translucent Paper Snowflake Ghost

Many non-Wiccans like to make ghost trees at Halloween. The ghosts are usually made of white rags with a cotton ball stuffed in for the head and a string knotted around the neck. When suspended from the branches, they look very much like they've been hanged. That's fine if you're trying to re-create the sacred oak at Uppsala, but it is not, I think, an appropriate way to greet the ancestors at Samhain.

Light and fluttery, these paper ghosts dance on the air. If you're expecting rain on the appointed night, make them out of wax paper so they'll hold up a little longer.

Tools and Materials

Tracing paper or wax paper
Plate, bowl, or saucer for making a circle
Scissors
Needle and thread

Cut a circle out of your paper: the larger the circle, the larger the ghost. I use a teacup saucer to make a ghost that fits in the palm of my hand. Fold the circle into eighths and cut as shown. It's just like making a paper snowflake. (You can use this same pattern for your stencil-spiced yogurt at Imbolc.) Unfold once and there's your ghost. Thread a loop through the pointed top of the head for hanging.

Halloween Hand Sign

If you grew up during the 1970s, you may be familiar with the "Helping Hand." This was a sticker showing a white hand on a red ground, displayed in the window of participating homes. The Helping Hand was a sign to kids in trouble that such a home was a safe haven.

My Halloween Hand Sign—a black hand on an orange ground—is a festive twist on the old idea. Display your hand in the window on Halloween to let potential trick-or-treaters know you're open for business, and that you're the real thing! For a smaller sign, make a reduced image of your hand on a scanner or photocopier, cut out, and use this as your template.

Tools and Materials
Your hand
White crayon
Construction paper: black, orange
Scissors
Glue
Metallic silver paint marker (optional)
Clear packing tape (optional)

Use the white crayon to trace the outline of your hand on the black construction paper. Cut out. Mount your black hand on the orange paper and mount this on a larger piece of black paper to create a black border. If you think the neighborhood can handle it, decorate hand and border with your favorite arcane symbols in silver paint marker. For a laminated look, cover the surface of your sign with strips of clear packing tape.

All One Family

Sandra Kynes

THE BLAZING HUES OF autumn have faded into Earth's more subtle tones, except for the witch hazel. Showing up after the leaves have disappeared, its spidery yellow flowers create a golden haze in twilight afternoons while shallow rays of sun seem to follow the last arrows of geese across the sky. If the days are cold enough here in New England, we can see the beautifully eerie sea smoke (columns of light fog) rising above the harbor.

Samhain can be a challenging time for Pagan parents because it is difficult to balance our sabbat of reverence with the decorating and costuming frenzy it has become. While it is tempting to hide in the proverbial broom closet until this is over, I have found that it works best to meet it gently head-on. I believe that it is important to keep the season enjoyable for children, otherwise they may feel like they're missing out on the fun things that other kids are doing.

Our family decorates the house for "Halloween," but in a simple way that is in keeping with our traditions. We have plenty of carved pumpkins, gourds, and Indian corn to represent the season and the end of the harvest. We also use the quintessentially popular black cats, bats, and moons, but to us, they represent the night of the year that begins with Samhain.

About a week before Samhain we set aside a Saturday for what we call our day of "pumpkining." (Yes, we turned pumpkin into a verb.) We drive out to a farm where there are hayrides and we can pick our own pumpkins. The first thing we do is the hayride around the perimeter of the fields, which we use as a reconnaissance of the pumpkin patches before we get down to the serious business of finding the right ones. Since ancestors are a focus of this sabbat, riding in a horse-drawn wagon has usually been a touch-point for talking about how our relatives lived and traveled long ago. The smell of hay, crunching of leaves underfoot, and apple cider after the ride helps us use all our senses to connect with this turning of the Wheel of the Year.

After much walking around the fields and decision-making over pumpkins we head home with our treasures to continue the next phase of our pumpkining day. Newspapers are spread over the top of the kitchen table as we assemble all our gear for carving and painting the pumpkins. Little children start the process by drawing faces, which will be used as guidelines to cut the big pumpkins. When cutting starts, they continue drawing and painting faces or designs on the tiny pumpkins that will not be carved. Children can also be in charge of the pumpkin seeds, which need to be separated from the pulp and washed for roasting.

During this activity, we often talk about how the tradition of carving pumpkins may have started. Some sources say that lanterns were created by hollowing out turnips, beets, cabbage heads, or potatoes. Instead of candles, burning pieces of coal were placed inside for illumination. These were used to light the way for people traveling the roads from one farm to another in rural areas of Ireland. Of course, there are many stories and one of the most popular is about a man called Stingy Jack who tried to cheat the devil and ended up wandering the roads with his turnip lantern. Jack of the Lantern was eventually shortened to Jack-o'-Lantern. Irish settlers in early America found the larger pumpkin more suitable for carving than turnips. It's fun to have the children relate their own ideas for the origin of jack-o'-lanterns.

One or two of the smaller carved pumpkins get special places on our family altar. The autumn leaves that we collected at Mabon and pressed in a book are scattered across the altar and stand out brilliantly on the black cloth. Also scattered about are hazelnuts, which in Celtic tradition, were associated with wisdom and used for divination at Samhain. In addition, they were found in burial mounds in the British Isles, so to us, the hazelnut whispers of ancient ways and seem like the appropriate tokens of tribute to our ancestors.

We begin the process of setting up our altar at least a week in advance. This gives us time to get out all the old family photographs and talk about them. We begin with grandparents and let the children talk about their memories of them: Summer afternoons on Poppy's boat and pulling up crab traps from the dock with Grandma. Memories of aunts and uncles and big family gatherings for summer cookouts and Thanksgiving dinners come next. Working backwards in time through the generations, we look at pictures of men in uniforms from both World Wars and women in long flowing dresses with hair in fancy chignons atop their heads. Finally, we get to a point where we need to relay secondhand stories, and eventually we can only put a name to a face. We take time and look at all of them.

On the wall behind the altar we hang a poster-size piece of paper on which we have drawn our family tree. Actually, it looks more like a technical schematic than a tree but it works for pointing out where each person whose photo we have looked at fits into our family. Following the lines of our "tree," we eventually come to those who are merely names that we found through research, but we include them in our remembrances just the same. With this tree we show how we, in turn, will be remembered. It so clearly illustrates the cycles of lives, marriages, births, and deaths and how we each have our part to play in holding on to and connecting the strands of a much larger family. In addition to family, we include pets in our remembrances because they have been an important part of our lives, too.

The Samhain altar gets a little crowded because not only do we display pictures of loved ones, we also put out objects that were passed down through the family. Some items are very personal, such as jewelry that ranges from my grandfather's pocket watch to my mother's wedding ring. A few pieces of pottery and a beautifully decorated teapot are too fragile to use. Like the photographs, we spend time handling and talking about them. For children, holding these belongings adds a different, more real, and deeper dimension than just viewing pictures. It's as though we can reach across time and touch those who have gone before.

On Samhain night we have an early meal and then head outside for the local festivities. There's a little bit of door-to-door trick-or-treating, but the Halloween parade around the neighborhood is the main event. People of all ages join in—some in costumes and others not—to walk or dance along to the drumming and share goodies. These activities end by seven o'clock, giving us time to unwind and get ready for our family Samhain observances. We begin with a slow procession from the kitchen, through several rooms to the altar to help us make the shift from secular activities to ritual mindset.

While it might be easier to do ritual the night before, keeping it on the sabbat emphasizes its importance. However, getting small Pagans to make the transition after trick-or-treating can certainly be challenging, so this is a personal decision that can be reversed as children grow older. Because of our pumpkining day and early altar set-up, it has become easier to balance the fun aspects of Halloween with enjoyable sabbat-related activities that bring deeper meaning to our lives.

Ritual: Banishing the Unwanted

Raven Digitalis

THIS SAMHAIN RITUAL IDEA should be modified to your liking. Add to it, alter it, and otherwise change it depending on where intuition leads you. Make it serious, make it joyful, make it a ceremony that reverberates with your deepest spirit!

This ceremony is written with a group of practitioners in mind, but can be easily modified for solitary observation. The ritual assumes that you (one person) are leading the group, but the rite can be easily expanded or modified for coven use with a priest or priestess, *or* for people who may be uninitiated and are simply playing the role of high priest and high priestess for the sake of the circle.

Because I assume that readers are familiar with methods of circle casting and energy raising, I'll skip those particular steps. If you have recently begun your journey of witchcraft, I ask that you read various books and articles focused on how to cast a circle, call the elemental quarters, and otherwise raise energy, before performing this rite.

Items Needed

Before performing the ceremony, ensure that all participants are carrying a poppet, spellbag, or other item to represent everything they wish to banish from their lives for the year and beyond. These items will be thrown to one of the two fires, which can be known as the "banishing fire." Members should also bring items for divination, such as tarot cards, runes, scrying mirrors, crystal or glass balls, and so on.

Ask all members to bring pictures or other mementos of their loved ones who have crossed beyond the veil—images and effigies can be of family members, friends, celebrities, pets, spiritual leaders who have passed, and so on. These should be put on an the other bonfire, which can be known as the "sharing fire." You should also have a plate of fresh food offerings prepared for the ancestors. It's ideal if the food you're offering is hot, fresh, and/or organic, but this isn't a requirement. If you are having members bring potluck food items for a post-ritual feast, feel free to incorporate bits of everyone's dish on the plate so the spirits can eat first. You may also wish to offer a lit jack-o'-lantern, homemade sugar skulls, or some liquor or juice!

Additionally, you may wish to set up a seasonal harvest altar or put small altars or tools in the four directional quadrants.

Just before gathering, safely kindle the two bonfires suitable enough to burn everyone's poppets. (In other words, a taper candle to represent a bonfire won't work in this instance). You may also wish to bring a bundle of sage and some communal wine or beer, if appropriate.

The Ritual

First, gather all participants around the bonfires on Halloween night. Do so in silence. The silent aspect will allow people to reflect on the season and draw their energies inward. Continue this silence by walking around the bonfires in the pattern of an infinity knot (∞), also called a lemniscate, for a few minutes. When you (or the leader) feel the time is right, cast the circle and call the quarters, and then have everyone gather near the ancestral altar.

Holding your hands to the altar, look upward and declare the following:

Greetings and blessings to the spirits of the land and all those who have gone before us! We gather as children of Mother Earth and Father Sky. We ask for your protection. Come to us through time and space this Hallow's Eve, as we leave this plate of offerings to all beings who have come before us. Holy ancestors, eat of this food. Partake of these libations. You are loved. Blessed be!

Group repeats: *Blessed be.*

At this point, sit around that fire (the "sharing fire") and invite everyone in the group to share stories about loved ones who have died. Whether they're discussing someone they knew personally or someone they only knew about, and whether they're sharing stories about humans or animals, make sure that they have an opportunity to share everything that's on their mind. After each person speaks, say: *"Rest in peace. Blessed be."* and have the group repeat the phrase.

Feel free to read any passages, poetry, or incantations you may have written or encountered specifically for Samhain. When this is performed, the group should be standing. Get creative and get into the moment!

Have participants make way to the other fire for banishing. Raise your athame or wand and shout:

Hail to the Dread Lord of Shadows; the Hidden One! Great God, be around us and within us as we lay to rest that which no longer serves us. We ask you to take these items to the underworld, away from us forever, as they are engulfed in sacred flame! Hail to the Wise Crone; the Lady of Mysteries! Great Goddess, be around us and within us as we banish these effigies and what they represent! Make our magick wise and our intentions pure. So mote it be!

Group repeats: *So mote it be.*

Going widdershins (counterclockwise), the person to your left should begin by tossing his or her poppet into the fire. Glaring at the flame, they should declare their intention, which should be different for everyone depending on what magick they imbued the poppet, sachet, or other items with. Here's an example:

This Samhain night, I banish from my life issues of low self-image and lack of confidence.

I banish my tendency to overreact to situations.

I banish the energetic and mental blockages that keep me in a state of fear.

As I will, so mote it be.

Group repeats: *So mote it be.*

This should continue with each member until it comes back to you. Allow each member to take as much time as necessary.

❦

Once all the dolls have been cast to flame, dance around the fire moving in a widdershins direction, with everyone forcefully directing energy into the fire and chanting something like:

Sacred flame, fire bright; banish all these things tonight!

When the energy peaks, yell, "*Down!*" and have everyone fall to the ground in silence.

When you feel the time is right—when you feel that everyone has reflected on what they've needed—have everyone move back to the "sharing fire" and allow the mood to lighten. Pass around a bundle of sage to cleanse the energy. Pass around a bottle of wine or beer if you wish.

Once everyone's had a good time and received special messages, give heartfelt gratitude to all the spirits, deities, and ancestors who attended the ritual. Do this *in your own words*. You may wish to have everyone in the circle do this individually; if so, have everyone speak one-by-one in a deosil (clockwise) direction, with everyone repeating "*Blessed be; hail and farewell*" after each person speaks. Thank the directions and close the circle as you normally would.

Finally, enjoy the night by having a feast, dancing and drumming, visiting a cemetery, or otherwise having fun with any friends or family members who attended—after all, Samhain is a time for community and love. If you are working solitarily, do whatever feels natural, depending on how energetic you feel. You may wish to take a walk, draw a bath, or do some arts and crafts. Whatever you do on Samhain night, be sure you dance with the spirits and welcome the New Year. Just don't get too spooked in the process!

Notes

Yule

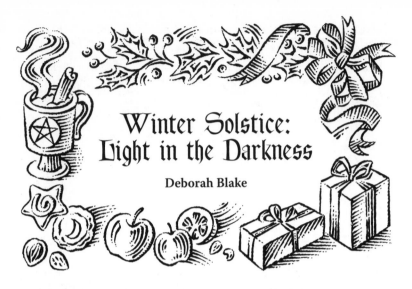

Winter Solstice: Light in the Darkness

Deborah Blake

THE WINTER SOLSTICE, ALSO known as Yule, falls on or around December 21. It is the longest day of the year, with the least amount of light and the most darkness—which is probably why our ancestors celebrated with gaiety, greenery, and plenty of candles blazing against the dark winter's night.

From this day forward, the days will grow a little longer and the days a little shorter, showing us the path out of the cold and darkness and into the spring. But for now, for many of us, it is still dark and chilly, with our energy at low ebb and our spirits struggling to find the light.

What better time to have a party with friends, family, and fellow Witches?

In the Wiccan symbolism of the Wheel of the Year, Yule marks the end of the Holly King's reign, representing the dark half of the year, as he is overthrown by the Oak King, who represents the light half of the year. This change in power ensures the slow return of light and warmth. The goddess, in her role as mother, gives birth to the infant sun; the god is reborn, bringing with him hope and completing the cycle of birth, growth, death, and rebirth. The Wheel has completed another turn.

Most of us grew up celebrating a different holiday at this time of year. For me, it was Chanukah, with eight nights of gifts to commemorate the miracle of the lamp that burned for eight days when there was only oil enough for one. The Jews call Chanukah the Festival of Lights, and eat potato pancakes (latkes), light the menorah, and gather round with family and friends. Starting to sound familiar?

For many, the holiday of their childhood was Christmas, which celebrates the birth of Christ, the son of God. (Again, the theme of birth and the sacred mother and the rebirth of hope.) Most of the traditions of Christmas have their roots in customs and folklore handed down from our Pagan ancestors. The colors of red and green come from the berries and evergreens that Pagans used to decorate their homes (mistletoe was sacred to the Druids); the Christmas tree and holly boughs originated as greenery brought inside to symbolize life in the midst of death.

Some theorize that Santa Claus was based on the Holly King (another jolly, bearded man), and the star at the top of the tree is the same as the Witch's five-pointed star that represents the elements of earth, air, fire, water, and spirit.

The original Yule was a fairly raucous holiday, celebrated by drinking wassail (an alcoholic punch as well as a toast that means "To your health!"), singing, and dancing in the streets. People would go from house to house—the origins of caroling. The holiday was so filled with merriment and misbehavior that it was banned by the Pilgrims for a while after they moved to the New World.

These days things aren't quite so rowdy, but we still gather together with those we love and celebrate in the traditional manner—with good food, beautiful decorations, and perhaps even some singing. If you want to make wassail for yourself and your guests, here is a simple recipe.

Winter Solstice Wassail

A gallon of apple cider (don't use apple juice; it won't have the right flavor)

1 to 2 cups of red wine *or* whiskey *or* brandy [note: if you are serving children or those with alcohol issues, just leave out this ingredient—wassail is perfectly lovely even with no alcohol].

Spices—if possible, use whole spices, such as cinnamon sticks, cloves, ginger, and allspice (powdered are okay if you don't have whole, but they won't look as nice or have as rich a flavor). These can be floated on top, placed in a tea ball, or placed in a piece of cheesecloth that is fished out before serving.

½ cup maple syrup or honey (you can use sugar, but the depth of flavor won't be as nice)—you might need more or less depending on the sweetness of the cider and/or the alcohol you're using. Add a small amount to start and then more as needed.

Optional: you can decorate the wassail with slices of apple (sliced across, the apple will show a pentacle in the middle) or pieces of orange with the peel on, which will also add a nice hint of citrus flavor.

Directions for cooking: Place all ingredients into a pot on the top of the stove or into a slow cooker. Adjust sweetener as needed. Let simmer at least 20 minutes. If necessary, skim spices off the top and decorate with apple or orange slices before serving.

Correspondences

If you will be having a ritual or gathering for the Winter Solstice, it is nice to know a few of the usual correspondences for the holiday. As with all things Pagan, these can vary from person to person and tradition to tradition, and you are welcome to use whatever feels right to you. However, these are a few of the more common items associated with Yule.

Colors: Red, green, gold, silver, white

Stones: Red and green gemstones such as garnet, ruby, and bloodstone

Incense/oils: Bayberry, cinnamon, pine, frankincense, juniper, myrrh, orange, wintergreen (you can see the Christmas traditions reflected here in the frankincense and myrrh, as well as the fir trees)

Herbs and foods: Cranberries, dried fruit (a traditional gift in countries where fresh fruit was unavailable at this time of year), oranges (also a traditional gift, since fresh fruit—especially those containing vitamin C, was prized in the days before supermarkets), fruitcake, gingerbread and gingerbread men, nuts, roasted meats (especially turkey or game birds such as duck or goose), apples, cookies

Animals: Reindeer, goats, stag, robin, wren, mouse

Symbols and decorations: Bayberry candles (which were originally made from actual bayberries, which have a waxy texture, but now are usually artificially scented and made from regular candle wax), candles and lights of all kinds, holly, mistletoe, wreaths and swags made of evergreens (real, if possible),Yule trees (live evergreen trees like pine or fir, if possible), poinsettia, gifts and ribbons, Yule log, bells, mother and child statues or pictures, pine cones [**Note:** as beautiful as the tradition is, it is unsafe to decorate a tree with real candles; it is better to put the candles separately on some fire-safe surface and use white lights to decorate the Yule tree]

Goddesses: All mother goddesses, including Freya, Gaia, Demeter, Lucina, and Isis (you can also just use a generic Mother Goddess figure)

Gods: All sun gods, including Apollo, Saturn, Cronos, Horus, as well as Janus, the god of beginnings, and father gods like Odin

Traditional customs and rituals: Exchange of gifts, kindling of lights/candles, burning the Yule log, singing, feasting, gathering with family and friends, kissing under mistletoe, decorating the Yule tree, joyous celebration

The Yule Log

The Yule log is a tradition that probably originated in Norway, although at the height of its popularity, variations could be found across Europe. In the beginning, an entire log was brought into the house and burned to bring prosperity and protection to the household throughout the year. These days, we usually use a section of log—oak, pine, or whichever type of tree has magickal meaning to you.

The Yule log can be decorated with pine cones, dried fruit such as cranberries, ribbons, or any other adornments that appeal to you. Then it can be used as a centerpiece on the feast table or altar, and/or burned outside in a bonfire (or inside in a fireplace, if you are lucky enough to have one). Traditionally, the Yule log was created on one Yule, then kept in the house for a year, and burned on the next Yule. Then one was created for the year to come. The new log would be lit off the remains of the old, to carry the magick through to another year.

Blue Moon Circle, my group, did a twist on this tradition one year that we really enjoyed. We gathered together earlier in the year and created our Yule log together. One member chopped a piece out of a tree that had fallen on her property (try to use an already dead and at least partially dried tree for this). The log was about a foot and a half long and almost a foot around, so it was quite hefty.

In ritual space, we took turns carving and drawing symbols on the log, then the original member took the log home with her and cut holes into the log to hold candles—one hole for each member of Blue Moon Circle. Every couple of weeks, when we saw each other at New Moons and Full Moons, the log would be handed off to another member of the coven. Each member would take the log home and let it absorb the positive energy of their household.

In each house, those who lived there would add more drawings, symbols, or written messages to the log, and spend time every day putting their own special energy into it. In the end, the log had traveled to each person's home, and then back again to my house for our Yule celebration.

On Yule, we lit the candles (plain white tapers) and sent out wishes for health, prosperity, and protection for the entire group and our families. We still use that same log every year on our Winter Solstice feast table.

You can start your own Yule log tradition, whether it is with a magickal group, your family, or friends. If you don't want the log to make the rounds, then just integrate decorating the log into your Solstice celebration. You can then burn it in a fire or keep it to add to every year.

Family Celebrations

Family means something different to each of us: for some, it is our actual immediate family (partners and children, and maybe a few other relatives), for others, it may be family-by-choice such as a coven or group of friends. Gatherings with family are usually smaller and more intimate than the larger holiday celebrations and often involve entertainment that is suitable for kids.

One of the most fun and traditional Winter Solstice activities is decorating the house and tree. This can be done in the weeks leading up to the holiday or during a party, with everyone working together. Easy decorations that kids can help make include stringing cranberries and/or popcorn, making a chain by gluing together loops of colorful paper, crafting a wreath from evergreen boughs, or buying a premade wreath and adorning it with ribbons, acorns, pine cones, dried flowers, cinnamon sticks, or anything else that appeals to you. Larger pine cones can be painted with seasonal colors and hung from pretty ribbons, or made into "gifts" for the birds and squirrels by rolling them in peanut butter and seeds, then hanging them outside.

Handmade cards can be created with colored paper, glue, glitter, crayons, and a bit of imagination, or the family can decorate a Yule log as described above. Older children can write a short play depicting the battle between the Holly King and the Oak King and perform it for family and guests. A child, with help and adult guidance, can light a candle that will burn through the rest of the evening. And, of course, small gifts can be exchanged.

If you want to help take the meaning of the holiday beyond the home, children (and adults) can be encouraged to decorate a small tree with gifts for the needy, which can be taken to a local shelter, food pantry, or Salvation Army the next day. A prayer of gratitude can be said in thanks for all the bounty of the year behind you, as well as thanks for the returning light.

A Spiritual Approach

We've talked mostly about ways to celebrate the holiday with joy and merriment, but there are deeper spiritual approaches that can be used instead, or integrated into a larger extended celebration. Blue Moon Circle often likes to start with serious ritual, and then move on to the fun and the frivolous!

Here are a few of the spiritual and magickal themes that we focus on at the Winter Solstice, any or all of which can become part of whatever ritual you do, whether it is solitary or with others.

Celebration of home and hearth: When the cold and dark times come, we appreciate warmth, shelter, and safety even more than usual. Our ancestors knew that a roof over their heads and abundant food stored away in the pantry could be the difference between life and death. Things may not be quite so dire for us, but these days, we still give thanks for security and home, and do protection work to ensure that they continue to be there for us.

Gathering with friends and family: More so than any other holiday, Yule is a festival that recognizes the importance of coming together with those you love. That is why even the most non-spiritual party still has an element of the sacred to at this time of year.

The return of the light: This is the prevailing theme of the Winter Solstice in cultures across the planet. The return of the Sun, the light within the darkness, and the rebirth of hope are all the focus of ancient ceremonies that took place on this night. Be sure to light a candle (as long as it is safe to do so), and whisper a prayer to welcome back the Sun as it grows stronger every day.

Honoring mother and child: Whether you celebrate the Mother goddess and the infant Sun god or Mary and the baby Jesus, this is a holiday that is sacred to mothers and children. If you know a new mother, be sure to treat her with extra care and honor on this of all nights.

Peace for all: Despite its raucous nature, at the core of this holiday filled with loud festivities is a sense of quiet, mystery, and peace. Take a moment from whatever it is you are doing to look at the night sky, taking in the peace of the long dark night and sending out a prayer for peace across the world. Just think how powerful it would be if everyone did that, all at once, on the same evening.

❧

Whether you observe the Winter Solstice alone under a starlit sky or with a hundred of your closest friends, or anything in between, I wish you these gifts for the holiday: may you have joy in your heart, be prosperous and healthy, and share a feast of good food with those that you love. Happy Yule and many bright blessings on the return of the sun.

Cosmic Sway

Daniel Pharr

YULE, THE SHORTEST DAY of the year, midwinter, and the Winter Solstice; all names for a turning point in global energies. This is the day when we turn toward the light, when we leave darkness behind, and every day experience longer and longer days. And, most special of all, this particular solstice, the Yule of 2012, according to many, marks the end of existence as we know it. According to the ancient Mayans, the world will end this day. If this Yule is the end of the world, there is not much point in writing about any days past Yule, but on the outside chance the end of the world is more of a metaphor, Christmas Eve and Christmas are also examined.

The season begins with the New Moon on December 13, followed a week later by Yule arriving on December 21, Christmas Eve and Christmas, and the Full Moon on December 28. Considering that Yule is a solar holiday, the Druids would have celebrated Yule on Yule, rather than moving the celebration to the New or Full Moon.

The New Moon in Sagittarius broadens the vision or perspective of future plans. Thoughts and actions may seem impulsive, but fit well into long-term plans when looked upon with a wide view. New opportunities abound, but look upon these with the power of intuition brought on by the Moon in the Third House rather than any bias that might be held. Communication will be key in any new venture or adventure, and the Sun and Mercury in the Third House will help with communication on a wide variety of topics. Philosophical discussions on religion and a new worldview may occupy a considerable amount of time. Mercury in Sagittarius will help to expand the already expansive worldview.

Yule officially arrives at 6:12 am EST on December 21, and it will bring in energy for taking the next step, from vision and communication to movement and action. The waxing first quarter Moon is about growing from new beginnings. Actions will get results when leading rather than pushing. The waxing Moon in Aries brings a strong desire for action and offers strength as a tool for achievement. Not only will strength come from the action and aggressiveness associated with fire, but also the strength of solidity that comes from the earthy energy of the Sun and Mars in Capricorn. The Moon is in the Tenth House, which may allow the world to recognize the achievements that result from action. The Moon trine Mercury will provide openness, allowing feelings and thoughts to be freely expressed. This easy expression releases the charmer within. Beware of losing the charm through vigorous debate about religious matters, as Mercury in Sagittarius will make religious debate seem joyful at first, but a price will be paid.

End of the World?

Yule 2012 is supposedly the end of the world as we know it. On the outside chance that this prediction is literal and not a metaphor, and on the same chance that the prophecy comes to pass, stay the night with whom you would prefer to spend this life and the next. If it goes badly, people who love each other will be together, if not, there will have been a great party. Yule is the high holiday that lasted all night. The Celts, like other societies, lit the fires and partied through the night, waiting for the first glimmer of the sun. Whether it was the first rays of the sun lighting a burial chamber in the rear of Newgrange or illuminating a stone orb at Machu Picchu, generations of people have been waiting and watching for the first ray of sun for thousands of years. Following in the footsteps of many tribes that came before, build a fire and collect enough extra wood to keep it burning all night.

Decorate the ritual circle, room, or area with a tree, boughs of holly, and objects resembling fruits, nuts, and berries to symbolize the coming bounty of summer. Make wreaths from cut flexible branches or tree trimmings by winding them around each other and in a circle. Hang mistletoe in conspicuous places. Sacred to the Druids, mistletoe was believed to heal all maladies, and kissing under the mistletoe, under the powerful berries, meant love and marriage were in the future. Use what remains of last year's Yule log to light this year's Yule fire. Select a log large enough to not fully burn through the night, so as to leave a piece for next year. Decorate this year's Yule log with holly, ivy, or fir boughs, lay upon the log the appropriate prayers or ritual asking for the return of the Sun and the warm days, and place the log in the fire built with last year's Yule log. Cast the circle, call the gods and goddesses, and light the fire. In the morning, collect the remaining piece of Yule log for next year, and collect the ashes from the fire for amulets.

As the Moon Waxes

The waxing Moon on Christmas Eve is in Taurus and will be a wonderful time for family, in part because of Taurean influence of stability and in part because of the Moon in the Eleventh House which is about safety and nurturing and emotional attachment. A family celebration of Christmas will be best had this day, Christmas Eve, while everyone is feeling the positive familial influences. Bolster the sense of family, and learn a lesson by serving the family's needs. Enjoy the family while joy is to be had, because the situation will change tomorrow.

The waxing Christmas Moon is in Gemini. The Gemini Moon's influence will be toward the talkative side, and more so about all subject matter, while less in depth about any particular subject. The Moon in Gemini adds a desire for intellectual stimulation, but this intellectual desire includes critique and does not support amicability in relationships. The Moon in the Third House will add a strong intuitive ability to the enhanced need for intellectual stimulation, but expressing the feelings gained from the sight will not be received well by others. Use the information for your own benefit.

Gemini in opposition to Venus brings individual needs into conflict with the needs of others. Giving in a relationship is the only chance at finding balance, but the Moon square Chiron and the Capricorn Sun will enhance self-serving. The Moon square Neptune influences emotional states to the negative, causing depression, and the Moon trine Mars offers aggressive behavior. Under the influence of Mars in Capricorn, people want to be dominant in groups, and Mars in the Tenth House will push those same people to fight to be top dog. Celebrate Christmas on Christmas Eve.

Full Moon in Cancer

The Full Moon on December 28 will be in Cancer. During this Moon, emotions and sensitivity will be at their peak, a time for nurturing and self-nurturing. This Full Moon is all about relationships. Intuition and empathy are strong right now. The Moon trine Chiron is like the patron saint of healers and gives the inclination to accept the negativity and pain that sometimes surfaces in life. The nature of this Moon coupled with Mars in Aquarius brings people to the aid and defense of other people and justified causes.

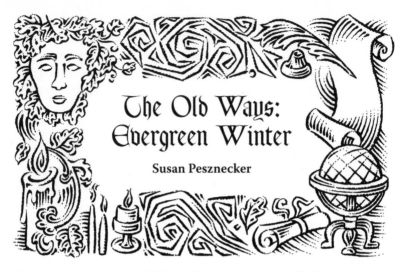

The Old Ways: Evergreen Winter

Susan Pesznecker

Second only to the Winter Solstice symbol of light comes the tradition of winter greenery. It has long been traditional to bring evergreens into the home at winter around the solstice. Because evergreens remain green year-round, the ancients regarded them as symbols of immortality, rebirth, and resurrection cast against barren winter. The wreaths and garlands we hang during winter harken back to these ancient beliefs.

In the legend of the evergreens, a tale is told of a small bird that breaks its wing while trying to fly south for the winter. The bird asks the deciduous trees to allow her to overwinter among their branches, but the trees are unkind. The birch tree is afraid of having its beauty spoiled, while the oak tree worries the bird will eat all of its acorns. Even the willow tree refuses to aid the small stranger.

The mighty spruce tree sees the small bird struggling and offers it a thick, warm branch for overwintering. A neighboring pine offers to shield the bird and the spruce from winter's north winds, and a juniper tree offers its berries for food. The Frost King is so impressed by the evergreen's generosity that he instructs the North Wind to leave the trees alone through the winter. The bird thus comes through the winter safely, and the evergreens are spared winter's effects without losing a single needle. In payment for their kindness, the spruce, pine, and juniper remain forever green and immune to winter's severity. The bird lives happily ever after. And the deciduous trees? Because of their selfishness, they lose their leaves every autumn and must suffer, naked, through the freezing winter.

Let's take a look at some beloved winter evergreens.

Holly and Ivy

Holly and ivy are known for protection and luck. The holly is considered to have a male correspondence—considered by Celts to be the "King of Winter"—while ivy corresponds with the female life force. Ivy is one of the last plants to bloom in the autumn, providing food for bees and insects into early winter. Together, holly and ivy are spoken of as the "Holly King and the Ivy Queen."

Holly is magically prized for decorating doors, windows, and fireplaces because of its prickliness, allowing it to either ward off or snag and capture evil spirits before they enter and harm a household—sort of like flypaper for faeries! Ivy dispels the evil eye, especially when woven into a wreath and hung over an entry.

The Yule Tree

Matthews notes the first written mention of Christmas trees in the writings of a German citizen: "At Christmas, they set up fir trees in the parlors of Strasbourg and hang thereon roses cut out of many colored paper, apples, wafers, gold-foil, sweets ... ."

But tree-decorating traditions weren't limited to the Germans. Greek farmers brought their landholders Christmas *rhamnas*, poles festooned with wreaths of myrtle, rosemary, olive, and bay and decorated with flowers and metallic papers. In Circassia, a young pear tree was laden with candles, topped with a cheese, and carried door to door throughout the solstice night for luck and good tidings.

In eighteenth century England and Germany, the traditional Yule tree was often replaced with a wood and dowel pyramid, decorated with ribbons, papers, candles, and evergreen boughs, with the spaces stuffed with fruit and nuts. The pyramid was carried throughout the home before being placed in the main parlor as a holiday focus. The triangular shape of the pyramid was a potent solar symbol, referencing the Winter Solstice and the return of sun and light to the world.

The tradition of bringing in and decorating a Yule tree endures. Cutting a tree for the holidays echoes the traditions of death and sacrifice that abound at Yule. It also makes us happy to have trees close by: studies show that being around trees creates feelings of relaxation and well-being. Those who eschew cutting a living tree could temporarily bring a living tree into the home during the holiday period.

Mistletoe

Some varieties of mistletoe are poisonous and parasitic, yet lore suggests it was sacred to the Druids. Mistletoe often grows in roundish bundles in oak trees. Legend says that Druids used golden sickles to cut mistletoe, ideally on the sixth night of the Full Moon before either solstice. Bolts of white linen were laid under the trees to catch the falling mistletoe; if the mistletoe was to touch the ground, the plant's sacred energy might pour back into the earth.

Believed to be a magickal aphrodisiac, bunches of mistletoe are still hung over doorways to bring luck and fertility. Mistletoe collected on Samhain is thought to confer protection and bring luck.

The Fir Tree

Fir trees are native to the Northern Hemisphere and are popular for their rich, resinous fragrance. The fir is one of the nine sacred woods and has masculine energy. Linked to Pan, Diana, Artemis, and Frigg, it's also sacred to dwarves, elves, faeries, and the forest devas. The tree attracts prosperity and offers magickal protection.

The fir was tragically commemorated in Hans Christian Anderson's tale, "The Fir Tree." In this story, a small fir lives in the forest but wishes to become a Christmas tree. One day, he's cut down and taken into the city, where he's erected in a Victorian parlor and becomes a splendid Christmas tree. He glories in the life, in the brilliant colors, trappings, and the warm candles that light up his branches. But then Christmas ends. He's hauled outside unceremoniously and his branches chopped off, after which he is burned away to nothing. The story ends, "Now all was past; the tree's life was past, and the story also, for all stories must come to an end at last." Interestingly, many pine species only release seeds when exposed to forest fires, perhaps giving hope that the above tree's ancestors are alive and thriving.

The Pine

The pine—with more than a hundred species worldwide—has a masculine correspondence and is sacred to Dionysus, Aphrodite, Venus, and Sylvanus, among others. Pine cones symbolize fertility and are often mounted atop phallic staffs. The ancient Romans would cut down a pine the night before Saturnalia, setting it up in the temple and decorating it as a celebration of joy and fertility.

Pine needles are burned for cleansing and purification. Boughs cut from the tree offer protection and prosperity to home and hearth, and pine is one of the world's most important timber trees. Put all of this together, and it's easy to see what a bountiful Yule a thick, gorgeous pine would provide.

The Spruce

The spruce's dense, symmetrical shape makes it a favorite Yule tree. This tree has feminine correspondence and is sacred to Cerridwen, Danu, and Poseidon. Like other evergreens, the fir brings prosperity and protection. To tell a spruce from a fir, remember, "Fir is friendly; Spruce is not." Fir boughs are soft to the touch, while spruce boughs have tiny points that are rough when stroked.

*

The evergreens of winter: a gift that keeps on giving.

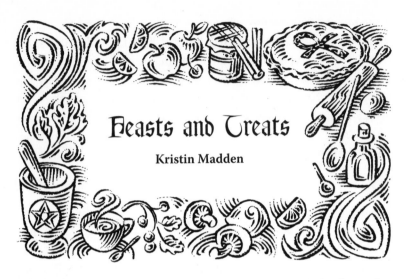

Feasts and Treats

Kristin Madden

ON THIS LONGEST NIGHT of the year, our ancestors joined together to celebrate bonds of community and the returning light. The recipes for this sabbat honor the traditional and the playful, focusing on dishes that both delight and sustain. They are quick to make or easy to prepare ahead of time, allowing for some much-needed downtime amidst the holiday stress.

Winter Pie

This versatile dish is something our ancestors might have made for the longest night, coming together with their communities to share in the best of the stored meats and root vegetables. It is easily adapted for vegetarians and should reflect your personal tastes.

Prep Time: 30 minutes
Cooking Time: 60 minutes
Serves: 6–8

5 medium potatoes, quartered
2½ tablespoons butter (divided)
½ cup cream
2 tablespoons olive oil

2 medium onions, chopped
2 pounds ground lamb, beef, or turkey
2 tomatoes, chopped
1 cup beef stock
½ teaspoon thyme, dried
¼ teaspoon sage, dried
1 tablespoon parsley, dried
Salt and pepper to taste

Quarter the potatoes and boil until tender. Drain. Add 1 tablespoon butter and the cream. Mash and set aside.

In a large frying pan, sauté onions in oil until translucent. Add the meat and brown. Add tomatoes, beef stock, and spices and cook on medium heat for 3 minutes.

Butter the bottom and sides of a casserole dish. Spread the frying pan ingredients on the bottom of the casserole dish. Top with mashed potatoes. Top with slices of the remaining butter. Bake at 350 degrees F for 40 minutes.

Winter Salad with Cranberry Vinaigrette

Combining traditional cranberry flavors with fresh, delicious ingredients from around the world, this is a light and healthy addition to your Yule celebrations.

Prep Time: 10 minutes
Cook time: 20 minutes
Chill time: 1 hour
Serves: 6–8

1 head red-tip leaf lettuce, chopped
½ cup arugula, chopped
1 carrot, sliced
4 radishes, sliced
½ head broccoli, chopped
½ cup feta or bleu cheese, crumbled
½ cup toasted walnuts

Dressing

½ cup red wine vinegar
¼ cup cranberries
¼ cup olive oil
Sea salt and pepper to taste

Cook vinegar and cranberries over medium heat in a saucepan until cranberries are soft. Add olive oil, salt, and pepper, and cook until warm. In blender, mix on medium until smooth. Refrigerate for at least 1 hour.

Combine lettuce, arugula, vegetables, and cheese in large bowl. Coat with dressing, top with walnuts, and serve.

Chocolate-Mint Milkshakes

These milkshakes are like delicious holiday gifts in a cup. Add a shot of peppermint liqueur and leave one of these out to help keep Santa warm as he (or she) travels the skies this night.

Prep Time: 5 minutes
Serves: 4

6 scoops vanilla ice cream, softened
¼ cup cream
½ cup chocolate syrup
1–2 drops peppermint syrup
Optional: chocolate chips or mint leaf

Combine all ingredients in blender and process until smooth. Serve in tall glasses and garnish with chocolate chips or mint leaf.

Holiday Fortune Cookies

You will be the hit of the party when you serve these edible presents. Take a little extra time to prepare heartfelt blessings for your guests or personalize the fortunes for your loved ones.

Prep Time: 15 minutes
Cooking Time: 5 minutes
Serves: 6–8

8 pieces of paper, 3–4 inches long by ½ inch wide
2 large egg whites
½ teaspoon almond extract
½ teaspoon lemon extract
4 tablespoons melted butter
8 tablespoons flour
¼ teaspoon salt
8 tablespoons sugar

Write the fortunes on the pieces of paper with a pencil or ballpoint pen.

Mix egg whites with almond and lemon extracts until foamy. Whisk in melted butter, flour, salt, and sugar.

Cover a cold baking sheet with parchment paper that has been sprayed with olive oil. For each cookie, spoon 1 tablespoon of batter onto sheet and spread into a thin circle. Bake at 400 degrees F for 5 minutes, until outer ½ inch of cookie is golden.

Place each cookie on a wooden board. Place the fortune in the center and fold cookie in half. While still very warm, pull folded corners toward each other and form into a "fortune cookie" shape. You have only about 15 to 20 seconds to complete this last step before the cookie is too hard to work with. Let cool in muffin pan until firm to retain shape.

Crafty Crafts

Linda Raedisch

IN THE GERMANIC WORLD, red and white are the traditional Christmas colors. *Stollen*, a sweet German fruit bread baked at this time of year, is always wrapped in white paper tied with a red ribbon. On Advent calendars, you can see little gnomes delivering white parcels sealed with red wax and dropping most of them in the snow! When I was growing up, we celebrated Advent at home with white candles in a red wooden candleholder. To this day, my mother would not dream of putting green, pink, or purple candles in it.

White, obviously, stands for snow. The red doesn't just stand for blood, it *was* blood. Yule came on the heels of the autumn slaughter. The slaying of the farm's fattest pig provided not just sausages, soap, and candles for the year, but also blood for mixing with cow's milk and making paint. That's why barns, as well as the traditional Swedish house, are red. Here in America, restorers of Colonial period furniture will tell you that this primitive paint is very hard to strip off.

Short of killing a pig, here are some ideas for bringing this ancient red and white aesthetic into your home at Yule. In addition to white candles and red apples, the Danes deck their sparse firs with strings of Danish flags: a white cross on a red field. I'm not wild about nationalistic trees, but you could use red and white bakery string to hang all your ornaments this year.

In Germany, another strikingly Pagan Christmas symbol is the red and white fly agaric mushroom. This mushroom has many German pet names, including "lucky mushroom," "little man on one foot," and "raven's bread." Yule is the season of the Wild Hunt, when Odin and his company of slain warriors are on the move through the skeletal winter forest. The fly agaric, it was said, was formed when the foam from Odin's eight-legged horse, Sleipnir, fell to the ground. The mushrooms were, perhaps, snacks for Odin's ravens Hugin and Munin.

You can buy delicate blown-glass versions of these lucky mushrooms to hang on your tree. I have also seen tiny ones made of papier-mâché for tying on packages, though these are harder to find. To make edible "fly agaric" for your Yule board, buy some small tomatoes and some fresh (not canned) whole white mushrooms at the grocery store. At home, cut the caps off the mushrooms and set aside for your favorite stuffed mushroom recipe. Cut the tomatoes in half widthwise with a sharp knife and set the bottoms on top of the mushroom stalks. Just before serving, dab the tomato skins with bits of cold butter.

Blazing Year Wheel

No one can be 100 percent certain what the term "Yule" originally meant. One prevalent theory is that it came from an old Germanic word, *hjul* or *hweol*, meaning "wheel." This makes a lot of sense to Wiccans whose calendar is the Wheel of the Year.

Like the term Yule itself, this craft is open to the interpretation of the user. The overall form can be seen as a Sun symbol or a Wodan's Cross. Celtic Witches might light the four candles in token of the four Celtic fire festivals—Samhain, Imbolc, Beltane, and Lughnasadh. On the other hand, Saxon Pagans might want to light the candles in honor of Eostre, Midsummer, Harvest Home, and Modranicht, leaving the sticks to represent the crossquarter days.

And then again, this centerpiece could be enjoyed as the Pagan answer to both the Advent wreath and the Chanukah Menorah. Light one candle each week starting three weeks before the Winter Solstice so that all four are burning on December 21. Continue to burn and replace the lights throughout Yule.

Tools and Materials

Bottom of one 11-centimeter box of soft cheese wedges, such as The Laughing Cow. (You can use the lid of the box for your Humble Henna Lamp at Imbolc.)

Pencil

Hole punch
4 dowels about 6 inches long and ¼ inch in diameter, or straight
    twigs of similar proportions
Acrylic paint
Paint brush
2–4 feet gold star wire garland, available at craft stores, usually in
    20 ft. lengths
4 white tealights

With a pencil, mark four equidistant points, i.e., the points of a
cross, on the rim of your box bottom. Punch holes at these points,
making one pair of opposite holes a little higher on the rim than the
other so that when the dowels are inserted they can rest one above
the other to form the cross.

Paint both the inside and the outside of the box bottom—red,
perhaps?

When the paint is dry, insert your dowels or twigs. Wind the star
garland around the box bottom, twisting it around the stick ends as
you go. Place the four white tealights inside the four quadrants.

Solstice Ornament

Once you've painted it, no one will be able to tell what this eight-
rayed star is made out of. For a larger ornament, use a paper towel
tube.

Tools and Materials
1 empty cardboard toilet paper tube
Masking or painter's tape (¾-inch width)
Scissors
Glue
Clothespin
Acrylic paint
Glitter

Wrap a piece of masking tape around the middle or "waist" of your tube. Don't press the tape down too firmly; you'll be peeling it off later. To make the rays of the sun, make eight evenly spaced cuts running from the edge of the tube to—but not through—the masking tape. Do this to both ends of the tube for a total of sixteen cuts, eight at each end, making sure that the cuts on one side of the tape line up with the cuts on the other side of the tape.

When you have finished making your cuts, you can peel off the masking tape. Now bend each strip of cardboard up to meet its "partner" on the other side of the tape. Glue the ends of each pair of strips together, clamping them with a clothespin until the glue is dry.

Paint your sun all over, even in the little nooks and crannies, and accent with glitter. When it's dry, loop a string through one of the holes and hang on the Solstice Tree.

All One Family

Sandra Kynes

THE WINTER SOLSTICE IS a time of joyous transformation as we await the return of the sun/son. This event has been celebrated by most civilizations throughout time; often one adapting from another. Current mainstream observances continue this overlay of customs from many cultures and faiths. As Pagans, we adopt or adapt the relevant ones and create some of our own.

My family's solstice activities include the traditional bringing in of sacred evergreens in the form of a Yule tree. We decorate it with solar and celestial ornaments, fairies, angels, and a host of seasonal treasures that we have collected over the years. The tree is topped by a shining star, a symbol of hope. To us, this star of wonder represents Sirius the Dog Star, one of the brightest in the heavens. In December, it rises in the southeast by mid-evening and arcs across to the southwest, riding low in the sky like the Sun at this time of year.

Each Yule we set up our tree on a Saturday morning and then spend the afternoon decorating it and making ornaments that are special for that year. My son had the idea to make little baskets as decorations that hold small candies and trinkets. He went a step further and suggested that the maker of a basket has to find a special place to nestle it deep within the branches of the tree, and then on Yule we each have to find two baskets that someone else made. The making and finding of these has become one of the highlights of our celebration.

A custom from the early 1800s involves hanging fruit and nuts on the tree, which represents abundance for the household in the coming year. We combine this with a nod to the tradition of wassailing by tying a few apples to the tree with bright, red ribbons. For a decorative garland, we make a couple of long strands with alternating cranberries and popcorn to echo the red and white berries of holly and mistletoe, which symbolize fertility and abundance as well as the Goddess and God.

After the popcorn and cranberry strands are wound around the tree, the baskets hidden amongst the branches, and all the other decorations in place, we return to the kitchen table. The last ornaments that we make are personal magic-wish charms. These can be created from magazine pictures, knick-knacks or practically anything small that represents something we want to manifest in our lives. Over the years these have ranged from pets and bicycles to travel (represented by a tiny airplane) and even a new home. Making these involves forethought and planning in order to gather the things needed to create the ornaments. When they are finished, we stand in our places, join hands across the table and say:

> *Dark days, soon are done, golden solstice, bring the sun.*
> *These our wishes we decree, thank you Goddess. Blessed be.*

Before placing them on the tree, we hold them with both hands, close our eyes, and visualize our wishes.

❧

Most of our sabbat celebrations include time outdoors so we can see, feel, and keep forever in our hearts a strong connection with the natural world. Either on the solstice or a few days before, we go for a walk around the neighborhood. December in coastal Maine is a slightly betwixt time, when nature is at an in-between stage of being clothed in foliage and blanketed by snow. The artist Andrew

Wyeth said that this is the time of year when you can "feel the bone structure of the landscape," and this is the focus of our walk. This focus is well illustrated in our garden under the walnut tree where from spring through autumn it's dressed with the greenery of day lilies, violets, and other plants. But in December, we can see the large protruding tree roots that contour the garden with small terraces. On our walk, we look at trees and admire the intricate structure of branches that give shape to their summer finery of leaves. On the ground, there are many more visual treasures awaiting discovery, which children are quick to spot in this hide-and-seek with nature. Usually recessed behind or beneath plants, rocks are revealed as the solid underpinnings in many gardens. Little sculptures, inuksuks (balanced, stacked stones), and other objects also emerge from their hiding places.

Yule is traditionally a time for song and dance and more outdoor activity. Originally, Christmas carols had no religious significance and were accompanied by a circle dance. On the night before the solstice, another Pagan family joins us for an evening of caroling. Many popular songs such as "Deck the Halls" are well suited for us, while others need a little tweaking. For example in "Here We Come A-Wassailing" we change "God bless" to "Goddess bless." We also use lyrics from the Winter Solstice CDs of the group Olympia's Daughters and sing "Good rest ye merry gentlefolk" and other carols. Children most enjoy the secular songs about Rudolph, Frosty, and, of course, Jingle Bells.

Before heading out into the neighborhood, we gather in the backyard, join hands, and enjoy the traditional circle dance to warm up our voices and our bodies. When the energy level seems right, we end the dance and distribute lyric sheets. Also in keeping with Yule traditions, we carry small boughs of evergreen, which carolers of old used as magical objects with which to bless the houses they visited. For children, the evergreen boughs add a touch of pageantry that makes the outing more interesting and fun. When we arrive at each residence, they lead us in touching the branches to

the house and saying: "Blessed be all within." We then start singing, which draws people to their front doors. The exchange of good
wishes afterward is a mixture of "Happy Solstice," "Merry Christmas" and "Happy Yule." We keep the caroling to about an hour to
give us plenty of time to return home and enjoy hot cocoa or mulled
cider before the youngest ones get too tired.

On solstice night our celebration begins by observing the sunset
in hopes of seeing the belt of Venus. This phenomenon appears as
a pinkish glow just above the dark shadow of the horizon. It can
be seen briefly before the sky melts into darker blues. The magical
thing about watching the belt of Venus is that a purplish haze seems
to envelop everything. When my son was small he loved to hear me
tell him that this was the Goddess tucking us in on the longest night
of the year so we would have sweet dreams.

Before our sabbat meal, we gather around the Yule tree to find
the little basket ornaments that we made and hid deep within the
branches. These then become additional decorations on the dining table. After dinner we return to the living room and sit on the
floor near the tree to exchange other gifts. When the presents are
opened and the oohing and aahing quiets down, we talk about the
special magic-wish ornaments we made and the thing we are wishing for most in the year ahead. Although something like a bicycle
may seem simple and straightforward, getting children to verbalize
why they really want something gets them to think about it. Want-
ing things for fun is okay, too, but this activity works for all of us;
not to just raise awareness about consumerism, but to be mindful of
what we bring into our lives.

When the calendar year comes to an end, we take down the Yule
tree and save a few of greens to burn at Imbolc. Linking our family sabbats helps us connect with the cycles in nature as well as the
greater spiral paths of our lives.

Ritual: Welcome Back the Light

Deborah Blake

Note: I recommend reading the entire ritual through before starting. It will go much more smoothly if you know exactly what to expect at each section of the rite.

When: It is best to do this ritual at dusk or full dark.

Who: This ritual is designed to be used by either a group or a solitary Witch. I have written it out to include the "welcome and explanation" speech that would customarily be given by the High Priest and/or High Priestess leading the ritual. Solitaries can leave that part out, or read it aloud to themselves if they so desire. All "group" instructions will be printed in bold, so that solitaries can spot them easily and skip over them. As necessary, substitute the word "we" for "I." If doing a group ritual, the quarter calls would usually be read by various group members, and the High Priestess and High Priest would invoke the gods and cast the circle.

Items Needed

Goddess and god candles (white or silver for the goddess and yellow or gold for the god)

Quarter candles (red, yellow, blue, green—or whatever colors you usually use)

White taper or votive candle (one per person taking part) in fire-
safe container(s)—if you don't have enough candleholders, you
can use small glass jars or even empty tin cans you have decorated for the holiday

Large white candle

Optional: bell (a string of sleigh bells or a hand bell)

Sage smudge stick (you can substitute the cleansing incense of your
choice)

Salt and water in separate containers and a small bowl to mix them

Chalice (this can be filled with wine or cider—use cider if there will
be children or anyone with alcohol issues present)

Cakes—decorated sugar cookies or cookies shaped like suns are
nice, but you could also use a loaf of fresh bread or gingerbread

Table to use as altar and a cloth to cover it

Matches or lighter/snuffer to put out candles as the end of the ritual
(if you have one)

Before Starting: Turn off as many lights as you can, leaving the
room in darkness or semi-darkness. Decorate your altar with seasonal items such as evergreens, pine cones, green, red, gold, and silver ribbons, mistletoe, and bells. Place the goddess and god candles
on the altar along with the quarter candles, unless you will be placing them around the room.

If doing this as a group, you may wish to process in from another room. Otherwise, gather in a circle and stand quietly.

Welcoming the Light

Cleanse yourself and your sacred space with the sage smudge stick.
As the smoke wafts over you and around the circle space, visualize
a glowing golden light washing away all negativity, and surrounding
you with clarity and serenity. **Pass the smudge stick around the
circle.** Take a few slow, deep breaths to help you ground and center.

Mix your salt and water together in a small bowl. If you want,
you can say aloud:

Salt into water, water into salt. Wash away all negativity, leaving only the positive and beneficial.

Anoint yourself at forehead, lips, heart and center, then sprinkle the salt and water mixture around the outline of your circle.

Cast the circle by walking around the perimeter deosil (clockwise) with an athame or your finger pointed at the ground, while saying:

*I cast the circle round and round, from earth to sky, from sky to ground. I conjure now this sacred place, outside time, and outside space. The circle is cast, I am (**we are**) between the worlds.*

Visualize the inside of the circle filled with light.

Invoke the Quarters

Invoke the four quarters by standing to face each direction (starting with the east), then lighting the appropriate candle after you have called that quarter.

East (yellow candle): I look to the east and invoke the power of air—cold breezes which chill the body, yet blow away the cobwebs of the year behind me (**us**). With the coming of the light, may you bring me (**us**) clarity and creativity. [*Light candle*]

South (red candle): I look to the south and invoke the power of fire—the warmth of hearth and home which shelters me (**us**) from the winter cold outside. With the coming of the light, may you bring me (**us**) passion to warm my life (**our lives**) in the seasons ahead. [*Light candle*]

West (blue candle): I look to the west and invoke the power of water—perfect crystals of water frozen into snow, each one different from the rest. With the coming of the light may you help me (**us**) to become more comfortable with my own (**our own**) individuality. [*Light candle*]

North (green candle): I turn to the north and invoke the power of earth—frozen beneath me (**us**) now, yet hiding still unseen the first small stirrings of life, readying itself for the warmth ahead. With the coming of the light, may you help me (**us**) give birth to the seeds of new beginnings that lie within me (**us**). [*Light candle*]

Invoke Goddess: Great goddess, I (**we**) honor you on this night as Mother, as you bring your child, the Sun, back into the world to share with us the gift of hope and light. Welcome and blessed be. [*Light candle.*]

Invoke God: Great Sun god, powerful and bright, join me (**us**) now as you begin your reign as the Oak King, and light my (**our**) path into the longer days to come. Welcome and blessed be. [*Light candle*]

[**Solitary** *or* **High Priest/ess** *lights the large white candle, saying:*] I (**We**) welcome back the light! Welcome and blessed be!

Welcome speech for group ritual, spoken by High Priest or High Priestess: It is the Winter Solstice, the longest night of the year. And yet, in the midst of the dark and the cold, we have hope. Because on this day, also known as Yule, we celebrate the rebirth of the Sun, born as the infant child of the Goddess, she who is mother of us all. We gather together and raise our voices in joyous harmony, and together we kindle a light in the darkness. So it has always been and so it will always be. Our ancestors, and those of many cultures across the world, observed this day with a special reverence, knowing that it marked the beginning of the slow return of the light. Yes, even as we plunge into winter, we look ahead to spring, knowing that the Wheel of the Year will turn and bring us back to warmth and sunlight. Until that time comes, we will create our own warmth and light—the warmth of love and the light of friendship—and find solace in our faith and in our community, even as our ancestors did.

All chant: The earth, the air, the fire, the water, return, return, return, return. (Repeat).

[*Note: The chant can be done whether solitary or in a group, and you can substitute any other chant you prefer. If you aren't familiar*

with this one, you can find a very nice example sung on YouTube
if you look under Pagan/Wiccan—Earth Air Fire Water Elemental
Chant or you can chant it without a melody.] **If doing as a group,
you may want to hold hands and sway or clap your hands. Repeat the chant until energy has built up in the circle, about five
minutes.**

[*Spoken by High Priestess/High Priest or out loud by solitary:*] It
is customary at Yule to give and receive gifts, but the most valuable
gifts cannot be wrapped and tied with ribbon, or purchased at the
local store. These are the gifts of the Winter Solstice, and I **(we)** will
light a candle **(one by one)** and speak of the true gifts of the holiday.

Light smaller candle(s) and say aloud the gifts you would wish
to give yourself, friend, **family,** and the world. These may include
health, happiness, prosperity, joy, peace, gratitude, understanding,
healing, etc. **If doing as a group, each person will take a turn
lighting a candle and speaking aloud.**

Moment of silence. Take as long as you want to gaze at the light
and feel the peace of the ritual washing over you.

Cakes and Ale

[*Hold "cakes" up to the sky and say:*] I **(we)** give thanks for the blessing of the harvest, and for the gift of food for me **(our)** table. [*Eat a
bit of cakes. Hold "ale" up to the sky and say:*] May the year to come
be as sweet as the drink in this cup. [*Drink, and pour a libation on
the ground for the gods, if outside.*]

Pass Speaking Stick if holding a group ritual.

Dismiss the quarters

Starting with North, turn toward each direction and snuffing out
the candle after saying thank you.

North: Powers of earth, I **(we)** thank you for being here today
and protecting my **(our)** circle. Stay if you will, go if you must, in
perfect love and perfect trust. So mote it be.

West: Powers of water, I (**we**) thank you for being here today and protecting my (**our**) circle. Stay if you will, go if you must, in perfect love and perfect trust. So mote it be.

South: Powers of fire, I (**we**) thank you for being here today and protecting my (**our**) circle. Stay if you will, go if you must, in perfect love and perfect trust. So mote it be.

East: Powers of the air, I (**we**) thank you for being here today and protecting my (**our**) circle. Stay if you will, go if you must, in perfect love and perfect trust. So mote it be.

Thank the god and goddess for their help by lifting your hands in the air and then snuffing out each candle after speaking.

*Great Mother Goddess, I (**we**) thank you for your presence here in this circle today, and always. May you guide me (**us**) through the long, dark nights ahead. Farewell, and blessed be.*

*Great Sun God, I (**we**) thank you for your presence here in this circle today, and always. May your strength and wisdom help me (**us**) to move forward in a positive and productive way. Farewell, and blessed be.*

Open the circle by walking widdershins (counterclockwise) around the circle or simply visualize the sacred space opening up and returning to the mundane world. **For a group ritual, you can all join hands and recite the Wiccan Rede, or simply say: "The circle is open, but never broken. Merry meet, merry part, and merry meet again!" Let go of each other's hands, and the circle is open.**

Notes

Notes

Imbolc

Imbolc:
Femininity & Fertility

Dallas Jennifer Cobb

IMBOLC, HALFWAY BETWEEN YULE and Ostara, Winter Solstice and Vernal Equinox, is celebrated on February 2. The third sabbat, Imbolc translates to mean "in the belly," symbolic of the seed planted in the womb of the Goddess at solstice, now growing and quickening, that she may bring forth a new son, a new year.

Imbolc is also known as Imbolg or Oimelc in the Gaelic; Brighid, Brigid's Day, and the Feast of Brigid; Bride and the Feast of Waxing Light. Catholics call it Candlemas, or St. Brigid's Day, and Groundhog Day is celebrated on Imbolc.

Brighid, the Celtic goddess of fire, crafts, healing, hearth, and home was known as a goddess of fertility and love, midwifery, and mothering. Protector of children and childbirth, she was the patron of blacksmiths, metalcrafts, fire, and tools. Brighid's shrine in Kildare, Ireland, is the ancient site where nineteen priestesses kept a fire burning perpetually in her honor.

Brighid was so loved by the Celts that Christian conquerors chose to deify her as Saint Brigit, because it was easier to assimilate her than to try to stamp out the love displayed for her. Alternately spelled Brighid, Brigid, Brigit, Bridget, and even Bride, it is said that Britain is a name derived from Brighid.

Saint Brigit was called the "foster mother" of Jesus, and the "Purification of the Virgin Mary" was held on this day, forty days after giving birth to Jesus. Saint Brigit was represented by a statue, and Brigit's Cross, a three- or four-armed cross made of rushes or reeds. It traditionally hung over children's beds or over the main door of the home, for protection.

Both goddess and saint are depicted wearing a cloak (symbolically represented by a mantle or altar cloth) and carrying a white wand made of birch or willow. Brigit is also associated with oak because of the traditional Druid's grove at Kildare.

Imbolc comes at the time of year when agrarian communities were running low on food after a long winter. It was both a celebration of making it through the worst of the season and anticipating the spring soon to come. It's a festival of light and fertility, and a time of purification. Traditionally it was a time for initiation ceremonies and self-dedication rituals.

Colors associated with Imbolc are red, white, and green, representing: life force, the hearth fire, and the rising sun; the pristine snow, purity, and milk; and faeries, sprouts, and new beginnings, respectively. Traditional Imbolc foods are those that might remain in a dwindling winter pantry such as nuts, grains, dried meats, and root vegetables, but also the food of new beginnings, like dairy foods derived from lactating livestock.

Animals associated with Imbolc and Brighid include the ewe, cattle, the raven, the serpent, and the white swan. The number nineteen is sacred, representing the nineteen priestesses who tended the perpetual flame in Kildare, and because Brighid is a triple goddess, the number three is also sacred.

Femininity and Fertility

In the desperate cold of winter, Imbolc comes like the sun, casting a bright light on the barren landscape, warming and enlivening people. The traditional fires warm our hearts, our hands, and our minds. We come alive with passion, creativity, and ideas. After several long months spent indoors, huddled close to the hearth in order to survive the cold darkness, we revel in Imbolc celebrations, a time to gather friends together to warm ourselves, affirming life.

While not popular with all Pagans, Imbolc occurs in early February, a time of year when we all need something to celebrate. In many areas, we have come through months of days so short that it is dark when we go to work and dark when we return. Whether it is a fire traditional to Imbolc in which family and friends burn old Christmas trees or a community gathering around the hearth or altar, celebrating Imbolc warms us.

In my family, Imbolc is a time to gather around our big harvest table, to feast, read poetry aloud, celebrate creativity and inspiration through craftmaking, and renew or rededicate ourselves. When I gather ritually with friends, family, and sacred circle mates, Imbolc is a time to purify ourselves, recharge our batteries with laughter and good food, and shape our visions for the coming spring. Indeed, in the darkness of early evening as we light the candles and turn on all the lights in the house, we are already dreaming of the coming spring, of days long with sun, and the ground rich with fertile produce.

Traditionally a women's ceremony associated with the Maiden aspect of the Triple Goddess, represented by Brighid, Imbolc sits on the Wheel of the Year opposite Lughanasadh or Lammas, which is a men's rite celebrating Lugh, the god of light. While I usually organize an Imbolc ritual honoring women, the men in my life and community are always welcome. At this time, and in preparation, I often urge men to contemplate the roles played by women in their lives in order to understand how women nurture and guide them, sustain and heal them; and I ask them to bring this energy to the ritual celebration.

Brighid's sacred day was celebrated with sacred fires, symbolizing inspiration, creativity, conception, birthing, and healing. Throughout Celtic countries, huge fires were lit to symbolically warm the spirit, inspire creativity, fan passion and fertility, and sustain us.

The Goddess

In the cycle of life, the Goddess has now recovered from giving birth to the God at Solstice. She nurtures him as he grows in strength, but he is still young. The God is not yet at full power, so Imbolc is a time to celebrate her femininity and fertility.

The Goddess' return to fertility is a remarkable event—something to be celebrated and prepared for. While fertility portends new life, abundance and continued survival, it also demands good health, great strength, and personal resources to sustain that life. And while the Goddess returns to a state of fertility, creativity, and great potential, she must also still care for her young son, nurturing and loving him. At Imbolc, the Goddess pauses, remembering that while she feeds and cares for her young son, she must also feed herself emotionally and physically so that she has the energy needed to nurture and love all her "children."

Symbolically, Imbolc is a time for purification of self, home, hearth and magical tools, and a time to clean out the old to make space for the new life to come. Imagine the young God graduating from the cradle to the bed, making room for the new baby that will be born. Balancing the care of her young son with the care of herself and the new life within, the Goddess must inventory where she "spends" her love and good energy. It is a practice of purifying her life through the process.

Modern goddesses may realize that they cannot sustain three part-time jobs, two volunteer positions, and endless community involvement in addition to taking care of herself and her family. She might realize that she needs to pull back in some areas of her life in order to focus on what means the most. This sorting helps her to see where, what, and whom she puts her energy into, and simultaneously enables her to see where she is fed, nurtured, and sustained.

Like the goddess Brighid, we must remember periodically to sort through our lives—to take stock of our energy levels, our health, and resources. Like our ancestors who inventoried the limited food remaining in their pantries, we must sort through our resources, getting rid of what is "soft" or "rotten," so that only nurturing and sustaining entities and activities remain.

While many women are taught to care for others before caring for themselves—and mothers are especially encouraged to do and be everything for their children—we must recognize that self-care provides for all that we do, everyone that we take care of, and those we love. Self-care is not selfish; it provides for the community that is intricately linked to us through care. As women, self-care is the fundamental fire that feeds and warms our families. At Imbolc, we must light our own fire within, one that will warm our spirit, inspire creativity, fan passion and fertility, and sustain us.

Our Deepest Needs

If caring for our own deepest needs is the way to ensure the survival of our community, then Imbolc is the ideal time to clarify what we want in our lives emotionally, spiritually, and socially. Beyond the rudimentary concerns of the season for survival, food, and warmth, now is the time to attempt to verbalize, picture, or envision our deeper desires. This clarification of our deepest needs, wants, and desires helps us direct our fertile energy. Like a cat having endless litters of kittens too close together, senseless fertility or creativity can drain and consume us. We must know what we want so we can direct our creative energy (fertility) into areas that will sustain and nurture our communities.

For a quick, personal practice, light a white candle (with three wicks for the Triple Goddess, if you can find one), and invoke Brighid. Envision her as a mother with a young, growing baby, contemplating the seed sewn within her. She stands at the hearth, with babe on one hip and one hand on her belly.

Know her joy and her fears. Speak to her.

Brighid, I am like you, sustaining those around me. My strength is my love and nurture, the fire of my heart, the water of my womb, the rock of my steadfast faith. I have love and strength to sustain my clan, but I worry about balancing all that I do. How can I be all that

I desire, create all that I want, and provide what my family needs?
Brighid, be with me as I sort and purify.

Make a quick list or what is working in your life, where you feel
sustained and nurtured. List the people, activities, and undertakings
you are involved with; list the projects, work, and creativity that you
put your energy into. And on a separate piece of paper quickly list
what is not working. Where do you feel your energy being sucking
out of you with nothing in return? Make the list, and know what
you must let go of.

Now, with lists in hand, it is time to get to work.

Over a large fireproof surface, ritually burn the list of what is not
working. If you made a Brighid's Cross last year, burn it too. As your
list burns, symbolically let go of the old. As the smoke rises up and
the paper turns to ash, whisper what you release. Say it out loud, let
go of the old.

I release you, I set you free. Live if you may, but not by me.
In your mind's eye, see these people, activities, or situations leav-
ing your life.
So mote it be.

Now, welcome the energy of this inspiration. Begin to clarify the
new goals and desires, so that the new may be born. Pull out the list
of what is working, then read it, and affirm these things in your life.
Now, put it away, and think about the new that is yet to come.

Brighid be with me, brighten my desire, let your creative juices
light my internal fires.

Crafting with words, use word-jamming, word association,
or improvising rhyming poems to help you to name your desires.
Trance work, meditation, and vision quests can help us envision
our needs. And crafting with pictures and images through collages,
sketches, and paintings can enable us to see what we really want.

Take time to craft, and reveal to yourself the deepest of desires,
capturing them in a word or image. Then take this energy into your
daily life. Hang your poems or images somewhere you will see them

regularly, and use them to keep the vision alive. Plan your gardens, rearrange your hearth, home, or altar, and be inspired to tend to family, friends, and neighbors in a way fitting to your needs.

In this season of darkness, invoke the light of Brighid within you, to brighten your way as you care for self, family, and community. Be the Goddess' Handmaiden in your community.

Cosmic Sway

Daniel Pharr

IMBOLC IS THE FIRST day of Celtic spring and the last day of winter. Groundhog Day is rooted in this Celtic holiday with the tradition being that if the groundhog does not see his shadow on this day, spring begins immediately. February weather can fluctuate between extremes, from lovely to loathsome, especially in the northeastern part of the United States, where the Groundhog Day tradition was contrived. Spring did not always seem a sure thing in early February. If the groundhog did see his shadow, then six more weeks of winter is said to follow, making the first day of spring March 21. The Groundhog tradition did not exist during the time of the Celts, but the tradition does speak to the unsettled nature of February.

The Full Moon arrives a bit early in the season for Imbolc, on January 26, yet the New Moon arrives a bit late, on February 9. The Celts knew that the span of a season was about forty-five days, and would have calculated Imbolc to arrive on February 2, but probably would have moved the celebration to the dark night of the New Moon. Even setting the date for this Imbolc is unsettled.

The Full Leo Moon shines the evening of January 26. Like the Moon, personalities will shine this evening. Give praise and attention to everyone today. There are many conflicting energies from the astrological phenomena, making this day's efforts best spent on emotional pleasantries and away from decisions, difficulties, and drama. As for the unsettled nature of this early Imbolc, consider the lunar aspects associated with this Full Moon. With the Moon in opposition to the Sun, as occurs every Full Moon, the masculine and feminine can oppose each other when matters of import are at hand. The Moon opposing Mercury brings a struggle between head and heart, although the Moon sextile Jupiter offers kindness and optimism, while the Moon square Saturn breeds discontent and the Moon trine Uranus offers excitement. Venus in Capricorn brings shyness, and Mars in Aquarius promotes unpredictability. Unsettled. The Moon in the Seventh House is all about family, friends, and humanitarian organizations. This is the perfect opportunity to enjoy an Imbolc ritual with family and friends.

Daylight Ritual

This is a daylight ritual for the morning of January 27. Meet the family outdoors in the yard, a park, or, ideally, out in the country. Bring drums and rattles or other celebratory noisemakers. Bring or create a symbol of spring and locate this symbol in an open space. Create your sacred space as is your custom. Begin drumming, or clapping, and moving in a circular fashion; walking, hopping, skipping, dancing around the symbol for spring. After a round or two, and once everyone feels warmed up and ready, begin to chant a little ditty announcing your desire for spring to arrive. Chant at least three times around the symbol, and have fun with it. The more the merrier. Some chants might be, "Melt the snow, melt the snow, all this snow has got to go"; or "Bring the sun, bring the sun, sun and fun for everyone"; or maybe, "Rain, sleet, snow, and ice, warmer days would be real nice." Making up your own chants in the moment will be fun. Afterward, enjoy a warm beverage together.

Evening Tradition

The traditional evening for celebrating Imbolc is February 1, and carrying over to Groundhog Day, February 2. In the tradition, this high holiday is for honoring the goddess Brighid, goddess of fire and childbirth. The Libra Moon will offer peace and tranquility during this time of the goddess and Mars in Pisces will help to clearly delineate spiritual paths. The Moon in the third house promotes intuition, the Moon trine Mercury adds to the ability to communicate thoughts and feelings, and the Moon trine Neptune will increase intuitive sensitivity. This is a great opportunity for divination. Light candles or build a fire, and keep them burning through the New Moon on February 9 to honor Brighid. In the ancient times, a fire was kept burning year-round by the priestesses dedicated to Brighid. After the Catholic Church took over the Brighid's Fire Temple, the nuns continued the tradition of honoring Saint Brigit with an ever-burning fire, even when ordered not to do so by Church leadership. The flame burned for more than one thousand years, until the temple was destroyed. Read the runes.

Astrological Imbolc

The calculated date for Imbolc 2013 is 10:57 am, February 3. This high holiday could promote some drama in the world of relationships, love affairs, sexuality, and adventure. The waning Scorpio Moon is about drama and emotional intensity. The Moon in the Ninth House brings comfort to the adventurer, to the explorer, to the traveler, and to any higher-learning opportunity outside of the comfort zone. The Moon rules the Fifth House and empowers artistic pursuits, joy, creativity, and procreation. The Moon also rules the Sixth House and is about supporting your daily routine and habits, your daily pursuits, and your service to others. The Aquarius Sun enhances originality, innovation, and unpredictability, while the Sun in the Twelfth House releases the sense of boundaries between people. Mercury in Aquarius and in the First House will support all of these activities by increasing the ability to originate ideas, think freely, and communicate the unique and unconventional in a manner that will be understood by the masses. This is a remarkable time to unbridle creativity and let it run free and in any direction that feels right. The Aquarian Venus in the Twelfth House allows the free expression of the self in relationships that exist outside of the norm, the sort of relationships that stretch boundaries and exist in an abandonment of normalcy.

New Moon Ethereal Travel

With the New Moon in Aquarius on February 9, emotions give way to intellect. The Aquarius Moon rules the Ninth House and, as such, promotes higher learning—the sort of philosophical, spiritual, and cultural learning that is best accessed through travel. Traveling might also bring about a new beginning due in part to the Moon conjunct with the Sun. Mercury in Pisces mixes intuition with imagination and in the mix with the Aquarian Moon will be conducive to personal growth through spiritual travel. Catch a flight and visit a shaman, magus, or Druid or Pagan priest. Learn through experience and absorb the energy surrounding such an individual. Allow a mental vision of day-to-day life to be molded by the imaginative injection of magical methodology. Fueled by the fantastic, Mars in Pisces will advance the spiritual seeker further down the path and will help bring the spiritual into the mundane. There should not be a worry of getting so caught up in the world of fantasy that reality vanishes for time, as can happen under the right celestial influences, because Mercury in Pisces will help to separate reality from fantasy. Creativity will be important after such adventures. Mercury in the Fifth House, Venus in the Fourth House, and Mars in the Fifth House, all promote creative expression. Self-expression through a creative outlet strengthens the bond between the self-image and the experience so that over time the experiences are integrated into the self rather than excluded as a "once in a lifetime thing." The ascending Libra brings balance to all beings, and harmony and happiness come from balance.

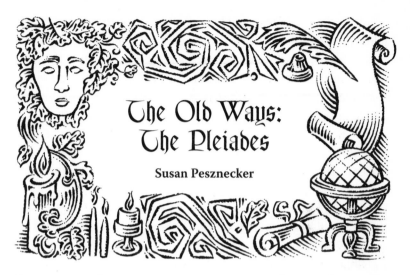

The Old Ways: The Pleiades

Susan Pesznecker

PERHAPS YOU'VE NOTICED A gorgeous star cluster when you've been outdoors on a cold winter night. Perched high overhead in the Taurus constellation, it looks like a blur of bright blue. As your eyes adjust to the dark, individual stars jump out of the blur, and if your eyes are really sharp, you might see what looks like a teeny "Big Dipper." You're looking at the Pleiades, one of the most richly visible star clusters in our northern night sky.

The Pleiades (PLAY-uh-dees) is an open star cluster visible to the naked eye. Open clusters normally contain only a few to several hundred stars, most of which are young and "hot" (active) and within 10 parsecs (32.6 light years) of each other, which is rather close in astronomical terms. Open clusters are believed to originate from cosmic gas and dust clouds (diffuse nebulae) in galaxies. The Pleiades is one of the closest star clusters to Earth, and it's the cluster easiest to spot in our night sky.

The Pleiades contains at least 1,000 significant stars. Nine of these are easy to see with the naked eye or minor magnification (binoculars). Because the Pleiades' stars are so easy to see, the cluster is known throughout a wide range of cultures and was seen in ancient times by ancient Australian, Aztec, Babylonian, Chinese,

Egyptian, Greek, Japanese, Maori, Native American, and Persian cultures, to name only a few. The earliest known graphic depiction of the cluster is in the Nebra Sky Disk, which dates to 1600 BCE. The Nebra Disk, found in Germany in 1999, is a shield of bronze with inlaid gold symbols representing the stars and heavenly bodies; the Pleiades are closely depicted.

The nine brightest stars in the Pleiades have names from Greek mythology: the seven daughters of Atlas and Pleione—Alcyone, Celaeno, Electra, Maia, Merope, Sterope, and Taygeta—plus Atlas and Pleione themselves. The cluster is often simply referred to as "The Seven Sisters." The Pleiades are a common sight in the winter night sky in the Northern Hemisphere and the summer skies in the Southern Hemisphere. Astronomers suggest the cluster will probably remain as is for up to 250 million years before gradually dispersing.

In mythological terms, the cluster has come to mean different things to many different cultures. In particular, the heliacal rising of the constellation—the point at which it first becomes visible above the eastern horizon of the morning sky, just before dawn—serves as an important marker for agriculture and for cultural rituals in many locations. The Aztecs based their entire calendar on the Pleiades' celestial movements.

Ancient Cosmology

In Greek mythos, the seven "daughters" were the Pleiades, daughters of Atlas and Pleione. Many of the early Greek astronomers actually considered the Pleiades to be a constellation, which is how they were described in Homer's *Iliad* and *Odyssey.* The Greek Hecatompedon temple and Parthenon were oriented to align with the rising Pleiades.

To the Bronze Age Celtic peoples, the cluster's acronychal rising—its first appearance in the eastern night sky just after twilight—heralded the arrival of the crossquarter day of Samhain. Precession-caused changes in star positions since then have changed this relationship, but the Pleiades are still associated with Samhain.

The cluster even made an appearance in religious texts. Some Islam scholars believe that the cluster is referred to in the Quran. The Pleiades are mentioned a number of times in the Christian Bible.

Ancient Astrology

Heinrich Cornelius Agrippa first described the cluster astrologically in his *Three Books of the Occult Philosophy* in the early 1500s. In more recent astrological symbolism, the Pleiades is considered one of the fixed medieval stars and is often associated with sorrow or longing. In Indian astrology, the Pleiades are collectively called the star of fire and are associated with anger, stubbornness, and fury.

Folkloric Tradition and Mythos

Ukrainian legend tells of seven sisters who lived their lives dancing and singing to honor the gods; after their deaths, they were given a home in the sky where they could continue their dance. In Hindu mythology, the six brightest stars in the Pleiades were revered as the six mothers of the war god, Skanda.

Some cultures attached a creationist tilt to the Pleiades. The Sioux of North America saw the star cluster as seven women giving birth. Australian legend links the Pleiades to seven sisters who brought fire to the aborigines, while some Nepalese people look upon the Pleiades cluster as representing their ancient kin.

Others draw a connection between the stars and the land. At least two North American tribes—the Lakota and Kiowa—associated the Pleiades legends with the Devil's Tower formation in North Dakota. In the latter legend, a group of seven young women climbed the Devil's Tower to escape hungry bears; the bears' claw marks remain visible on the rock formation to this day.

Many cultures and tribes associated the Pleiades cluster with agriculture or hunting. In the Maori culture of New Zealand, the Pleiades cluster was known as Matariki, and the heliacal rising in early

June heralded the arrival of the planting season. Tribes in the Andes and sub-Saharan African tribes also viewed the nighttime rising of the cluster as an agriculture marker. Disappearance of the cluster likewise signaled the end of the growth period and the arrival of harvest. The North American Blackfoot tribe used the final setting of the cluster in late spring as a signal to begin their hunting season. Some cultures associated the cluster with animals: the Vikings referred to the Pleiades' stars as "Freyja's hens," and the cluster's name in Old English is roughly akin to "hen with chicks."

Other tribes used the cluster for marking important rituals. North America's Hopi people built ceremonial structures known as kivas. When the Pleiades appeared in the hole in the kiva's ceiling, it was time to enact certain ceremonies. Guatemalan tribes used the cluster as an important reference point for their cosmological viewing and also used it to time important rituals and blessings.

Spotting the Pleiades

Regardless of its mythic connections, we regard the Pleiades as a wonderful gem in our winter skies. Go outdoors on a cold, clear late autumn or winter night in the Northern Hemisphere and look for the constellation Taurus, which is more or less directly overhead and located above the easily visible constellation Orion. The brightest star in Taurus—with a yellow tint—is Aldebaran. The Pleiades cluster is about 10 degrees (the distance of a closed fist held at arm's length) from Aldebaran. If you still need more help finding it, look online for a star chart, or use a planisphere. Once you find the cluster, try looking at it again with a pair of binoculars or a telescope— you'll see hundreds of stars!

For Further Reading:

Freedman, Roger, Robert Geller, and William J. Kauffman. *Universe (9th Ed.)* New York: Freeman, 2010.

Mythology. Myths, Legends, & Fantasies. New South Wales; Global, 2003.

Feasts and Treats

Kristin Madden

WITH AN EYE TO THE colors of the season, red and white, the recipes for this sabbat embody new life and joy. In these dishes, we blend traditional with trendy as we honor the goddess Brighid, her white cow companion, and the lactating ewes for whom this holiday is named.

Buttermilk Pot Roast

By Imbolc in the Northern Hemisphere, our ancestors' supplies could be expected to be in short supply. Game animals, or remaining livestock, might have helped them survive to see the spring. Buttermilk is not only a wonderful celebration of the season of lactating ewes, but it is a wonderful marinade to tenderize meat.

Prep Time: 5½ hours
Cooking Time: 4½ hours
Serves: 6–8

Buttermilk Marinade
2 cups buttermilk
1 teaspoon salt
1 teaspoon pepper

Pot Roast

3½ lb. boneless chuck roast

4–5 carrots, chopped

3 bell peppers, chopped

2 zucchinis, chopped

2 small potatoes, chopped

1 large onion, chopped

4 cloves garlic, chopped

1 tablespoon olive oil

1 teaspoon (each) salt, pepper, oregano, rosemary, thyme

½ cup dry red wine

Mix buttermilk, salt, and pepper in a large soup pot, pour marinade over meat and refrigerate at least 5 hours. Chop vegetables and garlic.

Remove roast from marinade, drain, dry with paper towels, and rub with spices. Brown in oil in a heavy roasting pan over medium heat.

Lift roast to place onions, garlic, and red wine on bottom of pan. Replace roast and cover. Bring to boil, then simmer for 4 hours. Add remaining vegetables for the final 20 minutes of cooking.

White Bean Salad

Perfect for potlucks, this colorful salad honors the colors of the season and will keep you going through the lingering cold.

Prep Time: 10 minutes

Cooking Time: 5–10 minutes

Serves: 4–6

1 cup walnuts

2 cans cannellini beans, drained

1 cup cherry tomatoes

¼ cup green onions, chopped

½ cup red bell pepper, chopped

2 cups baby spinach

¼ cup crumbled cheese (bleu, feta, goat)

Dressing
3 tablespoons olive oil
Juice of 1 lemon
1½ tablespoons red wine vinegar
2 teaspoons roasted garlic, mashed
1 teaspoon honey
Salt and pepper to taste

Toast walnuts in the oven at 350 degrees F for 5 to 10 minutes. Combine dressing ingredients in blender and mix well. Combine beans and vegetables in large bowl and toss with dressing mixture. Top with crumbled cheese and walnuts.

White Hot Cocoa

In her form as Saint Brigid, the goddess of Imbolc went about the countryside blessing households, accompanied by a white cow with red ears. In honor of her and her companion, share this delicious white and red warm beverage with your friends and family.

Prep Time: 15 minutes
Cooking Time: 45 minutes
Serves: 12

1 cup milk
1 cup half & half
7 ounces white chocolate, grated
1½ teaspoons vanilla extract
½ cup heavy cream
½ teaspoon sugar
Cherry or chopped strawberry garnish

Heat milk and half & half in saucepan over medium heat. Gradually add chocolate until it melts and begins to bubble. Add 1 teaspoon vanilla extract and remove from heat.

Mix ½ cup cream, ½ teaspoon vanilla, and sugar on high in a bowl until stiff peaks form.

Pour chocolate mixture in mugs and top with whipped cream. Garnish with cherry or chopped strawberry. Serve immediately.

Strawberry Tiramisu

The name of this traditional Italian dessert means "pick me up." Give it a try and let this fabulous dish of cream and fresh strawberries brighten your spirits for Imbolc. Feel free to add chocolate sprinkles, hazelnut liqueur, or anything else your heart desires.

Prep Time: 20 minutes
Chill Time: 4 hours
Serves: 4–6

1⅓ cups heavy cream
⅓ cup sugar
2 teaspoons vanilla extract
16 ounces mascarpone cheese, room temperature
⅓ cup orange juice
16–20 ladyfinger cookies
1½ pounds sliced strawberries

Beat cream, sugar, and vanilla until soft peaks form. Fold mascarpone into whipped cream. Cover bottom of casserole dish with ladyfingers, dipped first in orange juice. Cover with a layer of strawberries and top with half the mascarpone mix.

Add another layer of dipped ladyfingers, followed by strawberries and the remaining mascarpone mix.

Top with remaining strawberries. Cover and refrigerate for at least 4 hours.

Crafty Crafts

Linda Raedisch

IF YOU HAVEN'T ALREADY done so, it's time to take down the Yule greens! Throw them in the fireplace, or better yet, build a bonfire. It might warm the earth sufficiently to bring out a carpet of snowdrops as in *The Country Diary of an Edwardian Lady*. In England, the snowdrop is the star of Candlemas, a sign that spring is on its way. If you live where the winters are more severe, you can force a pot of snowdrops indoors. At the very least, you should try to incorporate the magical colors of green and white into your celebration.

Green is widely accepted as the color of fairy garments. There is a story from Gloucestershire in England about a lone traveler lost in a snowstorm. Much to his relief, at dusk he makes out warm lights shining over the white hills. He soon arrives at a well-appointed inn where all the servants are dressed in green. They serve him a good dinner and put him up comfortably for the night. The traveler wakes while it is still dark, anxious to set off again. As there is no one to draw up the bill, he leaves two gold coins on the table before departing.

When he finally arrives at his destination and tells his story, his friends inform him that he could not possibly have spent the night at an inn because no such inn exists. Returning to the scene of the night before, the bemused traveler finds that this is true: the only evidence of his stay is the two gold coins and his footprints in the snow.

Were the green-garbed innkeepers the spirits of the snowdrops? They took no payment, so what was the point of the illusion? It is well known that fairies like to amuse themselves at the expense of mortals, but this time they were thwarted by their unknowing guest, for he left before the dawn. Had he lazed in bed a little longer, he would probably have woken in the snow, as had other travelers before him. One wonders if they could hear the tinkling laughter of the snowdrops at the edge of the wood.

Humble "Henna" Lamp

This project is inspired by those very dramatic Moroccan henna lamps made of parchment and cast iron. Our lamp is made of humbler materials. Though the directions call for a tealight, the design can easily be converted to electricity. Just use a larger box lid, such as a hatbox, for your base, or make your own out of cardboard. Enlarge the shade size accordingly and, before assembly, remember to cut a hole in the lamp base large enough for the plug of a 35-light string of "fairy lights" to pass through. Also, use large wooden knobs for the feet.

There's some waiting involved in this craft, first for the watercolor paint and then for the coating of vegetable oil to dry, but the result will be a warmly glowing jewel-toned lamp that you'll be proud to put on your coffee table.

Tools and Materials

1 sheet decent quality watercolor paper, 15 inches long, 8 inches
   wide
Ruler
Pencil
Scissors
Black fine liner
Wide paint brush or clean sponge
Watercolor paints (the cheap kids' watercolors that come in little
   palettes will do)

Vegetable oil

Top lid from an 11 cm round box (see Blazing Year Wheel under "Yule")

3 wooden beads, ½-inch diameter or larger

Glue

1 3 oz. paper bathroom cup

Tealight

Once you have cut (or, if you are a very serious artist, *torn*) your paper to the proper size, use your ruler to draw a straight pencil line 1⅛ inches from the short end of the paper. Sketch and cut out a row of "teeth" between the pencil line and the edge of the paper.

Draw a swooping line from corner to corner on the long side of the paper. Cut along the line. This is to give your lamp a little panache when it is assembled. Who wants a boring cylinder?

Before you can assemble your lampshade, however, you have to decorate it. Wet the paper all over with a wide brush, wet paper towel, or very clean sponge. Apply paint immediately while the paper is still quite damp. To avoid muddiness, choose just one color of paint. Thin the paint well with water, blobbing it onto the damp paper where it will spread and bleed to create an irregular parchmenty effect.

When the paper is completely dry, which may take a few hours if you're using very high-quality paper, decorate the painted side with your fine liner. Use swooping lines, paisleys, spirals, or whatever designs fire you up.

When you're all drawn out, brush the painted, decorated surface with oil. Let the oiled paper dry overnight or longer in a warm place, but not near a flame. While you're waiting, you can prepare the lamp base. Cut off the top 1½ inches of your paper bathroom cup and glue what's left in the center of the inside of your box lid. This is where you'll place the tealight to prevent it sliding around dangerously inside the lamp. Glue your three wooden beads to the outside of the box lid in a triangular formation. These are the lamp's "feet."

Now it's time to assemble your lamp. Curl the shade into a cylinder, letting the teeth slide one over, one under, interlocking with the straight edge. Dab the points of the teeth with glue, pressing for a few seconds as the glue dries.

Slide your lamp base inside the finished lampshade, pushing it all the way down to the bottom. It should fit snugly.

Use one of those clicky candlelighters or a long fireplace match to light the tealight and please do be careful! This lamp should not be used outdoors or anywhere the wind might blow it over.

Stencil-Spiced Yogurt

Imbolc is not just about fire. Its very name means "ewe milk," so it's appropriate to celebrate with dairy products. With all the snow still lying around outside, it's hard to think of spring at all, but English sheep seem to think it's a good time to bear their lambs, and it was this miracle that our ancestors celebrated.

People don't honor dairy products the way they used to. Not so long ago it was considered vulgar to bring milk to the table in the bottle or carton it came in; you had to pour it into an attractive pitcher first. My German grandmother used to force the square pats of butter she bought at the store into her round china butter dish, and she didn't stop there. Though she never owned a butter stamp, she would create designs with the tip of a knife, scoring and lifting up curls of the cold butter to make stars and rosettes.

The best kind of yogurt to use for the following activity is the homemade kind that has set smooth and glossy in the bowl, but you can also use thick Greek yogurt spread out evenly. You can use your spices straight out of their jars, but heating them gently beforehand will help release their flavors. In a frying pan large enough to keep the spices separate, make a little mound of each one and heat for a

few minutes on low heat. Don't jiggle the pan. While the spices are cooling, you can make your stencil.

Tools and Materials
Bowl
Wax paper
Scissors
Plain yogurt
Spices: dried cilantro, onion powder, coriander, black pepper, curry
    powder, red chili powder—use this last one sparingly!
Salted pita chips

Cut out a circle of wax paper the same size as the mouth of your bowl. Leave on two tabs of paper opposite each other to use as handles later when you lift the stencil off the surface of the yogurt. Fold the circle into eighths and snip away as if you are making a paper snowflake. If, in your enthusiasm, you accidentally cut off the tabs, just replace them with two pieces of tape. Unfold the circle to see your design.

If you're pleased with it, lay the stencil you have made gently on the surface of the yogurt. Pick up a pinch of one of your spices between thumb and forefinger and let it trickle through one of the holes in the stencil as if you are making a sand painting or mandala. Apply one spice at a time, reserving the largest spaces in your design for the cilantro, since it has the coarsest consistency.

When you are done, lift the stencil carefully and throw it away. Serve your yogurt immediately with pita chips, and try not to feel too bad as your beautiful design is eaten. The most elaborate sand paintings, too, are ultimately swept away.

All One Family

Sandra Kynes

THIS IS MIDWINTER, WHEN days become just a little longer and winter's grip on the world begins to loosen. This is the time of hope and renewal: We have come through the dark into the quickening light.

While almost every television station in the United States and Canada mentions Groundhog Day, our little Pagans may wonder what it's really all about. I remember as a child trying to figure out why an animal would be afraid of its own shadow and why would a sunny day mean a longer winter? Of course, there are a number of explanations, but this is a good opportunity to introduce children to Celtic mythology.

Cailleach Bheur, as she was known in Scotland, was the personification of winter and ruled the weather from Samhain to Beltane. One of her tricks was to pound the earth with her long wooden staff to make the ground too hard for plants to grow. She especially liked snow, but by the beginning of February her store of wood ran low, which meant that it was time to collect fallen tree branches. If the day was bright and sunny, she would gather wood and be all set for more cold weather; however, if it was cloudy and wet, she would stay home and work her magic to bring winter to an end.

To help children remember this forecast, here's a rhyme based on an old Scottish poem about Candlemas: "If Imbolc be fair, more winter—beware! If Imbolc be gray, spring's not far away." A chalkboard or calendar in the kitchen is a good place to post this rhyme where it can be seen every day. This is also a good spot to post sunrise and sunset times to provide another reminder of this turning of the Wheel of the Year. A week or two before Imbolc, take a few minutes each day with your children recording the times. Teenagers could go online for the information, and younger children could write it on the calendar. This makes a fun pre-dinner activity that helps focus conversation during the meal.

Even though the days are growing longer, the hardest part of winter may lie ahead. While we might be reluctant to leave a cozy, warm house, this harsh side of nature has a beauty and magic all its own. This is a time of anticipation when the earth rests and holds its secrets for the splendor of spring. Bundle up the family and go for a walk—even it's just around your neighborhood. Ask children if they think Cailleach will bring snow. Look for sheltered areas around bushes where you might see that first tantalizing haze of green, heralding the snowdrops or crocus to come. Depending on where you live, you might find the tops of daffodils poking up through the soil. In New England, we usually don't see bare ground at this time of year, so my family and I like to take turns guessing where flowers will eventually emerge. While keeping the whereabouts of some plants secret, snow reveals something else: footprints. We usually find a network of prints and try to figure out what animals passed by. Was it the neighbor's cat or a little gray fox? In the woods, we look for deer and moose prints, but no matter where we walk, there are always a lot of footprints from birds.

This is an important time of year to maintain a birdfeeder, which can be a family activity that keeps everyone in touch with the natural world. We have ours located where we can sit comfortably on the window seat in the living room to watch the activity. We can even hear the loud squawking of blue jays and the piercing whistle of cardinals from inside the house. It may be a surprise, but robins stay right through the winter. Because they're ground feeders, we make sure to scatter food for them. We also see sparrows and the tufted titmouse, a cute little gray bird with a crest on its head like a cardinal. Another small bird we look for is the yellow-rumped warbler, who is affectionately nicknamed the "butter butt." He may be tiny, but stands his ground against the bigger birds. Although they don't come to the feeder, there are always seagulls to be heard overhead year-round here on the coast of Maine. Some seasons we keep our Yule tree and set it near the feeder to serve as a bird shelter.

Even if we don't keep the whole tree, we usually clip off some small branches to burn on Imbolc morning. This sabbat is a festival of the family and Brigid presides over the celebration of new beginnings. A fireplace is a good safe place indoors, but we prefer to use our iron cauldron outside. While we employ Brigid's power of fire to symbolically purify and prepare for Imbolc, mundane wishes are okay, too—we don't want to be so earnest that we spoil a fun time. One by one we pick up a sprig of greenery and name something new that we want to come in to our lives and then drop the green into the cauldron. For small children, have an adult place the branch in the fire for them. Depending on age, wishes range from toys to girlfriends to new careers. A few sprigs are saved for the end and get tossed in the fire together as we say: "Winter be gone, sun grow strong. Let spring stay, this Imbloc day."

On Imbolc, we have dinner by candlelight and begin with a few minutes of silence. The winter world is quieter with windows closed, fewer people outside and snow muffling sounds. This hushed world helps us move inward and have time with our thoughts. We then take turns with each person having a chance to share what the quiet time meant to them. If small children are present, ask them to listen, and then ask what they heard in the silence.

In addition to the candles with flames representing Brigid's power, consider decorating the dinner table with at least one of her crosses. The Brigid cross represents the four directions and unites them symbolically creating a crossroads. Because she is a goddess of crossroads and can see where a person has come and where he or she may be going, her sabbat is a time for divination.

After dinner, we leave four candles on the table and clear everything else away for our divination time. We place our crystal ball in the center of the table with a candle in each of the cardinal directions. A scrying mirror would work, too, or you can create a device by placing a piece of black paper or cloth in the center of the table and then setting a clear glass bowl filled with water on it. Younger children are more in tune with magical power and can tap into psychic abilities more easily than adults. Their innocent minds do not readily act as filters, and they are less inhibited to report what they see and feel. Make it a game to visualize good things in store for the family in the year ahead. Sometimes this turns into a conversation of hopes and dreams, but it usually comes full circle into the deeper meanings of our Pagan path.

The name Imbolc is thought to come from a Gaelic or Anglo-Saxon word meaning "ewe's milk." To people long ago, milk from their sheep was very important because even if winter continued and food stores ran low, this new source of nourishment was confirmation that spring's renewal was not far away. To end a busy Imbolc day, give the children or the whole family mugs of warm milk with honey before bedtime in celebration of continued abundance and the sweetness of life.

Imbolc Ritual: Handmaidens' Night

Dallas Jennifer Cobb

IN THE MIDDLE OF a cold Canadian winter, a night of poetry, laughter, food, and craftmaking heals the isolation and blues that often come with the season. Evoking inspiration, the Imbolc celebration leaves people feeling like they have something to take away with them, something more than a craft—a touchstone, hope, and light.

In my family, we honor Brigid at Imbolc, welcoming, cultivating, and celebrating the Celtic goddess of feminine fertility, children and childbirth, love and fire. Our Imbolc celebrations have long been known as Handmaidens' Night. Playing on the words of "handmade" and "maiden," Handmaidens' Night is a time for invoking our creative fires and inspiration, and rekindling Brigid's qualities of love and healing in our community. Every year I choose a different craft to do after the ritual.

Preparation

I overprepare, and that helps me feel relaxed on the day of the ritual. I prepare myself, my tools and supplies, and I prepare my space. With everything done, I feel confident and calm, and can let go and follow the flow.

Invitations are sent in advance, asking people to confirm attendance so that you can ensure there are ample craft supplies. The invitation asks them to bring a candle and a holder (if you are not going to supply these for each person), a few old magazines, and their warmth of spirit. This last one is a most important ingredient to the evening, so it is important to ask directly that everyone brings it. I also ask a few specific people to bring a food contribution, so anyone coming from work doesn't have to.

I like people to arrive in the dark, so Handmaidens' Night can easily be celebrated on a weeknight after work. Here in Canada, it is usually dark by the end of the workday when people arrive.

☘

For the ritual, scads of candles are needed. If you're on a budget, ask people to bring their own candle, in a holder. I prefer beeswax, and know where to buy them in bulk, so I usually supply candles. Do what best suits you. Candles must be contained in a fireproof container that won't tip or fall over, will collect melting wax, and won't explode if it gets hot. Yes, some of those cute glass candleholders—especially those made in China from the dollar store—have a habit of exploding. Opt instead for a suitable, safe candleholder.

For the ritual, purchase sea salt, Epsom salts, and lavender essential oil. You can get the salts in any bulk store, or if you live in a rural area, farm supply stores sell large quantities of Epsom salts (magnesium sulfate) at very affordable prices. You need about three cups of each salt and a few drops of essential oil.

For the craft, collect recycled cardboard or boxboard, and cut a variety of hearts in different sizes—anywhere from about 5 inches across to 20 inches across. You'll also need lots of magazines. If you haven't amassed a collection as a diversion to get through the dark months, visit your local library and ask if they have discards. Alternately, you can ask people to bring a couple of magazines.

You also need scissors and glue, three or four of each, which can be shared. I prefer glue sticks because they aren't quite as messy as a bottle of glue. Last, but not to be forgotten, find some ribbon, sparkles, or little paper shapes (stars and hearts are nice!) that can be glued on to decorate the craft.

In my home, I prepare the biggest room by pushing back the furniture to create space for an altar on the floor in the middle. Large bolts of cloth in red, white, and bright green lie in the midst. On them, I place eight sacred stones in a circle, resembling the sacred stones of Stonehenge. I have a collection of stones, one for each sabbat: fossils spiraling out, amethyst for emotional healing and strength, amber for insight and intuition, and stones from sacred places and special days. In a small pile next to the stone representing Imbolc, I place a pile of smaller stones, one for each person attending.

A large earthenware bowl sits in the middle of the sacred rock circle, filled with the salt and Epsom salt mixed together. The essential oil sits near my place in the circle.

Before people arrive, I take time to personally invoke Brighid, welcoming her into my home. I light three candles on the altar for the Triple Goddess, gently illuminating the ritual space. Then I purposefully turn off all the lights in my house, except for one in the entryway.

At the door, I greet guests, show them where to hang coats, leave boots, and place food. I take their magazines for later, and instruct them take their candle and find a spot in the ritual room.

The Ritual

When everyone is assembled, I take my spot in the circle, sitting near the Imbolc stone placed on the altar.

Welcome. We are gathered here to share our warmth of spirit, the essential ingredient for winter survival, and to celebrate the growing light, and bright sun.

I light my candle.

With this candle, I bring light, to this circle and to my life.
With this candle, I share my light, I share my magic, I share my life.

Turning to the person on my left, I light their candle from mine, asking them to chant with me.

With this candle, I share my light, I share my magic, I share my life.

Passing from person to person, the flame is shared and moves around the circle as the chanting grows, each voice weaving into the mix. When it comes to the person on my right, I symbolically touch my candle to theirs, the flames mixing for a moment, then make a motion for silence.

The circle is cast, and we are in the light, we let go of the darkness, and work magic tonight.

I instruct people to put their candle (in its holder) in front of them around the altar cloth.

We invoke Brighid, Goddess of healing, creativity, fertility and femininity. Be with us tonight. Bring your warm spirit, protector of children and childbirth, as we have brought our warm spirits here tonight. We're creeping out of the dark, ready to welcome new light, new life. Brighid, may your fires burn bright.

We invoke the Young Lord, the Sun God, young god, beautiful boy. Join us with your growing strength, your youthful energy and growing length of days. Bring us your light.

The Goddess has recovered from birthing her son. She is fertile and ready to create anew. She knows she must feed herself physically and emotionally so that she has love enough for all her children. She releases some responsibilities, and limits where her energy goes, so she can best sustain herself, and new life.

Think now, what doesn't work in your life? What do you feed that does not feed you, what do you care for that is careless to you? Know where your darkness lays. And be ready to surrender it. People, situations, activities or jobs, roles and responsibilities - think about what you need to let go of, purify, transform or release, in order to feed yourself.

Let the silence stretch out as people conjure up what doesn't work, and know where darkness lays within their life. Quietly pass a small stone to each person.

Take this stone, a piece of the earth, and fill it with your darkness. Release what no longer works, let go of what you cannot carry, and let the stone absorb it. When you're ready, slide your stone into the bowl of salt, for it to be cleansed. The salt of the earth purifies, banishing the darkness that has consumed you. Let go of the old so you can welcome the new.

When everyone has placed their stone into the bowl, stir it widdershins, or counterclockwise, saying:

Sacred fires in us burn bright, illuminating darkness on this night,
We release our troubles, worries and blight, transform their energy into light.

Speaking to everyone in the circle:

Goddesses and Gods, here tonight, time to illuminate desires, and rekindle light,
Meditate now on your deepest desires, what will feed you and rekindle your fire.

Let people sit in silence for a few moments, envisioning their own bright wants, needs and desires.

Now, leave this circle, but just for a bit, and go to a room that is not lit,
Turn on the switch and summon the light, throughout this house let spirit burn bright.
Leave the lights on and come back here, to the light of community let us draw near.

When everyone has returned:

What was hidden in the dark, comes into the light,
Purified and released, wrong becomes right,
The house once dark, is filled with light,
The Maiden once weary, is filled with delight.

From the salts, choose a symbol of strength (reach in to the bowl and extract one stone). Anoint and bless it, and hold it at arm's length. (Use your finger to spread a drop of lavender essential oil on the stone and say: "*Brighid bless me.*")

Each stone purified, transformed, and renewed,
The deepest of magic is working through you,
The old is gone, and now comes new
Choose a talisman to carry with you.

Pass the essential oil to your left so that it can circle and be used by all. Remember to cap the oil after.

I tuck my talisman safely away, it is with me for the coming days.
Farewell Brighid and young Son bright,
We extinguish our candles, and stay in your light,
We close this circle, but do it right,
Stay to feast and in Brighid's crafts, delight.

Extinguish candles in the reverse order they were lit, so that the energy moves counterclockwise around the circle.

After the ritual we move to the harvest table where the craft supplies lay. Each person gets to pick a heart that they like and is told to "tear through the magazines" to find images (and words) that represent their deep desires. Collages made in the shape of a heart symbolizes their "heart's desire." Decorated with glitter and ribbon, each person can take their collage home so they remember their heart's desire and have an image to work with in the coming days.

And after the crafts (sometimes during), we feast. Imbolc feast foods include those common to the season. Last year I made a beef stew with root vegetables, roasted squash, quinoa with onion and garlic, and a hazelnut spice cake served with warm custard sauce.

This year I plan on making a huge cheesecake, convinced that this is what I need to feed body, mind, and spirit.

Later, when people leave with their "touchstone" in their pocket, clutching their "heart's desire" and sporting a full belly, I revel in Brighid's blessing. My house, and my life, is filled with the "warmth of spirit" that is generated when my community gathers together.

Notes

Ostara

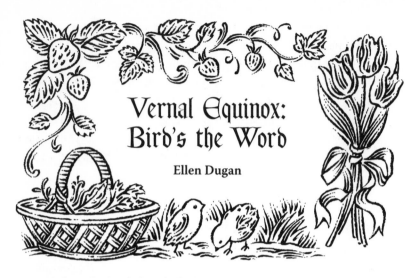

Vernal Equinox: Bird's the Word

Ellen Dugan

Faith is the bird that feels the light and sings when the dawn is still dark.

—Rabindranath Tagore

THE VERNAL EQUINOX IN the Northern Hemisphere will occur on March 20, 2013. Classically, this is considered to be the day of equal night and daylight hours. However, if you want to get technical, that equal day/night thing is only a moment in time called the equiluxe.

Remember that back in the old days, the majority of Pagan folks could not calculate that *exact* moment, and yet they still celebrated the festival successfully. So I think it's a safe bet to go about your celebrations on the date marked as the Vernal Equinox. Enjoy the beginning of spring and the balance of the day and night. Celebrate the sabbat without worrying that the world will fall on your head.

The equinox is a magickal time, and on an interesting note, the days of the vernal and autumnal equinoxes allow us to view the Sun rising at true east and setting at true west. So, if you ever wondered exactly where true east and true west are at your house, here is your big chance to mark it.

The Vernal Equinox in the Northern Hemisphere begins as the Sun moves into the astrological sign of Aries. This is a fire sign, and all that fiery energy is welcome at this time of year as the days begin to warm up and life returns to the land.

The earth is finally waking up, the grass is starting to peep through, and the trees are budding. The earliest bulbs are blooming. Crocus have broken through and are chuckling at the muddy snow in their colors of purple, yellow, and bright white while the spring-green spears of the daffodils get a bit taller every day. The earliest tulips are breaking the ground, the forsythia is showing hints of the yellow flowers to come, and the willows are misted in pale green. Birds are returning from their winter homes. Spring has arrived!

For this year's sabbat, instead of trotting out the traditional Ostara goddess Eostre, the sacred hare, I thought I'd focus on other harbingers of spring, namely birds, birds nests, and eggs. The egg is an alchemical symbol. Think about all the transformation that goes on inside of an egg. No doubt about it; the creation of new life is magickal.

A nest filled with bird eggs is a universal symbol for spring. It represents fertility and potential. Eggs are linked to this sabbat in particular as the classic symbols for new life, as well as rebirth and new beginnings. There is something so soft, pretty, and happy about a little bird's nest with softly colored eggs tucked in a tree.

A bird's nest is classic symbol for the family home. When pregnant women feel the need to get the home ready for the baby, it's called "nesting." Of course, years later when the kids are grown and move out to start their own lives and homes, suddenly you have an "empty nest." In the language of dreams, a nest full of eggs can symbolize prosperity or a loving home. While an empty nest may symbolize the feelings of loneliness, it can also stand for the freedom that comes once your chicks finally fly the nest.

Birds and magick have been intertwined forever. The practice of augury, which is divination by observing the flight and the behavior of birds, is an ancient practice that the Greeks and Roman priests once used. Bird augury follows the idea that since birds are much closer to nature than people, that they are more sensitive to the natural energies of the weather and the earth.

The physical reaction of the birds (and other animals) before a storm or natural disaster such as an earthquake is well documented by science. A few years ago, I was woken up in the middle of the night by very loud birdsong. I lay in bed a moment, wondering why the birds were singing so loud at three o'clock in the morning.

The cat screeched and jumped off the bed and took off down the hall, and then the earthquake started. Here in the Midwest, due to the New Madrid fault, earthquakes are not unheard of, but big ones are unusual. The birds got louder and louder with the rumbling of the earth and the popping and groaning of the house. But when the quake subsided, the birds settled down. For the Midwest, this was a good-sized quake. We had strong tremors for days afterward. But the birds going ballistic in the middle of the night, just before the quake, was fascinating to me.

Farmers have watched the migratory patterns of the birds and the behavior of the earth's creatures for eons. They know it is wise to pay attention to the clues and omens the animals share. Anyone who has a birdfeeder in the winter months has observed that the birds hit the feeders hard right before a snowfall. And in the spring, when the weather can swing back and forth from mild to cold, the birds will clue you in on what to expect.

Bird divination can be done anytime and anywhere. All you need is access to the outdoors and to pay attention to the birds that live in your neck of the woods.

Spontaneous bird appearances and their fallen feathers can also have messages for you as well. A fallen feather that you discover on your path is no accident. It is a message. Feathers are an obvious representation of the element of air. This element is also linked to the season of spring. Please keep in mind that some feathers from protected species may be illegal to posses. Check with your local conservation department to be sure.

Indulge in a little bird-watching this spring: Watch the local pigeons in the park; check out the native habitats as you walk reverently through the woods, meadows, or plains; or simply enjoying the songbirds flocking for a snack at your backyard birdfeeder. Use your intuition and listen to your own instincts. See what you learn. Here are a few bird omens to get you started reading the signs in nature this spring.

Bird Augury

The very idea of a bird is a symbol and a suggestion to the poet.
—John Burroughs

Spotting a species of bird you have never seen before close to your home can be signal happy news or an unexpected opportunity.

An **all-white bird** landing nearby that regards you silently and seems to keep you company for a time, is a symbol of the goddess.

The **bluebird** is a symbol of happiness and joy.

Blue jays defend your territory. This feisty songbird demands that you walk your talk and speak up for yourself!

Cardinal symbolizes vitality and beauty. According to Ozark folklore, if a redbird (cardinal) crosses quickly in front of you while you are out walking, you can expect to be kissed before nightfall.

Crane is a symbol of patience and long life. The crane is honored in many magickal cultures across the globe.

A pair of **doves** cooing away outside your window may mean love is coming or that peace and contentment is needed in your life.

Eagle is a classic symbol of the divine, independence, and of the human spirit.

Hawk is a messenger. When the hawk swoops into your life, it is a call to embrace your more regal qualities and to rise above and to watch for the coming messages.

Hummingbird stands for energy and joy. If you have hummingbirds hovering around you this means you are deeply connected to your garden and the magick of the Fey and of nature. Hummers are smart and very territorial. For them to flit around without dive-bombing you means that they have accepted you.

The **goldfinch** embodies magick and knowledge. The goldfinch is a faery bird. Wherever the goldfinches happily live you can count on lots of faery activity.

The **goose** reminds you of the rewards and challenges of parenting and raising a brood.

The **owl** signifies secrets, wisdom, and magick.

Ravens and **crows** also represent magick and the Crone goddess. They also remind you to be aware, and if necessary, to work protection magick.

The **robin** is a harbinger of spring and new beginnings.

Swan symbolizes magick, beauty, inspiration, the faerie realm, and dreams. Yes, it is possible to see swans in the wild.

The **wren** is associated with enchantment, cunning, prophecy, and gentleness. The wren is a sacred to the Druids and is associated with the Fey.

If you would like to practice your divinatory skills with augury, go sit someplace quiet in nature and observe the birds. If you like, take a bird identification guide along with you. Remember to do more than just categorize the birds. What color birds did you see most often? Apply color magick to that and ask yourself what that color means to you, and most importantly, what does your heart tell you about this experience?

Here is a little spell verse for you to aid in augury. Recite this verse three times as you sit quietly enjoying nature, and see what sort of messages you can divine by observing the natural magick of the birds in the outdoors.

Creatures of the air, beautiful birds hear my call,
I value the messages you bring, one and all.
Brave raptor or sweet songbird, I call you near,
Through augury, your wisdom will become clear.
Wisdom to gain that brings harm to none,
With a simple rhyme this spell is spun.

The Bird Goddess

A religion without a goddess is halfway to atheism.

—Dion Fortune

There are many goddesses associated with birds. Actually, the Bird Goddess is one of our earliest symbols of the divine feminine. A Neolithic goddess, this famous figurine has arms that are curved up and back, much like the wings of a bird. She is feminine and elegantly simple. The figurine even has a subtle beak on her face.

Once, many years ago when the kids were small, I took my family a local art museum. The exhibit was called "Splendor of the Pharaohs," and it featured many artifacts from Egypt. My kids, though young, were fascinated. While we worked our way through the exhibit, I turned a corner and came face to face with the very Egyptian Bird Goddess figurine I had only ever seen in books.

Tears welled up in my eyes and I took a shaky breath. It was everything I had to keep my hands off the display case. My kids even wandered over to see what I was so enraptured with. My daughter Erin, who was I think about five years old at the time, immediately piped up and said "Hey it's the Bird Goddess!" I have had a fondness for that ancient representation of the Goddess ever since.

This spring, why not consider incorporating these deities into your magick and get to know their feathered friends a little better? Here is a list the deity, their associated magicks, and their bird.

Aphrodite: Greek goddess of beauty and physical love; the dove

Astarte: Ancient Mediterranean goddess of sexuality, fertility, and war; the dove

Athena: Greek goddess of wisdom; the owl

Blodeuwedd (Flower face): Celtic maiden goddess of flowers and the spring; the owl

Freya: Norse goddess of magick, seers, and prophecy; the falcon

Hera: Greek goddess of women and marriage; the peacock

Inanna: Sumerian goddess of sexual love, fertility and battle; the owl, the dove, and the swallow

Isis: the Egyptian mother goddess of magick; the falcon

Lakshmi: The Hindu goddess of wealth and prosperity; the owl

Lilith: Sumerian goddess of magick and sorcery; the screech owl

Macha: Celtic goddess of battle; the crow

Minerva: Roman goddess of wisdom and war; the owl

Morrigan Celtic Triple Goddess: the raven

Nephthys: Egyptian goddess of protection, prophecy, and the dark moon; the falcon and the vulture

Sarasvati: The Hindu goddess of knowledge, music, and the arts; the swan and the peacock

Venus: Roman goddess of love and beauty; the dove

Cosmic Sway

Daniel Pharr

THE MIDDAY OF SPRING arrives early this year at 7:02 am EST March 20, meaning the celebration begins on Ostara Eve, March 19. Considering the New Moon precedes Ostara by eight days and the Full Moon celebration would begin on evening of March 26, a week after Ostara, this equinox celebration would have probably been moved to the Full Moon. However, many of the celebrations that happen on this high holiday involve the balance of energies which dictates the observation of Ostara be on the day, sometimes to the hour and minute.

The New Moon is a time of new beginnings, and Ostara is often considered a time of renewal. Many rituals involve symbolizing nature's rebirth, which is evident is every part of the Northern Hemisphere. Animals are birthing, flowers are opening, sprouts are popping up. This is an appropriate time to birth a new project or business venture. The New Moon is in Pisces and will enhance your innate empathy. Use your empathic abilities in the social realms to achieve greater success. The Moon in the Tenth House will help. The Moon rules the First House, which is all about the personality and identity. This is a time of new beginnings, so it is a good time to make some changes in the way the self is presented to the world.

As an example, if you see yourself as a poet but haven't penned a poem in ten years, consider sitting down to write and renew the poet within. Or consider those days long gone and quit adding stress to your life. There is nothing wrong with being a former poet. Life changes. The feminine and masculine energies are in balance so it is not surprising to see two lunar aspects supplying opposing energies. The Moon conjunct Venus instills a desire for beauty, to follow musical and artistic pursuits, and to approach life with a calm, spiritual demeanor. In juxtaposition, the Moon conjunct Mars offers emotional impulsivity, and a desire to be a hard-nosed leader with very little empathy.

The Sun in Pisces will aid your imaginative efforts to change dreams into reality. Mercury in Pisces will ignite the imagination by enhancing intuitive communication. Venus in Pisces asks for a commitment to the dreamed reality—to be "all in"—to be fully, completely, and in every way committed to your cause. Mars in Pisces further boosts intuition and guides the efforts to parallel the spiritual path.

The calculated date of Ostara, March 20, is the date general society and media consider to be the Spring Equinox. The Moon is waxing and in Cancer. This day is about self-care. As a person of action, care for the self usually rates low on the list of priorities. In this Cancer Moon, seek out nurturing. Care for yourself in all situations, even if you must withdraw. The Moon in the Fifth House will help guide the momentum toward self-care in the form of joy. The Moon rules the Sixth House and is about everyday life. It asks how others are served. The answer is by serving the self. Only through caring for the self is there enough life energy created to serve others. Mars has moved into Aries and with it comes spontaneity, hustle, and a high tolerance for risk. High quality self-care provides a foundation for risk-taking. Venus and Mars are in the Second House, the house of money. Mars brings the aggressive pursuit of money and Venus works the results into the comfort zone. The consistent curiosity and the quest for information brought on by Mercury in the First House supports aggressive action and monetary gain.

Full Moon–March 27

The Full Moon arrives at 5:27 am, March 27, and in Libra, bringing peace and harmony to all manner of relationships, including business, personal, family. Dealing with an issue, problem, or opportunity will be improved by capturing the global view, according to the Moon in the Ninth House, and always considering lessons learned through philosophy and education. The Moon rules the Seventh House, which is also about relationships—both personal and business partnerships. Intra-personal relationships, such as between ego and emotions, are also affected. These relationships will be made available for personal critique, similar to looking in the mirror. The masculine and feminine internal relationship will also be examined if it is not in balance.

This may not be the best time to indulge in social activities. The Moon opposes Mars, which will create personal struggles that may be met with assertive responses. This assertive behavior may then be met with anger from loved ones, and this aggression may be supported by Venus in Aries. Personal relaxation, like a massage, will help to relieve the pressure of an irritated relationship. The Moon also opposes Venus, which may add energy to the conflicts in your relationships. Some conflicts are due to the Moon opposing Uranus, which causes distrust in the emotional reaction, the gut reaction, to a situation. Pay attention to the inner voice. Rely on the enhanced intuition available from Mercury still in Pisces.

Celebrations of Hope

The Daylight Labyrinth

Sprinkle birdseed in a labyrinth pattern on the ground. The birdseed can either be a trail or the edges of the trail, whichever works for the folks that will walk. Get a stick with a long string attached and plant it in the middle to keep the pathway somewhat round. In the center, place an Altar of Hope. Once the group gathers, cast the circle and walk the labyrinth, separating each walker by about ten steps. Walk with intent and openness. Keep questions that need answers in the mind. Place an object representing the questions. Once everyone has completed the walk, gather in a circle and share the experience, questions, and answers.

The Evening Dance and Dinner

Build a fire, but do not light it. Decorate the fire and pit with the essence of spring—flowers, paper ribbons, and sprigs of green. Cast the circle and call the deities as is the custom. This holiday is about hope in all forms: hope the birthing of livestock produces healthy offspring, hope this year's sowing produces a bounty of crops, hope that the coming year is better than the last. Each person takes a turn lighting a piece of the fire and in doing so, speaks aloud what they hope to achieve or obtain over the coming summer and autumn. Move closer and away from the fire in unison, moving energy into the fire, helping the fire to burn. Once the fire is established, spread the fire out to allow for cooking. Place fish, fowl, lamb, pork, potatoes, soup, and egg dishes like quiche and custard in the coals to cook. Join hands move in a line snaking around the fire, spiraling in and spiraling out, follow-the-leader style. Chant the spiral dance: "Spiraling in, spiraling out, spiraling up, spiraling down, spiraling round and round," while the meal cooks. The fish will cook quickly, the eggs dishes will take a bit longer, and some of the meats longer still. Sing songs. Tell stories. This is a celebration of the return of warmth and light. Joy is the best representation. Serve the meal in courses allowing the quickest cooking foods to be eaten while the other items finish cooking.

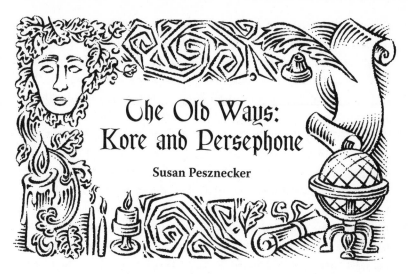

The Old Ways: Kore and Persephone

Susan Pesznecker

MOST PEOPLE KNOW THE Greek myth of Zeus' daughter Persephone in terms of her being abducted by Hades and carried off into the underworld, where she became its queen and a symbol of the cold, dark half of the year. So why are we talking about her in March? Because there's another "half" to the story. Persephone's alter ego, Kore, is the flower-maiden goddess of spring and rules over the springtime just as her other half rules over winter.

Here's the short version of the story: Zeus (ZOOS), the father of all gods, and Demeter (duh-MEE-tur), goddess of the grain and earth, married and produced a daughter: Kore (KOE-ray). Kore was the lovely, innocent, and virginal goddess of the flowers world—the flower maiden incarnate. Her name actually means "girl." Kore lived a gentle, peaceful life and loved nothing more that to spend time out in the fields filling her baskets with flowers.

Let's go back for a moment and meet the players. Demeter, daughter of Cronos and Rhea, was responsible for the Earth's fertility. Content to do her job, she paid little attention to the gossip and jockeying of the Olympian gods and goddesses. She was particularly revered by women, who prayed for her and left tributes to her through the festival of Thesmophoria, a ceremony for women who wished for fertility. Demeter's symbol was a sheaf of wheat.

Zeus was, of course, King of the Gods, Supreme God, God of Gods, etc. (I imagine he had a bit of an ego, wouldn't you think?) He was also the child of Cronos and Rhea, which means that he and his wife, Demeter, were siblings. (These kinds of relationships weren't unusual among the gods.) Zeus was mediator among the gods, protector of the human race, and interlocutor between the gods, humans, and demigods (beings born of a union between a human and a god). He controlled the weather and meted out justice. Oh—and he was in charge of good and evil, too.

Variations of the story are many, but here's the one I like best. Kore was out in the fields one day, picking her flowers, when she spotted a single, big, beautiful black flower—some sources say this was a poppy, others a narcissus. Unable to resist, Kore picked the flower, and the minute she did, there came a tremendous cracking sound. The earth shook and rolled and split open before her. Out through the split came Hades, god of the underworld, driving his black chariot pulled by (of course) black horses that were said to have eyes burning with fire.

Let's meet Hades. He was also a child of Cronos and Rhea and thus was Zeus' (and Demeter's) brother. (It keeps getting more complicated, doesn't it?) Long before this story, Zeus, Hades, and their brother, Poseidon, had defeated the Titans and claimed all lands as their own. Poseidon took custody of the seas, Zeus of the land and sky, and Hades of the underworld. Hades really wasn't such a bad guy—in fact, he ruled fairly and was even seen by his brothers as being somewhat passive. But he was rather possessive and would become enraged if anyone tried to leave his realm or take something that was his. He was also quite lonely.

Hades carried Kore off to his underworld, where he forced her to become his consort and queen. As part of this, she was given a new underworld name: Persephone (pur-SEFF-oh-nee). Rumor has it that Hades was actually rather nice to her—after all, he'd been very lonesome. But it didn't matter, because Persephone was bereft and missing her mother, father, and, most importantly, her beautiful flowers. After all, not many flowers grow in Hades, right?

Meanwhile, back on Earth, Demeter was overcome with grief. She walked the lands constantly, searching for her daughter. In her anger, she retaliated by cursing the land and refusing to let the Earth produce its usual fruits until her daughter was restored to her. As a result, the land grew cold and barren, plants died, and people began to starve. With no crops, the people were unable to make offerings to the gods, and the situation grew worse and worse. The gods didn't like this at all. One by one, they approached Demeter, asking her to lift her curse, but she refused.

Zeus finally sat Demeter down and appealed to her, but she held firm. No Kore? No plant life. From that untenable position, Zeus went and appealed directly to Hades, asking for Persephone's release. There was only one condition: Zeus wanted no connections to remain between Persephone/Kore and Hades, so he insisted that while she was in the underworld, Persephone could not have eaten anything. (Up to this time, she had, surprisingly, not eaten anything in the underworld. How she could have managed to be there for so long without eating seems kind of unlikely, but that's a myth for you.)

Here's where the story gets interesting. In an attempt to make it impossible for Persephone to leave him, Hades quickly fed her a number of pomegranate seeds. By doing this, a connection was created between Persephone and Hades, and she was forever bound to remain at least part-time in the dark realm.

Fortunately, a compromise was reached between the brothers, Zeus and Hades. Persephone would spend one-third of the year with Hades, reigning through the winter as Queen of the Dead. Then, each spring, she would be allowed to emerge and return to the Earth, where she would once again be Kore, the flower maiden, free to walk her fields.

It was a decent solution, and everyone was happy, mostly. Demeter was true to her word and returned the world to fecundity.

The plants grew, the people thrived, and the gods were appeased. All was right with the world. And the underworld.

✻

Persephone's story symbolizes the cyclical give and take between spring and winter and between darkness and light. It's also a neat little lesson about cooperation and perhaps one of the first examples of legal practice in the ancient world. Persephone/Kore's story is one of the Grecian initiatory mysteries and was enacted through the Elysian Mysteries, with initiates sworn to secrecy. Persephone is still symbolized today by the pomegranate (a unique fruit that ripens in late autumn and into the winter) and the poppy (associated with opium), symbols of the underworld.

Next time you think of spring or appreciate the flowers and greenery emerging around you, remember the story of Kore, the flower maiden. And if you're out in a meadow and see a pretty black flower, don't pick it. Especially if it's a poppy.

For Further Reading:

Mythology. Myths, Legends, & Fantasies. New South Wales; Global, 2003.

Feasts and Treats

Kristin Madden

ON THE SPRING EQUINOX, we honor balance, once again. The recipes for this sabbat celebrate sweet and savory, tradition and experimentation, sustenance and pleasure. Like the pumpkin at Samhain, the egg has become forever entwined with the holiday as an iconic and playful symbol of the season, and so we share some of our favorite egg delights.

Lamb Chops with Blackberry Sauce

Balance is the theme of the season, and this dish balances sweet with savory—preserved blackberries from last season and fresh spring lamb. This is a hearty main course for your equinox feast.

Prep Time: 10 minutes
Cooking Time: 20 minutes
Serves: 4

1 tablespoon cumin
½ tablespoon (each) granulated garlic, turmeric, sage, and thyme
1 teaspoon kosher salt
4 lamb chops

Sauce

1 teaspoon olive oil
1 garlic clove, minced
1 onion, minced
2 cups blackberry preserves
1 teaspoon cardamom
1 clove
2 teaspoons honey
1 cup port wine

Sauté minced garlic and onion in olive oil until soft. Add preserves, cardamom, clove, honey, and port wine. Bring to boil and reduce heat. Simmer and reduce by half.

While sauce is simmering, combine cumin, granulated garlic, turmeric, sage, thyme, and salt. Rub onto lamb chops. Cook chops on grill (or in a shallow pan with 1 tablespoon oil over medium-high heat) until brown, which takes about 4 minutes per side.

Serve lamb chops topped with warm sauce.

Baked Parsnips

While waiting for fresh fruits and vegetables, our ancestors took advantage of healthy and tasty root vegetables. Step outside of the ordinary and entice your friends with the traditional sweetness of parsnips.

Prep Time: 5 minutes
Cooking Time: 40 minutes
Serves: 6–8

4 cups parsnips, diced
4 cups chicken broth
Salt and pepper to taste
¼ teaspoon nutmeg
¼ teaspoon cinnamon
¼ cup butter

Parboil parsnips for 15 minutes. Drain. Place in ovenproof dish and cover with chicken broth. Sprinkle with spices and dot top with butter. Bake at 400 degrees F for 25 minutes.

Egg Cream

Surprisingly, a true egg cream doesn't contain any egg. Nonetheless, this is an ideal Ostara beverage to share.

Prep Time: 5 minutes
Serves: 1

½ cup whole milk, cold
1 cup seltzer water
2 tablespoons chocolate syrup

Pour milk into tall glass. Add seltzer water and stir quickly until it foams. Gently add chocolate syrup down the side of the glass and stir at the bottom of the glass. Serve immediately.

Egg Custard

What would Ostara be without eggs? Egg custard takes this symbol of the season to comfort-food status.

Prep Time: 15 minutes
Cooking Time: 15 minutes
Chill Time: 1 hour
Serves: 4–6

1½ cups heavy cream
6 egg yolks
1 teaspoon vanilla extract
¼ cup sugar

Bring cream to a boil in a small saucepan. Remove from heat and add vanilla. Allow to sit for 10 minutes. Beat egg yolks until creamy. Add yolks to cream gradually, mixing on low. Add sugar and simmer gently over low heat, stirring constantly, until it thickens. Refrigerate at least an hour.

Crafty Crafts

Linda Raedisch

ALONG WITH SAMHAIN/HALLOWEEN, Ostara/Easter is an occasion when both Witches and mainstream Christians are engaging in many of the same activities: we're coloring eggs, preparing baskets, buying chocolate bunnies and putting up egg trees. You might, therefore, feel the need to witch it up a notch. A basket of black stones adorned with Neolithic moon signs, a few flickering lanterns, and an egg tree mobbed by Swedish witches should do the trick.

Ostara Moonstones

You can use plain wooden eggs from a craft store, but I prefer beach or river stones. They don't have to be perfectly egg-shaped. Stones are the bones of Mother Earth, and any irregularities will add to the visual interest of the final product. The Moon symbols I've used come from *The Myth of the Goddess* by Anne Baring and Jules Cashford.

Tools and Materials
A variety of more or less smooth, vaguely egg-shaped stones
Black paint: matte, not glossy
Paintbrush
Silver metallic paint marker, the finer the better

Paint the stones black all over. When dry, draw on your Moon symbols. Make a whole clutch of moonstones and display them in a round basket filled with real grass or straw.

Egg-Striped Lantern

My absolute favorite German city is Eckernfoerde. For one thing, its name means "firth of the squirrels," and it has a reputation as one of the top squirrel rescue centers in Europe. In the summer, they have "Pirate Days," during which the mayor is sometimes led away in chains, and at Easter they have a huge bonfire.

Easter fires were once common throughout northern Germany, especially along the Baltic Coast. Ostara, it should be remembered, is not only the goddess of springtime and fertility, she is also the goddess of light, specifically the first ruddy light of dawn. Those of us who cannot build a bonfire in the sand on the Spring Equinox can at least have our own Ostara fire in a jar.

This craft requires some time and patience, but the results are oh, so pretty.

Tools and Materials

1 large, wide-mouthed glass jar such as an applesauce or pickle jar
Tissue paper: white and a variety of pastel colors
Glue
Pencil
Tealight or votive candle

Cut a piece of white tissue paper long enough to wrap around your jar and wide enough to cover the whole jar from rim to bottom. Drizzle glue over the surface of the jar and apply the tissue paper, scrunching it to cover the threaded neck and any curves the jar might have.

While the glue is drying, tear your colored tissue papers into tiny scraps about the size of your fingernail. Keep colors separate to make your life easier. An egg carton is helpful if you have lot of different colors. When the white tissue paper no longer feels moist, draw some light pencil lines on the jar to define your stripes. The best way to do this is to cut a band of paper the width you want your stripe to be, position it on the jar and trace around it with the pencil. A combination of wide and narrow stripes looks best.

Now fill in the stripes by gluing the torn strips of tissue paper one by one onto your jar. Neatness counts: try not to stray over the lines! When you're done, place the candle inside and light with a long match.

Egg-Shaped Easter Witch

A black cat, a besom, and a copper kettle: that's all you need to be an Easter Witch, a folkloric icon of the Swedish springtime. I hope you'll try your hand at these painted ornaments, but don't be surprised if they suddenly disappear from your egg tree on Maundy

Thursday. That's when the Swedish Easter Witches fly off to Blakulla to dance around the bonfire, eat, and drink coffee, growing rounder and fatter all the while—they sometimes get stuck in their own chimneys when they come home on Easter Eve!

Where is Blakulla, you ask? That's a matter still open to debate, but some believe it is the same mountain to which German Witches fly on Walpurgis Night (April 30).

When painting your Witch, remember: no pointy hats! Swedish witches wear gaily patterned kerchiefs. They are also said to have red cheeks, probably from all that drinking and dancing. If you want to Americanize your Easter Witch, give her a bandana and a blue spackleware coffee pot.

Tools and Materials

1 flat wooden egg, 2¼ inches by 3¼ inches, available at craft stores
    at this time of year

Pencil

Tracing paper (optional)

Acrylic paints

Fine paintbrush

Small scrap of white tissue paper

Glue

String

Paint both sides of your egg with a base coat of white. When it's dry, you can sketch and then paint your witch on. Make her as realistic or as abstract as you like. If you're lacking in confidence, you can use tracing paper and a soft lead pencil to transfer the design directly from this book to the white surface of your egg. Just trace the illustration, turn over the paper and draw over the lines again so there's lead on both sides of the paper. Now place the paper right-side up on your egg and, pressing firmly, draw over the lines once more. When you lift up the paper, there will be the outline of your witch.

Before painting the back of your witch's kerchief, glue a loop of string to the back of the egg. Glue a scrap of tissue paper over the bottom of the loop to hide it, then simply paint over the tissue paper. Don't forget the witch's black cat!

All One Family

Sandra Kynes

AS SPRING ARRIVES, THE natural world seems to vibrate with quickening energy and signs of reawakening come forth. Halfway between the solstices, this is a time of balance when day and night are equal. Although Ostara is one of the solar sabbats, it is a celebration of both the Earth and Sun. The Earth represents female energy and the Sun represents male energy, and when they are in balance, things blossom and grow—plants on the earth, new life in the womb, and creativity of the spirit.

Getting eggs to stand on their own is a fun activity that illustrates balance. Even though I had seen pictures of this, I have to admit I was a bit skeptical until we tried it. First, you need to know the time the solstice actually occurs in your area, which can be found online. Because it's difficult to be absolutely exact, you will want to start about five minutes before the given time and continue to about five minutes after. Next, you need a flat, level surface.

When it's time to begin, position an uncooked egg with its narrow end downward. Hold it upright loosely and gently with your fingers forming a cage around it. Smaller children may need to work with an adult or older sibling. The eggs will stand on their own when the Sun is right over the equator, bringing the magnetic poles into balance. You may want to have a camera ready to capture the moment—not so much for the eggs, but for the facial expressions. The look on my son's face the first time we did this was one of those things parents remember forever.

If the time of the solstice occurs in the middle of the night or doesn't fit your family's schedule, another fun activity involving balance is to do the classic yoga posture called "tree." We like to do this standing in a circle so we can all see each other. You can expect lots of giggles with this. Begin by shifting your weight on to one foot, and then as you turn the knee of the other leg out to the side, place the sole of that foot against the calf of the standing leg. If small children are a little too wobbly, have them keep the toes of that foot on the floor and the heel against the other ankle. When everyone is fairly steady, lift your arms up and out to the sides to represent full leafy branches. One at a time, each person tells what kind of tree they are. We usually follow this with a discussion about the Celtic tree calendar. Beginning with alder, the tree for this time of year, we try to see who can name all the trees in order. Because balance is the theme for the day, we switch sides and do the tree pose again with the opposite leg as support. This time, on the count of three, we say what tree we are all at the same moment. We've been surprised at how many times we have chosen the same tree.

Food is an important component of celebrations, and spring has its traditions and treats. We like to have eggs for breakfast on Ostara because they are the quintessential symbol of spring—not just for balancing them. For many ancient peoples the egg was central to their creation myths, representing sacred life and its mysteries. The yolk symbolized the bright yellow sun, and the white protective shell the white goddess herself bringing new life and sustenance.

Of course, a fried egg can represent the sun, but we like to make what we call a "bird's nest." We cut a fairly large circle out of the center of a piece of bread to make the basket. This goes into the frying pan first and then the egg is cracked open into the circle. It's a little trickier to flip over, but is a fun variation of the fried egg. Although hot cross buns are part of the Christian celebration of Easter, we like to include them in our sabbat breakfast. They are easily adapted for Ostara by carving or using icing to make a circle near the center turning the cross into a Celtic Sun symbol.

March is a good time to start work in the backyard, and it is an activity that our whole family shares just after Ostara. While it's too early to plant anything here in northern New England, there is plenty of cleaning up to do that keeps us outdoors and in touch with nature. Picking up twigs and branches brought down by winter storms is a project small children can handle, and it serves to gather fuel for future use for a Beltane fire. We also look for longer twigs we can bundle together to create besom brooms. It may be necessary to remove some smaller twigs to create a less bushy end to the bundle, so it can be bound together with twine and serve as a handle. One year it became a quest for my son to find just the right straight branch to attach the twigs to so it would look more like a regular broom. Unfortunately it didn't function all that well for actually sweeping, but it was beautiful for ritual purposes.

In addition to tidying up the garden, this is a traditional time of year for a major house cleaning, which is an affirmation of making ready for growth and transformation. We use our new besoms from this year's yard cleanup to add a magical start to the Spring cleaning project. We start at the front door and move through each room in a procession lead by the youngest member of the family carrying the broom if there's only one besom that year. Along with making sweeping movements with the besoms, we chant the following as we go through the house: "As we sweep to and fro, Winter's staleness now must go. Springtime enter mild and fair, bring the magic of element air." We end at the back door with one final synchronized sweeping motion to send winter and any negativity away.

Early spring also provides an opportunity to find branches for making wands. Make the suggestion to your children that they look at the branches they've collected during the yard cleanup and imagine what they may look like as wands. Years ago I had not considered using a wand until the branch that was to become my first one found me. I was out for my morning walk and happened to look at a maple branch on the ground. For just a moment, I saw it as a wand. Of course, I had to take it home with me to create what I had seen.

If just the right branch can't be found on the ground and your trees are still dormant, spring is a good time for pruning (which also might yield a natural wand, so be sure to keep a few branches). Older children can help by holding branches steady while you cut, but to safely include younger children, have them join in saying a cutting blessing: "Thank you spirits of this tree, for gifting this branch to me. Give it power for spells of good, blessed be this sacred wood." Sometimes we tie a small white ribbon on the tree as a reminder of our connection with the tree spirit. By summer, the ribbon disappears behind foliage, but will become visible again in the autumn.

Being able to spend more time outside helps us celebrate the return of spring and keeps us in touch with the cycle of renewal as we give thanks to the Mother Goddess for the wonder of her power and her unfolding beauty.

Ostara Ritual: Soaring Ambition

Ellen Dugan

If I keep a green bough in my heart, the singing bird will come.
—Chinese proverb

This springtime ritual may be performed as a solitary or with your circle or coven. This ritual relies on the folklore and the magick of both birds and the symbolism of birds' nests. If you like, you could incorporate pictures of birds in your altar setup. Quarter candles are not necessary, but you may use them if you wish.

For your altar setup, I suggest classic spring-fresh flowers from the garden, such as tulips and daffodils and perhaps a few soft and fuzzy branches of pussy willow or bright yellow blooming forsythia in a simple glass jar. This would be a lovely addition to your altar. If weather permits, I recommend working this ritual outdoors.

Note: For this ritual, you will want to incorporate little artificial eggs and small decorative birds' nests. (Both are available at craft stores.) You will want one nest for each person. You can add little colored eggs or a silk bird to the decorative nest if you like.

Don't forget to add to your central workspace a few fallen feathers that you have found on your augury quests and illuminator candles in soft green and other pastel spring shades. Bottom line: make a beautiful altar set up with whatever you have.

Items Needed

Spring flowers, fresh

Glass jar

Artificial eggs (available at craft stores)

Decorative bird's nest (available at craft stores)

Feathers, fallen and recovered

Illuminator candles, pastels, soft green, etc.

Quarter candles

Silk bird/ picture of birds (optional)

Songbird food (optional)

Take the time to set the stage and get in the mood for some springtime magick. Also, as a thoughtful touch, add a small dish of good songbird food to your altar setup. You will be leaving that outdoors as an offering when the ritual is finished.

If you have a group, you may assign speaking parts for this ritual or simply all say them together. If you work alone, then just do all of the speaking parts.

The Spring Equinox Ritual

To begin have all of the participants gather in a circle around the central altar.

Call the quarters, begin in the east. Say: *I call to the element of air, may the goldfinches send us fresh inspiration and wisdom during this spring season. Blessed be.*

Turn to the right and face the south. Say: *I call upon the element of fire, may the cardinals fly in and brighten our lives with passion and the energy to complete all of our goals. Blessed be.*

Turn to the right and face the west. Say: *I call to the element of water, may the bluebirds bless us with joy, health and love during this season of growth. Blessed be.*

Finally turn right and face the north. Say: *I call upon the element of earth, may the robins gift us with determination and abundance as we celebrate the earth's rebirth. Blessed be.*

Have all the participants turn and face the center and the altar. Join hands and cast the circle, say:

As above now so below. The elemental powers spin and our magick holds.

Allow the joined hands to drop and continue with the ritual by saying together:

Now begins the lovely season of the spring,
Good luck, joy and cheer this enchantment will bring.
As the birds fly around me/ us, the magick begins,
Bringing opportunity, rebirth and wisdom.

May new possibilities hatch today,
Leaving room for blessings to soar my/ our way.

Have everyone pick up their own little bird's nest. Hold it with both hands and fill the nest with all of the positive thoughts, wishes for success and growth that you can manage. Imagine that the little nest is filled with warmth, love, and possibilities that are absolutely brimming over. Raise your energy high. Once you have done that, hold out the nest and say:

May this magickal goal now take wing,
Soaring higher even as the birds do sing.

Now release that energy and your goals out into the universe where they will go about their business. Ground and center yourself. Sit on the ground and hold your nest in your lap. Now say together:

This small bird's nest will now act as a talisman true,
May I/ we be happy and successful in all that I/ we do.

Break for Cakes and Ale

Have someone or the high priestess of the group hold up the chalice of wine or cider, and the plate of cookies and then say:

> *In the name of the Bird Goddess of old,*
> *I bless these seasonal cakes and wine/ juice.*
> *May they imbue us with health, happiness and prosperity,*
> *By the powers of the moon and the sun, as I will it so mote it be.*

Pass the chalice and then the cookies around to the participants with a blessing. As each person takes a sip of the liquid and takes a cookie, they pass them along to their neighbor with a blessing. They could say something like, *"Blessed be the spring," "May the birds grant you knowledge and success,"* or *"May you never thirst/ hunger."*

Let everyone enjoy the snack and relax for a bit. Then it is time to conclude the ritual. When everyone is finished, return the chalice and plate to the altar. Have everybody stand up and place their little decorative bird nest on the altar again. Then everyone should all join hands again for a moment. Feel the energy and fellowship of your group.

If there are any special requests for magick from individuals in the group, it should be done now. Be sure to keep it positive and the mood upbeat. Afterward, have **everyone** say together:

> *The ritual of spring is now done. May the Goddess bless us all.*
> *May we all know happiness, wisdom, well-being and growth in the coming season.*
> *Blessed be.*

Allow the joined hands to drop. Prepare to open the quarters.

Start in the north. Say: *Brother robin and the element of earth, we thank you for your strength and purpose during our ritual. Blessed be.*

Turn to the left and face the west. Say: *Sister bluebird and the element of water, we thank you for your healing and affection during our ritual. Blessed be.*

Turn to the left and face the south. Say: *Brother cardinal, and the element of fire, we thank you for your light, and energy during our ritual. Blessed be.*

Finally, turn to the left and face the east. Say: *Sister goldfinch, and the element of air, we thank you for your wisdom and flow during our ritual. Blessed be.*

To close up the ritual have everyone join hands one final time and face the center and the Equinox altar again. Then **all** say:

The circle is open, but unbroken. Merry meet, merry part and merry meet again!
Blessed be the spring!

Clean up your ritual area. Extinguish any candles, and be sure to leave the bird food offering outdoors for the local song birds. Have everyone take home their little decorative nests as a keepsake and as a talisman for growth and success. May this springtime bring you and yours every happiness.

Notes

Beltane

Beltane: The Beautiful Season

Suzanne Ress

THE FLORALIA WAS AN ancient Roman festival that took place from around April 28 through May 3, celebrating fecundity, blooming flowers, and the goddess Flora. Women, young and old, decorated their hair, clothes, and homes with flowers, and there was much feasting, drinking, and erotic gaming for everyone.

Later, the powerful Christian church desired so much to eradicate any trace of paganism and its festivals that in Italy the month of May was proclaimed *La Mese della Madonna*—The Madonna's Month, when one was supposed to stay celibate and chaste. It was generally believed (and still is, in some parts of Italy) that bad luck and barrenness would come to couples that married (or copulated) during the month of May.

Ancient Germanic pagan people celebrated the start of the light half of the year, fertility, and flowers as Walpurgisnacht, April 30 to May 1. This was also believed to be the most important of all the Witches' sabbats. Here again, the Church eventually transformed this festival of joy into a Christian Saint's Day—Saint Walpurga—who is supposed to protect one against witchcraft!

Modern Pagan sabbats derive from the original archaic celebrations of the changing seasons in nature. They are the human group response to the earth's seasonal transformation, and the dates they occur are pretty consistent with our current awareness of nature having taken a major new step along the Wheel of the Year. I find it really interesting that even traditional Christian and Jewish holidays celebrated in modern Western civilization have their roots in these same ancient pagan nature worship festivals. If we are deeply aware of the natural world, we respond with our spirits, and this is, in essence, what sabbats are all about.

One of the four great Celtic fire festivals is Beltane, May 1. In years gone by, huge bonfires were lit at Beltane, to cleanse and renew the earth, livestock, and human beings alike, ensuring their health and fertility for the growing season.

Together with Midsummer's Eve and Samhain, Beltane Eve was considered to be one of the three Celtic Spirit Nights, when one could most easily find and commune with the spirits of dead friends and relatives, because the veil between the spirit world and the mundane one was at its thinnest. At both Beltane and Midsummer, fairies and fairy spirits were supposed to be at their most accessible to human seekers!

🌿

Beltane Eve, April 30, was considered a traditional time for Witches to congregate, which may have scared some non-Witches, but the holiday certainly must have been happily anticipated by pretty much everyone, because it offered a break from cultural norms and conventional behavior.

At Beltane, then, as now, the Earth's reproductive energies are at their peak. Thus, the original intent of this sabbat was to celebrate the earth's forces of sexuality and reproduction in a state of joy. Couples, whether old, young, or middle-aged would retreat to the woods at sundown on the last day of April for a night of unbridled erotic pleasure. This was an act of copulation for human fertility as well as a symbolic reenactment of the marriage of Flora (Queen of the May) to her lover, who was called, among other names, the Horned God, the Green Man, or Lord of the Greenwood.

On the morning on the first of May, everyone returned from the woods carrying bunches of flowers, especially hawthorn blossoms, which are also known as mayflowers. These would be set atop or at the base of the phallic maypole, or woven into one another's hair, and then everyone would dance naked around the pole, holding one of the attached colored streamers, until all of the streamers were woven around the pole. Then the dancers reversed direction to unwind the streamers and unbind the pole. At the end of the celebration the pole was taken down and burnt to ashes. Some of these ashes were saved to use in fertility amulets.

An old Scottish ritual for Beltane called for a bannock cake to be divided into pieces, one of which was marked with charcoal. With participants blindfolded, the pieces of cake were selected, and he or she who got the charcoaled morsel became the "Beltane Carline" (Hag). The "hag" would be tossed around by the others, sometimes dangerously close, or even into, the fire, or else forced to run several times back and forth between two large bonfires. Sometimes the others would stage a mock mobbing, at the end of which the "hag" was supposed to play dead. For an entire year after the celebrations the person designated as the Beltane Carline was considered to be dead, and spoken of as if he or she was actually no longer alive!

This sort of Beltane celebration continued until the fourth century, when all pagan festivals were banned throughout the Holy Roman Empire. Nonetheless, people continued to celebrate May as the month of sexual freedom throughout rural Europe, until the sixteenth century, and, in a lesser way, into the eighteenth century.

⚜

Nowadays at Beltane, few people can manage to run off naked into the forest with their latest crush for a night of wild lovemaking and follow that with a day of raucous and bawdy group gaming, but everyone, even non-Pagans, still celebrate fertility, perhaps without even knowing it! We all love to see and smell the flowering fruit trees (apple, almond, plum, pear, cherry, etc.), enjoy the new green shoots in herb and perennial flower gardens, and experience the overwhelmingly joyous feeling that life is developing and growing everywhere all around and within us.

The seasons are mild where I live in northern Italy, near the Alps. Crocus come up faithfully every year in mid-February, and, by the very end of April, the sweet perfume of black locust (*Robinia pseudoacacia*) blossoms permeates the soft evening breezes that come down from the mountains, through the woods, and into the village.

Standing at the high edge of one valley and looking over the void to the next hill where springy green foliage is spattered with white blooms, the mere act of breathing the scent in the air fills me with the dizzy, happy feel of springtime.

As a beekeeper, I especially look forward to the blooming of the black locust each year right around May 1, as this signals one of the main honey flows of the season. The air smells like honey! I hear the buzzing of thousands of bees overhead in the treetops, busy gathering nectar from early morning until late afternoon.

As in the rest of Europe, May 1 is celebrated as Labor Day, but in Italy it also marks the start of what is called *La Bella Stagione*, or "the Beautiful Season"—the lighter half of the year, from May through October—as opposed to the less beautiful, dark season from November through April.

I love the lighter half of the year, especially the start of it, for its greening up, its warmth, and blooming, buzzing, raucously sexual fecundity. Because I live and work on a small farm, I spend a good part of every day outdoors during all seasons, and when the Beautiful Season arrives, I rush to relish every moment of it, seeking out and seeing changes in my natural surroundings. These changes are constant: Flower buds appear on the azalea bushes one day, a new generation of bees are orienting themselves to the hive the next, a hen begins to brood on a clutch of eggs, the horses' coats shed out to become glossy and fine, the strange red leaf shoots of the rhubarb poke out from the earth and their rhizomic underground homes. Seeing and smelling, and being generally aware of the all-around presence of flowers, flowering plants, and blossoming trees are greatly responsible for the energy-boosting high we all feel at Beltane.

❧

In the traditional Beltane festival of the British Isles, the hawthorn tree (*Crataegus monogyna*) played and still plays a central role. The name hawthorn means literally "hedge thorn," or thorny hedge. The hawthorn is usually a smallish tree, and its tight thorny branches make an excellent barrier hedge. Right around May 1 the tree blooms with bunches of five-petaled white flowers dotted inside with red or pink. These will be fertilized by bees (who then produce hawthorn honey), and in the fall the tree will sport brilliant red berries, called haws.

In days of yore, the hawthorn tree was known as the "bread and cheese tree" because chewing the leaves takes away hunger pangs and gives one a feeling of well-being. One of the world's greatest sacred trees was the Glastonbury Holy Thorn, which was purported to be more than 700 years old. Normally, hawthorn trees can live as long as 400 years. The hawthorn is one of the Druids' sacred trees, and was known as the fairy tree, because it was believed that fairies dwelt in and around it. A powerful protective amulet can be made by taking a small twig each from the oak, the ash, and the hawthorn and tying them together with a red ribbon. Wands made of hawthorn are also extremely powerful.

The hawthorn is a symbol of fertility, love, and the heart. Amazingly, its leaves, flowers, and berries contain chemical compounds that are used in modern blood pressure medicines. Drinking hawthorn tea regularly over a long period of time tones and strengthens the heart muscle. Hawthorn flowers can be used in salads and to make jam, and the haw berries, too, can be made into jam, or macerated in brandy or grappa to make liquor.

The hawthorn tree, in Italian, is called *biancospino*, or "white thorn." I find it now and then whilst horse-riding through the woods, but it is not so widespread nor as common as in other parts of the world. The two main trees types of trees in my neck of the woods are chestnut and black locust.

The black locust was only brought to Italy from the United States in the eighteenth century as an ornamental tree. It is an extremely fast-growing tree, so fast that it is often considered an invasive species. It can reach a height of seventy feet, but is not particularly long-lived. Black locust flowers are intensely fragrant and bloom in clusters like grapes. These are edible; they are, in fact, a legume, and are dipped in batter and sold as fritters at local fairs and festivals in early May. The flowers can also be used in jams.

I see the bees' year as a replica of the Pagan sabbat year in miniature. When the days become short and the outside temperature falls at night, around Samhain, the bees form a cluster. They must have a store of honey in their hive to last through the winter, for when temperatures are this low, even if there were something blooming (and there is not!) they are unable to move enough to fly out and get it. They are just like us, or anyway, as we used to be before we became dependent on supermarkets for food, in that they harvest as much as they can when it is available, and put it away in their wax combs, where it cannot spoil. They are able to move only enough to change positions in the cluster, and to eat a little food. On very bright sunny days their bodies may become warm enough so they can fly just outside the hive to defecate, but mostly they will stay huddled up inside through Yule, and until about Imbolc.

At Imbolc, with the first few warm days when the outside temperature reaches about 57 degrees Fahrenheit and early blooming plants begin to bud, the bees who have made it through the winter begin to fly again at the warmest part of the day. They will find their first few morsels of pollen as some trees and flowers bloom, and bring this, along with whatever nectar they can get, back to the hive. The queen will start depositing eggs in the brood nest area of the hive.

With the arrival of Ostara, life in the hive begins to go into full swing. The bee population is growing rapidly, and, if there are not enough flowers in bloom, the beekeeper must provide additional food in the form of fructose syrup or leftover supers of the hive's own honey, to keep the family healthy and growing.

Beltane, festival of flowers and fecundity, is when the bees and their hives become the central part of my daily activity. Flowering trees and plants are busting out all over. The hives hum with happy and excited activity, and the population inside each hive will reach its maximum of around 80,000 to 100,000 bees between Beltane and Litha. I must be on constant watch for swarms, checking each hive frequently to monitor its population, general health, activity, and honey production. Worker bees will spend up to fifteen hours a day gathering nectar to make honey. With a source, bees will continue to make honey indefinitely, so I must know when it's time to put another super (framed box beekeepers use) on the hive to give them space to store it. Once the first honey flow is over (when the flowers on the black locust trees begin to turn brown and fall, like fairy snow, to the ground), I can remove the extra supers and steal some honey for my own uses.

Lammas and Mabon see a gradual winding down of fecundity in the queen, and a great lessening of hive activity, as the bees once again begin to prepare for winter.

Both bees and trees have always been, and continue to be, important to human beings, and whether we realize it or not, they continue to be essential to our survival. The trees' roots, bark, leaves, sap, seeds, nuts, berries, fruit, and their flowers provide us with food, drink, medicine, potions, and aphrodisiacs; their bark, branches, and trunks provide building materials for boats, buildings, fences, furniture, jewelry, and wands. Their exhalations are our inhalations, and without them, we would have difficulty breathing.

Honeybees, of course, are irreplaceable as pollinators, and, without them, trees could produce neither flowers nor fruit. To me, Beltane is a joyous celebration of flowering trees and bees!

Cosmic Sway

Daniel Pharr

THE FIRST DAY OF Celtic summer and the last day of Celtic winter, Beltaine was one of the two most important days of the year, the other being Samhain. The Celtic Wheel began with two seasons, winter and summer. Spring and autumn were added later as the Celts settled into agrarianism. The solstices and equinoxes entered the lexicon of high holidays after the Celts came to recognize midseason days and the astronomical alignments of the prehistoric installations such as Stonehenge and many other pre-Celtic stone circles.

The traditional solar calendar has Beltaine beginning at sundown on April 30 and continuing overnight to May 1, although the calculated date this year is the night of May 4. However, the Celts would have considered the night of the Full Scorpio Moon, April 25, to be the evening for celebrating Beltaine. The New Moon doesn't arrive until May 9 and would have been too far removed from the Beltaine energies to host the celebration.

Beltaine was celebrated with a huge fire, which fits in well with the aspects of the Scorpio Full Moon. Even though Scorpio is of the element water, the intensity of the Scorpio Full Moon has fiery energy. The Scorpio Moon will bring emotional intensity to everything you do, and emotional intensity can lead to drama and stress. The

Full Moon will further intensify the lunar influences. The Moon in the Fourth House provides us with refuge and security. The easiest places to be in this Moon are home and hearth. The most sustaining activities are those involving family and friends. The Twelfth House is ruled by the moon, and in this Scorpio arena, the dark side steps onto the floor. All that is normally hidden in shadow—fears, failures, fights, spirituality, sexuality, and, the esoteric—moves temporarily into the light to be seen. Hidden strengths and hidden enemies, along with the hidden weakness of karmic debt waiting to be paid, demonstrate a need for balance. This a time for ending the controlled self-image and letting your assertiveness meet your empathy to battle on the floor of the coliseum in front of your family, friends, and the very gods themselves, and find the balanced place that lets them both exist in harmony and in light. The Moon trines Chiron right now giving you the inner strength to face your painful personal plights and the Neptune trine allows your creativity and artistic sides flourish. Use these two lunar aspects to recognize the existence of your shadow nature, accept that piece of your personality, and commit to living in the light. The Taurus Sun in the Tenth House will help you shine privately, publicly, and professionally. An ascending Leo also makes you powerful.

Scorpio Full Moon

Under the Full Scorpio Moon, build a fire, a big one—no, a huge one. Write the aspects of yourself that you prefer to remain hidden on a piece of paper, or many pieces of paper. Be brutally honest, even if tears or screaming are involved. Sit with the fire and visualize your life without the shadow of your hidden self following you everywhere, without caring if anyone or everyone knows your deepest, darkest secrets. Stand before the fire and read your many faults and fears aloud, so that even the gods may hear over the crackling of the fire. Announce that those aspects of your life will no longer hold you back or influence your future, and ask your friends and family, as well as the deities you hold dear, to help you in this brave endeavor by reminding you of your commitment should they, at some future moment, see hesitation in your eyes. Burn the papers so that the shadow may be illuminated, and jump the fire. If you are in a group, each person takes their turn. If a fire cannot be built and burned, use a cauldron or candles.

May Day

May Day, the first day of May, the traditional day of Beltaine, actually begins at sundown on April 30, night before day, darkness before light. The Capricorn Moon will remind you of the sense of security you experience in a structured environment, and the waning phase of the moon will help you to let that feeling go. It does not serve you. Libra on the ascent, the Moon square Mercury and trine Venus, will all help you to find and achieve the balance that comes from strong familial ties and self-confidence in the face of an ever-changing life experience. Others want to share in your experiences and the wisdom that has come from your experiences. You must be in balance in yourself in order to effectively impart such knowledge. The strength of Mars in Taurus will provide significant emotional strength.

Astrological Beltaine

The Druids were talented mathematicians and astronomers, but the advancement of science beyond the Druidic realm has given us the ability to calculate the exact day and time of Beltaine when measured to be midway between the Spring Equinox and the Summer Solstice, as well halfway through the year from Samhain. This calculated time is 10:05 pm EDT May 4, which means Beltaine actually begins at sundown.

The waning Moon in Pisces makes the energy around Beltaine deeply emotional for all. Know that your empathic qualities are strong right now, and following your heart will surely be the best course. The Moon is ruling the Seventh House, which is all about partnerships of all kinds: external and internal, loving and combative. You will be given the opportunity to take a look at the relationships in your life and decide which are working and which need improvement, and where you should be putting your energy and where you should not, be it in your marriage, your business, your inner animus or your outer enemies. Turn on the empathy and the charm. The Moon sextile Venus and the Moon conjunct Chiron will help with both. Mercury, Venus, and Mars are all in Taurus now, offering patience in your communication, your love, and your desires. Your methodical manner will prove motivating.

Beltaine New Moon

The Beltaine New Moon on May 9 brings a fresh start. Residing in Taurus, the lunar influences will be on strength, stability, and sexuality. You may feel powerful and seductive. Mercury and Mars are also in Taurus bringing their influence of stability, while Venus in Gemini will bring out your flirtatious side. The Moon, Mars, Venus, and Mercury are in the Eighth House right now. These four will strongly influence you to seek out a better understanding of the meaning of life. Not the greater exoteric meaning in the planetary cycle of life, but the more focused and centralized question of the meaning of your individual life. This self-examination will undoubtedly lead to a study of the choices you have made and direction you are heading. Do not allow the various lunar aspects to cause you to worry about your life. Call down the power of ascending Libra to bring balance to your future. By changing the focus of your energies, you can positively influence any area of your life to become exactly that which makes you most happy. As you already know, you cannot change other people, but you can change yourself, and this ability gives you power over your entire world.

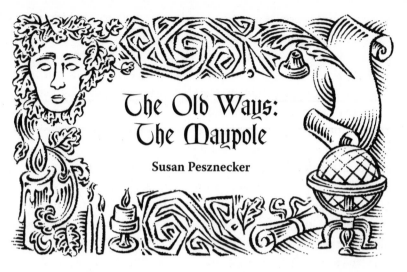

The Old Ways: The Maypole

Susan Pesznecker

It's BELTAINE TIME AGAIN.... And let's clear up a little bit of semantic confusion right here at the start. The word may also be spelled Beltane, Beltain, Beltine, Bealtaine, Bealltainn, Bealtuinn, and probably in some ways I haven't yet discovered. The word comes from Gaelic, and it's correctly pronounced BEE-yul-TIN-yuh.

Along with Lughnasadh (Lammas), Samhain, and Imbolc, Beltaine is one of the four crossquarter sabbats, i.e., one that falls between the quarter days—the equinoxes and solstices. Beltaine is generally celebrated on May 1, although the astronomical point between the Spring Equinox and the Summer Solstice is usually between May 5 and 7. To make this even a little more confusing, extant records suggest that the ancient Celtic Druids most likely didn't celebrate Beltaine on a specific date or according to the night sky, but rather according to what was happening in the agricultural world. When the hawthorn—or other spring-blooming white flowered tree—bloomed, Beltaine had arrived.

Yet another name for Beltaine is May Day, a holiday always celebrated on May 1. Whatever you call it, Beltaine or May Day has always symbolized the kickoff of summer. It's also a day strongly associated with fertility, sex, reproduction, and passion. This is the holiday where peoples past would celebrate raucously for hours (or days) and then pair off and steal into the fields, where they'd copulate as a way of insuring the earth's fertility in the coming season.

Carrying this ancient sexual allusion forward, it's no surprise that the most recognizable modern symbol of Beltaine is the maypole. The maypole is a tall wooden pole that is erected for Beltaine celebrations. Streams of ribbon are fastened to the top of the pole, and dancers grab the ends and dance round the pole, weaving in and out in patterns that literally weave the ribbons into a pattern around the pole. The dance can be done with a group as small as 6 and as large as 24; it works best with 12 to 16 dancers. The taller the pole, the longer the ribbons, and the wider the circle inscribed; therefore, a taller pole usually benefits from a larger number of dancers.

Most serious maypoles are 12 feet or more in height, and some of the really tall ones reached 50 to 60 feet. In many cases, the young men of the village were charged with finding the ideal tree for the maypole, a task they began weeks or even months before the event. The same young men would fell the tree, prepare it, and then sink and install the pole itself. Birch was commonly used for the pole and is one of the nine sacred Celtic woods. Spruce was sometimes used, too. The act of felling the tree, of course, became a type of sacrificial ritual and was enacted with solemnity and respect.

No one is really sure how the maypole ritual was started. There are scattered references to maypoles in Iron Age literature and in some medieval writings as well. One story links it to the Feast of Flora, goddess of flowers. Flora's feast was celebrated on April 30 to May 1 as part of traditional Rites of Spring. Young women who had reached physical maturity over the last year were chosen to dance (and sometimes to help prepare) the maypole. The day began with a dawn trip into forests and fields, where the young women picked vines and flowers to adorn their dancing costumes. The complete process became a rite of passage as well as a ritual.

The maypole dance has also been linked to old German Pagan customs, and was widely practiced throughout Europe in the Middle Ages and for a period after before being more or less quashed by the Christian church. Today, the practice of dancing the maypole is more commonly observed in Europe than in any other country.

The maypole is most commonly described as a phallic symbol, i.e., a representation of the erect penis that has been buried deeply in the (mother) earth—a clear symbol of fertility and reproduction. The idea of maypole-as-phallus also has a possible connection to Roman worship of the fertility god Priapus. There have been other attempts to explain the maypole's symbolism. For example, the poles have been linked to the "world axis" and possibly to demonstrating reverence for trees or for the World Tree, the Yggdrasil known in Norse Pagan traditions.

While most villages construct the maypole for Beltaine, some occasionally put it up for midsummer, the summer solstice. Towns that regularly include the maypole in their festivities often leave it in place from one season to the next, allowing it to become a focal point of sorts. In some locations, young men try to steal maypoles from neighboring communities, much as college mascot-stealing used to be held in vogue.

The actual maypole ceremony was usually just one part of a community-wide revel that may have involved singing, morris dancing, parades, food and drink, and other festivities. Many towns elected a "Queen of May" to rule over the festivities; a male corollary, the "Robin Hood," was also sometimes chosen. The actual maypole dancers were typically either children or young women and were often clad in white, giving rise again to symbols of procreation. It was typical for dancers to wear wreaths of vines and flowers in their hair, as well as adorning their outfits with colored ribbons. If the dance was completed without any ribbons coming loose from the pole or breaking during the dance, it was felt to be a sign of luck. Once the dance was done and the pole plaited with ribbons, some groups redid the dance in reverse to undo the weaving—the reasons for this are unclear.

The maypole ceremony has developed its own offshoots, too. In some European towns, young men plant miniature maypoles outside the homes of their fiancés or intended fiancés on the night before Beltaine. One version of the dance was immortalized in the film, *The Wicker Man*.

❦

At the end of the day on Beltaine, with dancing done and feasting complete, most groups built a giant bonfire to keep the revelry going. "Jumping the fire" was a common pastime for the young men of the village and was supposed to reveal their virility and courage.

Flowers and feasting, song and dance, parades and poles, crowns and Queens…. Just another Beltaine. May yours be merry!

Feasts and Treats

Kristin Madden

SYNONYMOUS WITH PASSION, LOVE, and sensuality, Beltane feasts demand an exceptional sensory experience. Each of these recipes awakens the senses in unique ways. The tastes and textures of each dish tantalizes and enchants with spice and ice. These are ideal for a Beltane feast alone, with your community, or simply shared with a lover.

Bacon-Wrapped Scallops

There is something so sensual about finger foods and these melt-in-your-mouth scallops wrapped in crispy bacon are sure to please all your senses. Add a Dijon mustard or Asian-inspired dipping sauce for a bit of a kick.

Prep Time: 10 minutes
Cooking Time: 15 minutes
Chill Time: 1 hour
Serves: 4

4 tablespoons soy sauce
½ cup olive oil (divided)
¼ cup sesame oil

¼ teaspoon (each) cumin, salt, and pepper
10 large scallops, halved
10 slices bacon, halved widthwise
20 toothpicks

Combine soy sauce, ¼ cup olive oil, sesame oil, and spices. Add scallops and toss to coat. Cover and refrigerate for at least 1 hour.

Fry bacon until cooked but still soft. Remove and drain on paper towels. Then sear scallops in ¼ cup olive oil, 4 to 5 minutes on each side, until browned. Wrap each scallop in a piece of bacon and secure with a toothpick. Broil on high for 2 minutes, turning once halfway through, until bacon is crispy.

Curried Shrimp Bites

Here is another sensual finger food that will ignite the fire within and stir some passions at your Beltane feast. This time, bring an Indian flavor to sweet seafood for the delight of all.

Prep Time: 15 minutes
Cooking Time: 50 minutes
Serves: 6–8

2 tablespoons olive oil
3 tablespoons butter
2 medium onions, chopped
2 garlic cloves, chopped
2 teaspoons (each) ground ginger and curry powder
1½ teaspoons (each) coriander and cumin
1 teaspoon red chili powder
½ teaspoon cloves
¼ teaspoon cinnamon
2 cups diced canned tomatoes
2 tablespoons lemon juice
2 pounds shrimp, peeled

Sauté onions in oil and butter until browned. Add garlic and spices. Cook for 3 minutes. Add tomatoes (including juice) and lemon juice. Cover and cook for 30 minutes, until sauce thickens. Add shrimp and cook for another 5 minutes. Serve with toothpicks or mini-forks.

Strawberry Margaritas

Temper the heat of Beltane a tad with these sensual yet cooling drinks. Frozen margaritas are the perfect beverage to relax mind and body while awakening all your senses.

> *Prep Time:* 5 minutes
> *Serves:* 4

3½ cups strawberries
2½ cups crushed ice
½ cup lime juice
¼ cup sugar
3 tablespoons orange juice
Optional: ½ cup tequila, 4 lime wedges

Combine all ingredients in a blender and blend until smooth. Pour into glasses and garnish with lime wedges.

Chocolate Lava Cakes

Nothing says passion and romance like chocolate. This edible language of love is elevated to near-Divinity in the form of a molten lava cake.

> *Prep Time:* 15 minutes
> *Cooking Time:* 25 minutes
> *Serves:* 4

½ cup butter
6 ounces semi-sweet chocolate
3 large eggs
⅓ cup brown sugar
¼ teaspoon vanilla extract
⅛ teaspoon cream of tartar
3 tablespoons white sugar (divided)

Melt the butter and chocolate in a double boiler over simmering water. Set aside.

Separate eggs and beat egg yolks with brown sugar and vanilla extract until fluffy. Fold into chocolate mixture.

Beat egg whites until fluffy. Add cream of tartar, and beat until soft peaks form. Add 1 tablespoon white sugar, and beat until stiff peaks form. Fold into chocolate mixture until just mixed.

Bake in buttered ramekins, dusted with the remaining white sugar, at 400 degrees F for 15 to 20 minutes, until the outside has set and the center is still wet. Remove from oven and set aside for 3 minutes before serving.

Crafty Crafts

Linda Raedisch

IF GERMAN WITCHES FLY to the Brocken on May Eve, then the ideal gathering place for Celtic Witches would presumably be Cliorcal Cloch na Bealtaine, a rather tumble-down, yet unbroken, stone circle in County Donegal in northwest Ireland. Known in English as Beltany, it is an early stone circle, meaning it was constructed sometime just before or during the Bronze Age. We can't be sure what these builders had in mind when they thrust these hulks in the ground, but one of the tallest pillars (nine feet) marks the point on the horizon where the Sun rises on—you guessed it!—Beltane. Beltany must have been a place of active worship for thousands of years, for it was also home to the Beltany Stone Head, an enigmatic sculpture (there's a little bit of neck attached) that has been dated to the Celtic Iron Age. From the Middle Ages onward, the jaunty pillars of the Beltany circle were said to be local parishioners turned to stone for dancing on the Sabbath.

If you live outside the Old World, standing stones are probably not an integral part of your tradition. Nor should they be, at least not in a big way. In a perfect world, we could all make pilgrimages to Avebury and Carnac and a Stonehenge free of barbed wire as soon as we wanted to. But for most of us, there are no plane tickets on the immediate horizon. In the meantime, here are some thoughts on celebrating that old megalithic magic, in a small way, at home.

On May Eve, my daughter and I like to go out and look for "witches." My daughter's concept of a witch is rather more like a fairy than a Halloween witch. As far as I can tell, it's a small, magical, emphatically feminine creature, possibly dangerous but also quite pretty, and not to be seen with everyday vision. When she was four years old, she identified a witch named Princess, also four, in the crown of a half-dead birch tree at the train station. Since then, she has pointed out to me the dark cave inside a yew, a circle of grass in the front yard and the diminutive, spreading branches of a Chinese maple as possible witch habitations.

Witches, fairies, sidhe, elementals: call them what you will, there are bound to be a handful dwelling in your own vicinity. Seek them out. If they're open to it, consider honoring their presence with a stone circle—a very small stone circle. Even if the stones you use are only six inches high, this can be a worthwhile experience, and one that will take longer than you think.

First you must gather your stones. Will you use rocks dug up from the garden or venture further afield to the beach or a mountaintop? Choose each stone carefully. Does the shape suggest something to you? How many will you use? Thirteen, to represent the fabled Witches' Coven, or sixty-four, as at Beltany? Maybe you want to position them trickily, like the Rollright Stones, so they can never be properly counted. I've never tried it, but they say you can't make it all the way around the circle without losing count.

You'll need a garden spade. Avebury, Carnac, and Cornwall's Merry Maidens are all still standing because so much of them is underground. Plant your stones deep—at least one-third of the total length should be buried.

Take care to build your circle a little distance from your spirit's abode. You wouldn't want to wake up in the morning to find a sarcen in the middle of your living room! Consider including the fairy-haunt in an alignment with the circle and a special feature of the landscape such as a high hill, your house, or an apple tree whose blossoms turn to fairy silver by the light of the Beltane Moon.

If you've failed to contact a fairy, don't despair. It could be that she just hasn't arrived yet. Go ahead and build your circle. As you work, imagine the joy of the four-year-old child who clears away the leaf mold and discovers it long after you are gone. "Who made this?" she will wonder, "And what for?" Try to guess what stories she might weave in and around your circle.

In addition to fairies, standing stones make me think of cows. Isn't it the same with you? To the Celts, cows were every bit as sacred as the massive stone groves (ancient already in Druid times) that hallowed the moors. The stone avenues of Carnac, for one, were the site of seasonal cattle blessings, perhaps of a year-round cattle cult. In the old days, blessing the cattle meant smudging them. This was accomplished by leading the herds between the roaring Beltane fires on which such herbs as rue, chervil, pennyroyal, thyme, chamomile and wild geranium were heaped and made to send out rolling puffs of cleansing blue smoke.

After that, the cows were led up to the summer pastures by the unmarried girls of the community. In Ireland, temporary shelters called booley huts were made for the girls to live in during the summer half of the year. There they kept themselves busy milking the cows and tending small gardens. Still energized by the spirit of Beltane, which is, after all, a fertility festival, they were open to visits from the young men of the village who came to drink and dance with them of a summer's night. Who knows what trysts might have taken place on the springy heather carpets of the booley huts?

If you find yourself without a young man or even a maypole round with which to dance on Beltane, you can at least light a stick of incense as a promise of what the summer might hold.

Silver Smoke Blossom

Since earliest times in India, the lotus blossom has symbolized the female principle, the womb, and the source of life itself. Here, we

co-opt the Japanese version of the lotus blossom for our observance of Beltane.

Tools and Materials
1 square foot standard aluminum foil, not the nonstick or heavy-
duty kind
Toothpick for poking hole
Stick incense

Fold your foil into quarters in order to find the center point. Unfold. With the shiny side against your work surface, fold all four corners in to the center point. Do this two more times. Turn the piece over and fold the corners in one more time. Turn the piece over again and lift the four outermost "petals" one by one, gently peeling them back so they stand up. This will reveal the next set of petals. Peel these up too.

Do the same with the last, innermost set of petals. Poke a hole in the center of the blossom. Insert and light your incense stick.

Beltany Mask

The initial inspiration for this craft is a product of the Celtic Iron Age, the Beltany Stone Head. The idea to transform it into a mask came from looking at illustrations of tal, carved Korean dance masks. And the method of decoration is the same used in Mexican yarn painting. The end result has a rather funky, 1960s feel to it.

Tools and Materials
Watercolor paper
Compass or pasta bowl for making a circle
Pencil
Scissors
X-acto or other craft/utility knife
Glue
Hole punch
Yarn

Draw an 8-inch diameter circle on your watercolor paper. Cut out. Fold your circle into quarters. Unfold. You will see two creases. We'll call them the "equator" and the "meridian." Fold the paper again along the meridian. Sketch a large, almond-shaped eye about an inch above the equator and cut out with your knife, pressing hard to go through both layers of the paper. Now sketch one half of the nose by drawing a line from the inner corner of the eye down to about an inch below the equator to form a wedge. You can use your scissors to cut out the nose, but don't cut it all the way out; leave it attached to the mask at the bridge of the nose.

Unfold the mask. Fold the bottom half inch of the nose in so that the nose sticks out and a mouth is formed just below it.

Now, on either side of the face, cut a slit from the edge of the paper inward about three quarters of an inch along the equator. Slide the edges of each slit over one another and glue in place to make the cheeks pop out. Repeat these steps on the meridian to give your mask a chin and forehead.

Though no longer a chinless wonder, your mask is still something of a moon face. To remedy this, punch two holes on either side of the face on the equator, where you glued your slits earlier. Pass a length of yarn through the holes and pull it to elongate the face. Knot the string behind the mask. Wet the paper and allow it to dry in its new shape. If you want to paint your mask, now is the time to do it.

When the paper is dry, outline the eyes, nose and open mouth with yarn in the color of your choice. Variegated yarn works nicely for this. Go around each feature at least three times. If you want to wear the mask instead of just hanging it on the wall, untie the yarn in back and adjust accordingly.

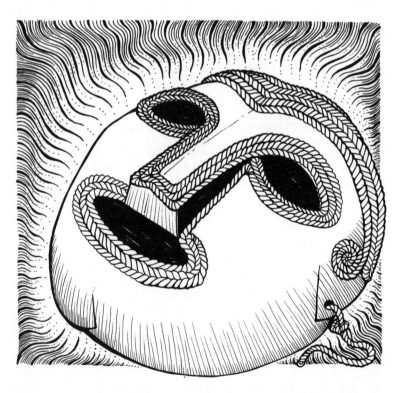

All One Family

Sandra Kynes

MAY IS A MONTH OF magic and flowers when the sun climbs higher and the forsythia persist on tender branches. Warm weather entices us outside to walk barefoot in the grass and enjoy nature's fragrances carried on gentle breezes. A woodland ramble on May Day is an age-old custom in England where it was called "a-maying." Its purpose was to collect flowers especially "May"—the flowers from hawthorn trees. When my family and I lived in England, we didn't have to go far for these flowers because we were blessed with a beautiful hawthorn in our backyard. Some years this tree served as the focus for our Beltane ritual, and we would decorate the trunk and branches with ribbons just for the day. Other years we added some of its flowers to the bundles of twigs that we tied up with white ribbons for the Beltane fire. Putting together these little bundles is a good task for children to keep them involved in the process of ritual preparation. No matter the age, they enjoy the creativity and responsibility.

It was also the custom to collect other flowers while "a-maying" that would be used for May baskets. By tradition these are very small—about the size and shape of an ice cream cone—and hung on the front door. A couple of times we had collected so many flowers that we had May baskets hanging on almost every doorknob in the house. It's another project for children to do because all it takes is a little construction paper, tape, and a few staples to secure the handles. These baskets also make nice little gifts for people who visit or share your Beltane ritual.

More than any other time of year, the waters of May are particularly potent. Springs and wells are considered holy because of the power of spirit that resides there. On our May Day ramble in the woods in New England, where we now live, we stop at a place that has a little flowing spring. We use some of the flowers we collect on the way and sometimes we fashion leaves and flowers into small wreaths for offerings. We also take along a jar to collect a little water. When we arrive at the spring we take a minute or two to listen to the water and other natural sounds. This gives us a chance to tune into the energy of the woods and the spring. With small children it's fun to make a guessing game about what's making the different sounds.

When it feels like the right moment, we walk deosil (clockwise) three times in silence around the spring. Also in silence, we each dip a finger into the spring and then touch it to our foreheads and heart centers as a symbolic ritual purification that unites the family with each other as well as the natural world. Sometimes we designate one of us to dip a finger in the water and then draw a pentagram on the forehead of each person. One by one after the anointing, we each place a flower offering beside the spring as we chant:

Water spirit, water fair, thank you for the gift you share. Water spirit, undine, sprite, be with us this Beltane night.

In addition to using some of the water we take with us for our Beltane ritual, we sprinkle some of it around our garden to unite the sacred spring with our home. We also add some water to our fairy pool. (More on this later.) Don't feel limited to finding a spring because any other body of water—a creek, pond, or even a well is appropriate. Trust your intuition. If you feel spirit of place at its location, then it's right.

On the Wheel of the Year, Beltane is directly opposite Samhain. Just as Samhain is associated with other worlds, so too, is Beltane, because this is when the fair folk return from fairyland. Because of this, Beltane is a good time to look for fairies. However, before you go, take a few things for offerings to show that you honor them and mean no harm. Offerings can include small pieces of cake or cookies, tiny quartz crystals or shiny trinkets.

We like to look for fairies during our woodland ramble, but you might also find them in a big park as long as it has a lot of trees. Hawthorn, elder, weeping willow, and apple trees are their favorites. Sometimes you may see them when you least expect it. Once when I was walking alone, I happened to look up and was startled to see a fairy about ten feet off the ground. She was as surprised as I was and immediately disappeared. That was the only time I saw a fairy, but we often find places where they have been. Circles of toadstools or flowers are called fairy rings and mark the places where they have danced. When we have found them, we step into the middle, join hands and say:

Fairies who have returned here, may you see us and draw near.
As you dance with merry grace, welcome back to this green place.

On several occasions when we've done this, we all felt an incredible rush of energy. Before we depart the circle, we always leave an offering in the center so the fairies will know that we were there with good intent when they come back to dance.

Throughout the spring and summer, we love visiting a wooded park on an island connected to the mainland by a causeway. Over the years people have been building fairy houses in an area along the footpath, and it's become a wonderfully magical place. A shift in energy around that one spot tells us that they are indeed there. The fairy village inspired us to make a few houses in our own garden. This is a project that requires imagination more than anything else. Fairy houses should be constructed of things from nature—nothing human-made and certainly not store-bought. Twigs, pieces of bark, stones, feathers, and seashells make good building material. First, we looked for well-sheltered spots in the garden to locate them. Another important consideration was plants. In addition to the trees already mentioned, their favorite shrubs include lilac and pussy willow, and their favorite plants include primrose, foxglove, jasmine, lavender, and ivy. However, don't worry if you don't have any of these because fairies love all types of plants. We built one between the lavender and ivy, and the other under the Tinkerbell lilac bush, which seemed more appropriate than the French lilac. It took a little trial and error to get them just right, but in the end we found that the small hands of children are much more adept at this. Throughout the summer and into autumn we leave treats and trinkets for them.

Fairies love being near water, so in addition to or instead of constructing a house for them a simple water feature is easy to create and adds enchantment to a garden on its own. We added a fairy pool in the middle of a patch of Lily of the Valley so it would be surrounded by flowers. A decorative font from a birdbath works well, but we decided to make it a little fancier with an old china bowl from a thrift shop. My son thought it would be attractive to fairies because the pink design inside has the scene of a castle on a lake. If you create a fairy pool, be sure to keep the water clean and to show them that you care. Whether you build a house or a little pool, leave gifts for the fairies to encourage them to visit your garden.

A Free-flowing Spring Rite

Suzanne Ress

Items Needed

An eight-foot-long red satin ribbon

A hard-boiled quail's egg for each person present (lacking this, the
    smallest size chicken eggs may be substituted)

A long slender pine cone for each person present

Closed candle lit lanterns

Closed candle lit garden lanterns on stakes

A beautiful consecrated goblet

Freshly picked wildflowers

A powerful, consecrated athame

Suggested Refreshments

A Tupperware container of freshly whipped cream

A quart of strawberries

A bottle of mead, and/or a closed pitcher of May wine

A homemade honey cake

When, as head Witch, I first began organizing our coven's sabbats, I
found it difficult to stick to plans from books. I couldn't remember
everything exactly as it was written, and it wasn't practical to bring
the book along with me to the celebration. It was much easier and

more fun to read through a plan, or several different ones, and then, with a clear idea in mind, improvise *in situ.*

The three core Witches in our coven speak and understand both English and Italian equally well, but others who join the group usually have knowledge of only one of those two languages. For this reason, and also because I am more kinetic than aural/verbal, I organize our sabbat celebrations that downplay the use of prepared spoken words, and rely more on movement and improvised chanting and singing.

At Beltane Eve, the woods where we meet is gloriously beautiful—the black locust trees are in full bloom with their sweet and strongly scented racemes of white flowers. If we are lucky enough to have a clear sky and a bright Moon, the paths that lead to our secret meeting place will be lit up by moonlight reflecting off the tiny snow-white petals which have already fallen to the ground.

Our secret grove in the woods is marked naturally by several oak trees around the west and north sides, a large chestnut tree to the south, and a grouping of black locusts along the east and northeast. Within this natural circle, eight enclosed tealight garden lanterns on stakes have been put in the ground. Because this wooded area is on my own property, where we will not be observed or disturbed by possibly unsympathetic passersby, I was able to construct a circle within a circle consisting of thirteen flagstones around a small in-ground fire pit.

The ground inside and around the flagstone circle is planted with ivy and bright-violet flowering myrtle. We almost never make a fire in the pit—even though it is functional, I feel it is dangerous to do so in the woods. Instead we use the pit to place our closed candlelit lanterns, along with any items we wish to bless.

Our Beltane sabbat can vary greatly from year to year, but this year it started with all participants gathering at the designated place shortly after sunset. Most people arrive via automobile, so once the cars are parked, we get out and those of us who have them don our white and silver sabbat cloaks. New members and guests are given white lab coats to wear over their clothes. Carrying enclosed candlelit torches, we make our way along the narrow path single file and up hill through the woods, to the secret grove.

In addition to a lantern, each person carries along a refreshment or any item she might wish to empower, such as a small hand mirror, a crystal, a ring, deck of tarot cards, or a pendulum. Each person also brings a small nosegay-sized bunch of wildflowers he or she has collected earlier that day. These may be locust blossoms, lawn daisies, woodruff, hawthorn, apple blossoms, dandelions, bluebells, myrtle, or whatever else one finds in bloom. We also bring all other necessary items. I keep a special white cotton bag for these things; other people prefer black.

Once we arrive at the grove, the candles around the outside of the circle in the garden-staked lanterns are lit. The hand-carried lanterns, plus all other items necessary for the ritual, are placed in the fire pit at the center of the circle. Refreshments (except the mead or May wine and the goblet) are put upon a table near the chestnut tree outside of the circle.

All members of the group take their places on the flagstone circle, and begin moving, slowly at first, in clockwise direction, making sure to step on each of the thirteen flagstones each time around. We may sing, chant, drum, or remain silent while circling ever faster until we are practically running around the circle. In my left hand, I hold the athame pointing downward toward the ground, and as we turn around and around, a circle of light begins, faintly at first, to rise up from the ground outside the flagstones. Initially this light is a mere glow of whitish-golden color, but as our speed and power increase, the light begins to rise up to knee height, then shoulder height, taking on a gentle whitish-pink color. Eventually, this light rises up over our heads, and then slightly inward to form a protective cone shape. The top of the cone is open to the sky. Whilst the cone of light is raised, no one of the group, lest he be an animal, may pass outside. Likewise no intruder, whether human or spirit, is able to enter into the cone of light and our magic circle.

Once the cone is raised, everyone gradually stops moving and sits down. Using the athame, I draw a pentagram in the air above the fire pit. This symbolizes fire, water, air, and earth, headed by the fifth point at the top, facing west: the spirit.

I take up my nosegay of wildflowers, and turning to the person to my left and instructing all others in the group to follow suit, I carefully weave all of my flowers into the hair of my neighbor. At the same time, he is weaving his flowers into the the hair of the person on his left. We take our time, enjoying the sensual experience of touching one another's hair whilst our own hair and head are being touched and played with. If one's neighbor has long enough hair, the flowers can be braided in; if he has short hair, they will have to be tucked in; if he is bald, most of the flowers must be placed behind his ears. At any rate, we spend some time doing it, perhaps even crushing some of the more fragrant blossoms in the other's hair to release their perfume.

Each member of the group is given a hard-boiled egg and a pine cone. We hold these items up before us, the eggs in our left hands, and the pine cones in our right, with arms outstretched toward the main source of light (whether it be the Moon, or the lanterns in the fire pit). In turn, each person may speak some words, sing, recite poetry, hum a resonating tone, or offer some precious moments of silence to the group. These offerings serve to request or celebrate each individual's fertility, be it actual reproductive fertility; creative, intellectual, or artistic fertility; or fertility for one's vegetable, herb, or flower garden. The pine cone and egg are then joined in a symbolic union, so that each person's arms form an oval shape, like a halo around his head.

The phallic pine cone is then tossed over one's left shoulder, where it soars through the cone of light and into the woods, to transmit its imbued power into the spirit realm. For the time being, the eggs are kept with each individual. Once the circle has been opened, these eggs will be buried nearby.

At this point, if anyone has a special request, for example for healing energy on behalf of a loved one or for spiritual support in a difficult endeavor, we all join hands, and with eyes all or half the way closed, the request is made. Anyone in the group may comment, add her blessings, or begin a syllabic chant. If weather and ground conditions permit, we may spend some time lying down, our feet touching around the circle, gazing at the sky visible through the top of the cone of light, and meditating on our place on Earth as a part of this great and mysterious universe.

When we return to sitting position, the goblet is filled with mead or May wine, and passed around the circle, so that everyone takes a sip. Using the athame, I draw the pentagram in reverse in the air above the fire pit. We all rise once again to our feet, and walk easily counterclockwise around the flagstones three times, to bring down the cone of light and open the circle.

Now the dish of whipped cream, the strawberries, the honey cakes, and more mead or May wine are distributed. Everyone finds a special place nearby to make a small hole in the earth and bury his egg.

The red ribbon is tied to a low branch of the smallest oak tree, close to its trunk. Each person takes a turn winding the ribbon around the trunk, and then unwinding it again, all the while visualizing and concentrating on her fertility wish. After everyone has had a turn around the tree, we gather up our belongings, and take off running downhill through the woods.

When we reach the (hopefully moonlit) field, we dance around like dervishes, swaying and swishing our white and silver cloaks in the pale light. Some people may feel like hugging one another, or climbing up into a tree. Others may run races, play ring-around-the-rosy, or do whatever else their spirits move them to.

When the time seems right, the party is broken up, white cloaks are removed and everyone returns home to their normal lives, spirits refreshed and greatly invigorated.

Notes

Litha

Magickal Midsummer

Melanie Marquis

As a devoted lover of sunshine, one of my favorite sabbats is Midsummer. Filled with magick and mayhem, the mysticism of Midsummer entices the Witch to let loose and celebrate, partying with the sun for one last hurrah before that solar body begins his annual dip back into the underworld of cold and darkness. One thing I love about Midsummer is how the prevalent energies of the earth switch and sway throughout the day. From the glory of sunrise to the power and strength of the daytime, from the letting go at sunset to the magick of the night, Midsummer takes us on a journey through the Mystery. I love every minute, and I try to make the most of each one.

While it would be awesome to have all day to practice elaborate magick at my leisure, reality doesn't pan out that way, so I find creative ways to weave a celebration of Midsummer into everything I do that day, be it drying the laundry or playing with my kids. Before I get started on the daily demands, however, I reserve a special moment for just me and the sun. I wake up while it's still dark, and I brew up a pot of coffee. I pour a cup for me and a cup for the sun, then I add a few dashes of cinnamon, associated with solar energies. I take the coffee outside and sit in the grass, sipping my cup while I wait for sunrise. As the darkness gives way to an inky blue, I think about my gratitude toward the sun. Not only does the sun provide warmth and light, it also essentially feeds us by helping plants grow and animals thrive. Life just wouldn't be possible without it! I contemplate these gifts, and I also think back on the many solar-powered spells and charms I've cast, reminding myself that sunshine is truly a blessing. My heart fills with love and gratitude, and it hold it there as the sun ascends over the horizon. I smile a greeting to the sun, raise skyward the coffee, and sip a merry and pleasant toast in honor of my brightest friend. I leave one of the cups outside as an offering, a way to share my symbolized strength with the sun, who does so much.

For breakfast at Midsummer, I serve solar foods if I'm lucky enough to have something appropriate. Oranges, cinnamon toast, and citrus juice make a great solar-packed combination that helps me feel united with the sun throughout the day. It seems to keep the kids feeling happy, too, especially when we enjoy our breakfast outside for a morning picnic! This allows the food to absorb even more solar energy, empowering it with a light, bright, shining strength.

After breakfast, it's time to face the pressing chores, play, work, and other daily duties, which can be kind of a drag when you'd rather be basking in the sunshine! That's why I keep the windows and doors open while I piddle around the house taking care of whatever needs to be done. If there is cleaning to do (and there always is!), I use it as an opportunity to further experience and attune with solar power. I add a little citrus juice to cleaning sprays, and as I wipe down the kitchen counters and such, I envision the solar energies of the juice seeping into the surfaces, infusing my home with happiness and positive energy. When heavy scrubbing is required, I sprinkle on a little solar-charged salt. Associated with purification and strength, this helps the cleaning process while adding to the magickal atmosphere of the day. If I have laundry to do, I shake the clothes out very hard before washing to remove any stale energies. After they're washed, I perform a Midsummer charm, hanging the clothes outside to dry in the sun. Whenever I wear sun-dried clothing, I find I feel more courageous, empowered, and joyful.

If I have any nondomestic work to do, such as writing or reading tarot for a client, I'll place my pen, deck, and other working tools outside to absorb the sunlight. Sometimes, I'll make a to-do list and set this outside, as well. This symbolic action and the resulting solar empowerment supercharges my ability to carry out my work swiftly and successfully.

After a while, I take a break from the daily grind to relax and work a little solstice magick. I encourage my kids to enjoy the sunshine as we all play outside. I light a yellow, white, or orange candle and place it on a table or tall tree stump. Inspired by the bonfires lit at Midsummer since ancient times, with the idea of adding to the power and brightness of the sun, the flame of the candle acts as a symbol of my own gratitude and allegiance both to the sun itself and to the deities and energies that sun represents. If I don't have an appropriately colored candle, I simply use any available candle and either scratch a sun symbol into the wax or anoint it with a solar oil such as frankincense. As the candle burns, and the children play, I feel the energy surrounding us growing and magnifying. I tell the kids to feel the sunshine soaking in to their bodies as they run around, and I channel as much solar power to myself as I can. Once the energy reaches its peak, I send it straight back to the Sun, adding to it my compliments and any wishes I have for the dawn of summer.

In the afternoon, I make some time to get out into nature, hiking in the wilderness and looking for magickal treasures. Many plants are at their height of power at Midsummer, making it an ideal day for harvesting herbs and replenishing your stock of magickal supplies. I even found my wand on a Midsummer—lying right in the middle of the path during an exploration of the woods behind my home, which was then in Georgia. Once I saw it, I knew instantly that this was a special solstice gift straight from the gods and just for me. In addition to finding magickal tools and replenishing my herb stocks, I look around for special rocks. These I save to mark out the circle when I perform solar-themed rituals throughout the year.

The outdoor "treasure" hunt is usually followed by a quick Midsummer lunch; lemonade or sun tea paired with round, solar disk–shaped sandwiches is a real treat. During the picnic, I think of all the blessings the sun gives us daily, and I think of the bounty of nature made manifest through the sacrifice of the earth. The sun has given us his full power, the fruits of our labors have ripened, and now it's time to say farewell as we enter the second half of the solar year. This is why I take any leftovers from the picnic and bury them deep in the ground as an offering of gratitude and also as a symbol of the sinking sun.

I spend the rest of the day preparing for a nighttime of magick. This includes making flower or leaf garlands for decoration and costuming, giving the cauldron a thorough cleaning, gathering wood for the fire, and preparing any herbs, potions, or oils I will need for my solstice spellwork. I also like to take a ritual bath, filling the tub with water and a mixture of solar-associated herbs and oils. Frankincense, orange oil, and a few sunflower petals are a great combination. As the water swirls around me, I envision the solar energies of the herbs and oils seeping into my body, charging me with the power of the sun so that I'll be more in tune once it's time for the ritual. I drain the tub and get dressed for magick, forgoing the everyday black for a sun-yellow robe perfect for Midsummer. I typically prefer silver jewelry, but on this day, I go for the gold, as this metal has solar correspondences. I also decorate my arms, feet, hands, and face with solar symbols like suns and stars.

After the bath, I take the family outside in the backyard just as the sun threatens to sink beneath the horizon. As the sky fills with pink and orange hues, I turn on a strand of holiday lights and light as many candles as possible. I give the children tiny bells to jingle, and I set out a few shallow dishes of water sweetened with honey. Thus equipped, my patio becomes a magickal place where any wayward fairies would feel comfortable and welcome—and on Midsummer, you never know who or what will come calling for a visit! Like Samhain, Midsummer is also a time when spirits and elementals find it easier to cross into our everyday world.

Next, I get the fire started, I hang up the leaf and flower garlands, and begin setting up the altar. Believing a direct route is best, I like to keep my rituals pretty simple, and my altar setup reflects this ideal. I usually place a silver candle on the altar in honor of the Goddess, then I add a yellow candle to symbolize the God's active, solar state. I also place a black or brown candle on the altar, but for the moment, I leave it unlit. This candle later becomes a symbol for the God's passive, more lunar state, mirroring nature and the old Celtic myth of the Oak King's defeat at the hands of the Holly King and his subsequent banishment to the underworld. I fill my cauldron with fresh water, and I sit it within the ritual area. I also place on the altar a bell and a cup of red wine.

By this time, I can usually trick the children to go back inside so that I can get down to some serious magick. The religious aspects of my Craft have always been very personal, and I simply prefer a solitary ritual for devotional ceremonies. Once the yard is cleared, I stand at the altar, the silver Goddess candle and the yellow God candle aflame. I cast the circle and invite the God and Goddess to join me for the ceremony. I begin by thinking of the great sacrifice of the Goddess.

In Wiccan mythos, the Goddess, pregnant with the God-child, must say goodbye to her beloved consort, the active aspects of the Horned God symbolized by the soon-to-be-waning sun. I find it helps me better understand and relate to this mystery if I think of how this same old story plays out in my own life. We've all sacrificed for the sake of love, for the sake of art, for the sake of life. The sun gives his power to the Earth, who then delivers up a mighty bounty that must be enjoyed at a high price—the days grow shorter and the sun's power becomes weaker, until once more the earth's tilt brings the brightest light back to our realm. And it goes on, a cycle never ending. With these thoughts in mind, I ring the bell and send out a loving, comforting energy, a way to soothe the Goddess's sorrow and clear away any lingering tensions of my own.

As the sun sinks further, I toss flower petals toward the horizon, with wishes for the God's well-being and happy return. When the sun is just about to completely disappear, I hold the cup of wine aloft and dedicate it to the gods:

For the Love of the Goddess, For the Life of the God; my Lord and Lady, I honor you!

I take a sip of the wine and then I pour the rest on the bare earth, a symbol of my gratitude to the deities and my willingness to nurture the land.

I then perform any solar-themed spellwork needed, typically focusing on positive goals like manifesting resources, success, and opportunity.

Once the sky is completely dark, I extinguish the yellow God candle and light the black or brown God candle. I then welcome back the Holly King, representative of the Horned God's shadow aspects. I congratulate the Holly King on his victory over the Oak King, and I take some time to think about what I would like to accomplish between Midsummer and Yule, when the Oak King (and the stronger sunlight) returns once more. After this, I spend some time divining, using tarot cards or scrying in a mirror or my water-filled cauldron. Then I bid farewell to the deities and cut the circle.

My Midsummer celebration might not be the most elaborate, but it works for me, and that's what matters. When we personalize our rituals and our worship, our religion becomes less abstract and much more real, accessible, and practical. Instead of pulling a ritual out of a book and following it to the letter, why not add your own ideas and adaptations to the mix? Your ceremony will be much more "you" as a result, and Midsummer will be all the more magickal!

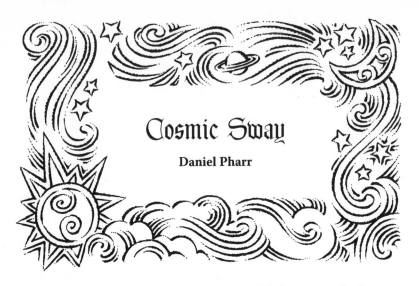

Cosmic Sway

Daniel Pharr

Litha, also known as High Summer, Midsummer, the longest day of the year, and the Summer Solstice, is traditionally set on June 21, but when calculated varies up to a couple days on both sides. This day is the most energetically masculine of the eight Celtic high holidays. Shakespeare used this day as the backdrop for his play *A Midsummer Night's Dream*. Fairies played a prominent role in the play, and may also play a prominent role our lives. As with Fairies, Pagans tend to prefer the dawn and dusk times more than the rest of the day, and enjoy the solstices and equinoxes more than the normal workdays. Signs that fairies may be present are all about the six senses. Walking through the scent of flowers floating in the air, hearing bells or voices in the breeze, sudden goosebumps or a chill down the spine, or simply feeling their presence are all signs of fairies saying hello. This holiday is a wonderful time to meet fairies.

The New Moon comes weeks before the solstice, on June 8, and will be in Gemini. The Gemini Moon is known for fast talking and inquisitiveness. The future comes into focus, and the feeling of owing destiny its due may shape the near future. The Moon is waxing from here, so energies are building. Start new projects, make new plans, prepare for the solstice celebration coming in a couple of weeks. The Moon and Mercury, both in the Twelfth House, can open the psyche to sensing other people's thoughts and emotional state. This much input can be intense, confusing, and overwhelming. Venus in the Twelfth House compensates for the massive input of psychic information through the ability and courage to give the self freely to this unknown place of overload. By giving in to the onslaught of psychic information—allowing the information to come in and go out, simply passing through the mind without judgment or emotion—this New Moon will be a very productive time for collecting information for future plans or doing some divination for others.

The exact calculation for this year's Midsummer is 1:04 am EDT, June 21. As with all Celtic high holidays, the solstice begins at sunset, often on the evening before. The waxing Scorpio Moon will welcome the waning of the year with resourcefulness, strength, and focus. Knowledge gained during this Moon will add meaning to life's direction and purpose. Seek truth and spiritual knowledge in deep conversation with your spouse or partner, and Mercury in the Seventh House will help. Venus in the Seventh House will help resolve conflicts in intimate relations. Celebrate this holiday with family. Searching the family archives and creating a family photo album, complete with captions and stories will be nice family activity. Mercury in Cancer will help with the mindset, while Venus in Cancer will turn this or any family activity into a family bonding event. Family time should take place before the Moon moves out of Scorpio. This will be a fabulous family activity for the afternoon and early evening before the main celebration begins just after sundown, which will come late in the day.

This year the traditional date for this esbat is the same day as the calculated date; however, the traditional date is some hours later, generally thought of beginning at sunset on June 21. The Moon will have moved from Scorpio into Sagittarius by this time and the lunar energies will have shifted dramatically. This astrological lunar shift will cause an energetic shift from family to adventure and regeneration. Normally, regeneration would look like rest and relaxation, and this may still be the case, but this renewing time will be spiced up with adventure. The sense of independence that comes with the need of adventure will be bolstered by the Moon in the Seventh House. The Eighth House is ruled by the Moon and is all about regeneration and recuperation. The idea of having an adventure is supported by the need to revitalize the metaphysical self. Mercury and Venus, now both in the Eighth House, support a quest for spiritual growth. Aspects of the Moon highlight some of the issues that are best brought into balance through independent and adventuresome renewal. These aspects include the Moon opposing Mars, which displays the struggles of life; the Moon trine Uranus, which brings unconventionality to self-expression; the Moon square Neptune and square Chiron, which both intensify the need for personal healing. In short, over these two days, enjoy some quality family time and also find some personal space for spiritual work.

Full Moon in Capricorn

The Full Moon comes two days later on June 23. The Moon in Capricorn appeals to the structured nature of living in our times. Those onerous detailed tasks, such as balancing the checkbook, are easier to tackle in this Moon. The Moon in the Eighth House brightens emotional and psychic sensitivity. The Third House is ruled by the Moon and as such stimulates intuition. The Moon sextile Neptune helps to focus the psychic sensitivity toward spiritual goals. Family is a priority again. The Sun, Mercury, and Venus are all in Cancer and provide nurturing energies and comfort within family gatherings and activities. Bonding with family is a priority.

Bonfire Celebration

The typical ritual celebration for the Summer Solstice involves an all-night bonfire. Gather the family, friends, coven, and others from the circle of relationships and build the fire in community, casting the circle and calling the deities as custom dictates. The celebratory fire is traditionally built on a hilltop with a view of the next hilltop to the west. The High Druid stood with a balefire farthest to the west in the land and waited until the moment of sunset and the beginning of the solstice. When the moment arrived, the Druid's bonfire was lit. Seeing the light of that fire, the group on the next hilltop would light their fire, signaling to the next hilltop and so on. Chances are most fires these days will not be built on a hilltop with a view of the High Druid, so light the fire just after the sun sets. If the horizon cannot be seen, use a clock, or wait to see three stars.

Once the fire is burning, spend a bit of time seeking out the fairies. Turn to face away from the fire and sit looking into the darkness. Allow enough time for your senses to adjust. Let your eyes peer into the darkness, let your nose smell everything but the fire, let your skin feel the air. Tell the fairies the fire site is occupied by good people—that it is a safe place. With the internal voice, ask the fairies to join the group.

Fairies, fairies, come to me, step to the light so I can see.

Repeat this chant several times. After a few rounds, begin to speak the chant in a whisper, and gradually speak more loudly, a soft, reverent voice, then an intimate voice, then a coffee shop voice, and louder and louder, until you are certain the fairies have heard you. Now sit quietly. Watch. Smell. Listen. When you experience a sign of a fairy presence, greet the fairy, say hello, and introduce yourself. Ask simple questions, yes or no, as in divination. The fairies know what will come and how to help. Just ask.

The Old Ways: Summertime Fruits

Susan Pesznecker

WOULD SUMMER REALLY BE summer without the berries? Without fresh biscuits topped with sliced red strawberries and clouds of whipped heavy cream? Without sun-warmed blackberries eaten as fast as they're picked? Without plump, juicy blueberries—so many of them that the bounty must be frozen and enjoyed year-round? Fresh berries are a gift of summer and have long been part of traditional lore and wisdom. Get your gathering basket ready—let's explore.

In botanical terms, a "berry" is a fruit produced from a single ovary—one part of a flower's female reproductive system. Using this definition, we can count a good many fruits as berries, including everything from a tiny currant to a tennis ball-sized persimmon or fist-sized tomato. However, the common definition considers berries to be small fruits that are juicy, brightly colored, taste sweetly tart, and a lack a center stone or pit.

Berries tend to have pronounced health benefits. Their deep hues are created by high levels of anthocyanins, flavonoids, and tannins, plant-based compounds that act as antioxidants when eaten, fighting the cellular changes associated with aging. Most berries are high in vitamin C and fiber, and several have positive effects on memory and cognition.

Berry plants are perennial and may grow via small plants (strawberries), canes (blackberries), shrubs (blueberries), or trees (hawthorn). Most ripen in the summer, but a few—like rowan and hawthorn berries—linger into fall and winter, providing an important food source for animals.

Berries play a role in a number of Earth-based traditions. Most berries are regarded as having a feminine nature and are used in spells invoking love or passion. Berry juice is often used as magickal ink. The ancient Celtic festival of Lughnasadh, named for the Celtic God Lugh, celebrates the first grains and fruits of the harvest. At ancient Lughnasadh, the entire community gathered berries and shared a berry-rich feast to celebrate the harvest. Today's Celtic Reconstructionist Druids celebrate Lughnasadh when summer's-end berries ripen, usually meaning blackberries on the West Coast and blueberries on the East.

The **blackberry** (*Rubus villosus, R. fructiosus*) goes by the folk names bly, bramble, bramble-kite, bumble, cloudberry, dewberry, goutberry, scaldhead, thimbleberry, and thornberry. Like most berries, it's usually given an elemental alliance of water, but its thorns suggest more than a little fire, too. My grandmother always told me to work carefully and thank the blackberry vines for the gift of fruit as I picked. By showing respect to the blackberries, she said, the thorns would prick less enthusiastically. (She was right!) Blackberries are associated with wealth and prosperity, strength, and the harvest. A natural arch of blackberry vines is a profoundly powerful passageway to the other realms, much like fairy circles.

However, the news isn't all cheery—some folkloric traditions link blackberries to bad omens, sorrow, death, and hubris. In Greek mythology, Bellerophon, a mortal, tries to ride Pegasus to Olympus, a forbidden act. Bellerphon falls, lands in a blackberry bush, and is blinded by the thorns, a punishment resulting from his arrogance in trying to take on the gods' power.

Medicinally, blackberries are astringent and tonic, while the leaf infusion treats diarrhea. An old legend warns against eating blackberries after October 11 (St. Michaelmas Day). Supposedly the devil urinates on them after this, rendering them inedible. This legend has medical credence, as berries picked this late in the season are prone to illness-inducing mold.

Blueberries (*Vaccinium* species) are also known as bilberries, blaeberries, bleuets, and whortleberries. Researchers call blueberries a medical superfood and a powerful memory booster as well as a potent antioxidant. Folk medicine espouses the blueberry's value in treating vision problems, while magick users eat blueberries to protect against psychic attack and boost mental clarity. Wild blueberries are wild versions of the domestic blueberry. Native Americans blended dried wild blueberries with animal fat to make a tasty pemmican.

The **cranberry** is a close relative of the blueberry and shares the genus *Vaccinium*. Also known as fenberry, mossberry, or crane berry, the berry may have been named for the crane-like shape of its blossoms. Cranberries were part of the early Thanksgiving celebrations in Colonial America and endure today as a fixture of the Thanksgiving table. The cranberry's acidity makes it valuable in treating kidney and urinary infections.

Gooseberries (*Ribes* species) are favorite foods of birds and butterflies, and Victorians told children that babies were found under gooseberry bushes. Folk medicine regards gooseberries as beneficial for kidney and "female" problems. Ancient people used the thorns to drain wounds and puncture warts.

The **huckleberry** (*Vaccinium sp.*) is a small, tart, wild relative of the blueberry. In the Pacific Northwest, the huckleberry is revered by local Indians as one of the sacred "first foods" and is a central part of annual roots feasts. Magickally, the leaves protect against evil, sever hexes and curses, and bring luck to gamblers.

According to Greek myth, the **raspberry** (*Rubus idaeus* and *R. strigosus*) was a discovery of the gods, made when the Olympians searched for berries on Mount Ida. Raspberries were subsequently known as bramble of Mount Ida, as well as by the folk names hindberry and hindbur. The berries were known to the ancients, appearing in Greek writings and throughout medieval herbal tomes.

Magickally, the raspberry appears in spells for love and passion and has connotations of protection and strength. The withered canes are hung over doors and windows to snag evil spirits as they enter. The leaves protect against snakebite. Medicinally, the leaves treat menstrual disorders.

Rowanberries grow on the mountain ash (mountain ash, *Sorbus americana*). In ancient Celtic culture, rowanberries were regarded as a deeply magickal plant and said to be the food of the fairies. The berries are a rich food for wintering birds, too. Rowan wood is strong physically and magickally and makes wonderful magickal tools. Necklaces of the berries were worn by Celtic people for protection. A rowan walking stick protects the user while wandering at night. High in vitamin C, rowanberries are used to treat cough and colds.

The **strawberry** (*Fragaria vesca*) is known for its sweet flavor, delicacy, and heart-like shape. What better berry to symbolize love and all things feminine? Also known as heartberry, the strawberry is sacred to Freya in Norse mythology and to mothers in many American Indian traditions. The leaves, growing in groups of three, are said to represent the mother goddess or Earth goddess. The name "strawberry" is a variation of the old Anglo-Saxon streoberie.

Magick users regard the heart shape as inspiring love and luck, and folk medicine claims that strawberries purify a woman's blood during pregnancy or menses. Eastern-European country dwellers leave strawberries out to appease the local elven folk. Pregnant women carry bundles of strawberry leaves to ease the pains of labor. Medicinally, strawberries may help fight dementia.

☙

Elves and fairies, sweetness and thorns, strength and passions, and a rich trove of tradition.... Next time you stop to pop that perfect berry into your mouth, pause and reflect on its story. There's a lot of history in each colorful little package.

For Further Reading:

Cunningham, Scott. *Cunningham's Encyclopedia of Magical Herbs.* Woodbury, MN: Llewellyn, 1985.

Drew, A.J. *A Wiccan Formulary and Herbal.* Pompton Plains, NJ: New Page, 2005.

Foster, Steven, and Christopher Hobbs. *Western Medicinal Plants and Herbs.* New York: Houghton, 2002.

Grieve, Maud. "A Modern Herbal." Botanical.com. 1995-2007. <http://www.botanical.com/index.html>.

Feasts and Treats

Kristin Madden

SINCE ANCIENT TIMES ON the Summer Solstice, societies around the world have honored the longest day in the Northern Hemisphere with feasts, storytelling, dances, and games. Dishes for this sabbat are light, energizing, and fun. Crafted using elements reminiscent of the sun and its power, these foods bring cool deliciousness and easy-to-transport sustenance to all your Litha activities.

Sun-Dried Tomato Pesto Chicken Wraps

On Midsummer Day, we celebrate the height of the sun's power and light. On this longest day, break out the grill and the sun-dried tomatoes to create a festive, handheld wrap that you can take with you on all of your fun summer travels.

Prep Time: 10 minutes
Serves: 4

Pesto
½ ounce sun-dried tomatoes
1 teaspoon basil
1 teaspoon parsley
½ teaspoon roasted garlic

2 teaspoons pine nuts
2 teaspoons onion, chopped
2 teaspoons balsamic vinegar
½ teaspoon tomato paste
2 teaspoons diced tomatoes
2 teaspoons red wine
4¼ teaspoons olive oil
4¼ teaspoons grated Parmesan cheese
Salt and pepper to taste

4 small tortillas
Spring lettuce mix
1 cup Monterey Jack cheese
4 grilled boneless chicken breasts, sliced

Place sun-dried tomatoes in a bowl and cover with warm water for 5 minutes. Drain. In a food processor or blender, make pesto by combining sun-dried tomatoes, basil, parsley, garlic, pine nuts, and onion; process until well blended.

Add vinegar, tomato paste, diced tomatoes, and red wine, and process. Stir in olive oil and Parmesan cheese. Season with salt and pepper to taste.

Warm tortillas in microwave for 12 seconds. On each tortilla, spread pesto. Add spring lettuce, cheese, and chicken. Roll and serve.

Pear and Goat Cheese Salad

Reminiscent of the summer sun, yet light and refreshing, pears are perfectly complemented by goat cheese. This unique salad is filling enough to stand on its own as a great Midsummer snack.

Prep Time: 10 minutes
Cooking Time: 25 minutes
Serves: 4–6

2 large Bosc pears, peeled and cored
2 tablespoons lemon juice
Olive oil
2 cups butter lettuce
4 cups spinach
4 ounces chèvre (goat cheese)
1 ounce toasted pine nuts
¼ cup balsamic vinaigrette

Cut pears in half. Brush with lemon juice and olive oil. Bake on a cookie sheet brushed with oil for 25 minutes at 400 degrees F.

Combine greens in salad bowl. Slice warm pears and toss into greens. Crumble goat cheese on top and add toasted pine nuts. Serve with vinaigrette.

Mint Mojitos

This may not be the hottest day of the year but we are celebrating the height of the sun's power. With that in mind, what could be better than a cooling, yet spicy mojito?

Prep Time: 10 minutes
Serves: 4

8 fresh mint leaves
Juice of 4 limes
1 teaspoon lemon zest
4 teaspoons powdered sugar
Ice cubes
8 ounces rum
8 ounces club soda
Optional garnish: 4 sprigs of mint

Chop mint leaves, or mash with a fork. Place in bottom of tall glass. Add lime juice, lemon zest, and sugar. Muddle, mix, and mash together with a wooden spoon. Stir in rum and club soda. Garnish with mint and ice cubes before serving.

Sun Cake Pops

These delightful cake pops are bright and fun and reminiscent of the sun at its height on this day.

Prep Time: 35 minutes
Cooking Time: 60 minutes
Chill Time: 1 hour
Serves: 40–50

1 box white or lemon cake mix
½ cup white frosting
24-ounce package of white candy melts/candy coating
50 lollipop sticks
Yellow or gold sprinkles
Small glasses or Styrofoam block, approx. 12 × 12 inches

Bake the cake according to package directions. Allow to cool, then grate in food processor. In a bowl, mix cake with ½ cup frosting, until thoroughly mixed and thick. Roll into small balls about ½-inch in diameter. Cover, and refrigerate for at least 1 hour.

Melt candy coating according to package directions. Dip the tip of each lollipop stick into candy then insert almost halfway into a cake ball.

Dip and gently roll each cake ball in candy coating. Immediately cover with sprinkles and allow to harden propped in small glasses or a Styrofoam block.

Crafty Crafts

Linda Raedisch

ARE YOU ACQUAINTED WITH the hordes of *Plantago Major*, those ubiquitous little green spirits of summer? Plantain, waybread, ribwort, white man's footprint: it goes by many names and it grows absolutely everywhere. Native to Europe, it probably started shooting up in the New World about fifteen minutes after the Mayflower landed. Hardy? This plant is irrepressible! It's one of the nine herbs sacred to Wodan, and the Romans associated it with Prosperina, goddess of the underworld. In Tibet, it's auspicious to eat the first shoots when you hear the first cuckoo's call of spring. By midsummer, our little friends are all over the place. Even if you live in a concrete jungle, you probably can't walk ten yards without meeting up with one. Greet it respectfully, for your ancestors held it in high regard.

Respecting it doesn't mean you can't pick it. Go ahead and pull up a couple of plantains by the roots; you won't be endangering the population in any way. I hesitate to call the greeny brown vertical protrusions "flower spikes," since the flowers are so tiny they are almost imperceptible. To me, these spikes look like skinny, hand-dipped candles. Display them in a fancy candleholder instead of a vase for a unique centerpiece.

Midsummer Sunlets

The fairies are out tonight as well as the Witches, so we must make our surroundings as magical as possible. This means lighting fires and, most importantly to those of us with quick and crafty fingers, festooning!

In Baltic lands, the traditions of maypole and Midsummer bonfire were sometimes combined at this time of year when flames were kindled atop a decorated post erected on a high hilltop. Meanwhile, in some parts of Siberia, male shamans repaired to mountain birch groves every third summer to kindle new fires. Meat cooked over the young flames was carried deosil around the grove while eagle feathers were tied to the branches of the tree with linen thread.

Saule, the Baltic goddess of the sun, the hearth fire, and the flax from which linen is made, was believed to inhabit the crown of a birch, which makes this tree a very good candidate for Midsummer festooning. Strung together, these diminutive sun symbols can be used both to define sacred space and to give your encampment the look of an English country fête. Woodsy Witches know that herbs and flowers picked at midnight on Midsummer Eve are especially potent. So if you're going out gathering—or simply seeking the fabled golden fern blossom that appears only on this night—you can leave individual sunlets behind as tokens of your thanks to the spirits of forest and meadow.

Tools and Materials

Double-sided origami paper in a variety of colors

Compass (or juice glass, tealight, small bowl, etc., for making circles)

Pencil

Scissors

X-acto or other craft/utility knife

Glue

String

To begin, you need to draw a smaller circle inside a larger circle. Since the idea is to make lots of little sunlets, I use the base of a juice glass for the larger circle and a tealight holder for the smaller inner circle.

Once you have drawn your large circle, you can cut it out with the scissors. Now, draw a smaller circle inside it. Use your knife to cut this smaller circle into eight "pie pieces." Fold the pie pieces back over the ring formed by the larger circle, creasing well, to make the rays of your sunlet. Make another sunlet and glue them back to back.

Hang your sunlets directly on the tree branches and hedgerows or string them together to make a garland.

Paper Votive Feather

Even if you do have a mountain birch grove at your disposal, you should not be tying genuine eagle feathers to the branches, as did the shamans of old. Eagles in North America have become quite

scarce, which is why you have to be a Native American to legally own an eagle feather. Fortunately, there are no laws governing the use of paper feathers.

The stylized paper feathers below, in which the markings are indicated by negative space, are adapted from Japanese tradition. The white paper "falcon feather" is one of myriad *shide*, cut and folded paper forms used in the Shinto religion to symbolize purity and to mark sacred precincts. Tie several feathers together at the end of a wand. They will make a reassuring rustling noise as you move about, hallowing your space. If you want to be old-fashioned, you can cut your feathers out of hempen or linen cloth as *shide* were made before the introduction of paper to Japan from China in AD 538.

Tools and Materials

White printer paper
Pencil
X-acto or other craft or utility knife
Scissors
Needle and thread

Fold your paper in half lengthwise and sketch half your feather close to the folded edge. Eagles are big and so are their feathers. Make yours at least 8½ inches long and 1½ inches wide. Don't forget to include the point of the quill at the end. Use your knife to cut out the "markings" and your scissors to cut out the overall feather shape. Poke a hole through the end of the quill and attach a loop of thread.

All One Family

Sandra Kynes

AT LITHA, THE SUN reaches its highest point in the sky as the North Pole tips toward the sun, giving us our longest day. This is "midday" on the Wheel of Year opposite Yule's "midnight."

As with the Winter Solstice, welcoming the dawn on the Summer Solstice has become a part of our family tradition. While my son is in charge of checking the time of sunrise, we all plan the location. Sometimes the backyard works out best. Although we have discussed it, we have not been inspired to drive the 4½ hours north and east to Quoddy Head in Lubec, Maine, which is the easternmost point in the United States. Most often we go to a local beach or one of the nearby lighthouses to watch the deep predawn sky fade into softer hues as the sun begins to rise over the water.

So we can get out of the house quickly, we take juice, coffee, and granola bars along with us. As we await the sun, we pass the time by drawing sun symbols in the sand or we create them with the plentiful periwinkle shells. This is a good way to keep younger children occupied and older ones busy seeing who can make the biggest one. We are often the only people on the beach, which is a magical experience. The expansiveness of ocean and sky, and the rhythm of the waves makes me feel connected with everything in universe. As

Pagans, we all have our special places of connection, so whether you can see a wide horizon or only a patch of sky, witnessing this sunrise with our children calls to something basic and enduring within us. While my son didn't always appreciate this type of outing when he was little, he came to believe in its significance as a teenager and was glad that he had grown up with it. Then of course, there are the rainy solstice days, but we get up early to carry on the tradition indoors even if we only see the sky lighten. On these occasions, I have taken out a basket of seashells to create our sun symbols on the carpet.

After the glorious bursting forth of spring, the world settles into summer's business of growth. Trees are in full leaf and the lavender, foxglove, and peonies create a colorful backdrop for brilliant marigolds. With their round golden heads, marigolds are associated with the sun and according to some, picking them at midday doubles their solar energy. Because of these associations, they are the perfect flower to incorporate into a Litha ritual or simply use on the altar. In England, it was a custom to weave garlands of ivy with marigolds and St. John's wort, but a simple "daisy chain" of marigolds makes a nice circlet to wear on the head. A few times we ended up with flower crowns, necklaces, and bracelets. Just as the sun is at its pinnacle of power, so too is the God, who in many ancient legends is often represented by the oak tree. Summer Solstice falls within the month of oak in the Celtic tree calendar (June 10 to July 7). Because we do not have an oak tree in our yard, we stop at a nearby park to leave an offering of marigolds at the base of a wonderfully big oak. Another association of the marigold comes into play from its having been the flower of the dead to the Aztecs and its modern use on Mexican Day of the Dead altars. As the Sun god begins his descent, we offer him this flower.

Getting children outdoors and into nature is good any time of year, and birds can be counted on as a focal point. Since ancient times, birds have been considered special creatures because they can soar to the heavens, and if you were lucky, bring back messages from goddesses and gods. I believe that bird feathers (like other things in nature) function as oracles at times to give us information. My best childhood memories are those from summers on the Delaware shore with the sound and sight of seagulls. When I moved to Maine as an adult and stepped out on the back porch for the first time, I found a seagull feather and felt that I had truly come home.

Sometimes instead of bird-watching, my family and I like to look for feathers. If you do this on the solstice, you might be lucky enough to find a shell from a hatchling. Eggshells symbolize beginnings and creativity and go well on a Litha altar to represent the fertility and growth aspects of this sabbat. However, feathers are a lot easier to find than eggshells, and they can show up almost anywhere. Of course, near trees where birds roost or feed is the best place to look. Some are distinctive, such as the blue jay's tail feather with its blue, black, and white pattern. A large black feather could be from a crow or a brown one from a robin. A seagull's feather can be pure white or multiple colors with brown, black or gray. A dark gray feather with white dots may be from a woodpecker or one with brown and white patterns from a hawk. If you're not familiar with the summer birds in your area, you may want to spend time online with your children to do a little research.

After we have found a few feathers and without searching for any deep hidden meanings, we simply say the first reason that comes to mind for finding a particular feather. Did I find a blue jay feather because I was squawky that morning? Or, if I had done yoga did I find a dove feather because I felt peaceful? Ask each child to tell the meaning of the feathers they find and encourage stories. When my son was little, he used to make up stories about the birds whose feathers we found, such as a robin on an errand for a friend or a crow looking for a restaurant. A couple of times we have followed a feather outing with the project of making Witches' ladders or wall hangings. Gather ribbons and yarn to string the feathers together or get creative and follow your imagination to make something more complex. Another method is to use color associations to create a feather hanging or a simple strand, which will hold special meaning for you. Following are some basic color meanings: black—inner strength, wisdom; blue—peace, mental abilities; brown—grounded, stability; green—growth, prosperity; red—vitality, energy; white—serenity, spirituality; yellow—cheerfulness, luck. Using this approach, I strung together brown and white hawk and seagull feathers with delicate green crocheting cord to symbolize grounded spirituality and growth. This has a permanent place on the wall above our altar. If you are pressed for time on the solstice, you can always arrange the feathers in a vase or pottery jar for the altar.

Another type of shell to look for comes from an insect called a cicada. My childhood summer treasure box always included them. From early- to mid-summer, cicadas emerge from underground, shed their skins, dry their wings then fly away. The "shells" of their old skins can be found on the sides of trees or garages as well as on the ground. Cicadas are symbols of transformation with their brief lives encompassing the underworld, the earthly plane, and the heavens. On a Summer Solstice altar, they represent the cycles and changes taking place in nature. Even though this sabbat marks the point at which the days will begin to shorten, we have time ahead to enjoy the richness and warmth of summer.

A Midsummer Night's Ritual

Melanie Marquis

THIS MIDSUMMER RITUAL IS inspired by William Shakespeare's *A Midsummer Night's Dream*, and you can make it every bit as theatrical and magickal as the work on which it's based. Though it's best if you can celebrate Midsummer with a group of trusted Witches, the particulars of this ceremony can be adapted for solo practice if needed.

The first thing to do is to get into character. If you're lucky enough to have friends joining you, you'll have a lot more leeway and variety. If you're carrying out the ritual solitary, you can choose to dress as any of the following roles. For a group ritual, the High Priestess can play the part of the fairy queen, Titania, donning wings and even sparkles if she likes. Likewise, the High Priest can become Oberon, king of the fairies and Titania's consort. You'll also need someone, male or female, to play the role of the Pan-inspired Puck, who should be bare-chested and decorated with leaves. If you like, round out the cast by having any additional coven members dress as fairies, or alternatively, as plainclothes actors or craftsmen who, in *A Midsummer Night's Dream*, are unintended parties to the night's magick. You might even find someone to play the role of the donkey-headed Bottom.

Once everyone is in costume, set up the ritual space. First, build a small fire. Then fill a cauldron or other female-representative vessel with fresh water, symbolic of the goddess and her cauldron of life and death, the sacred source from which all things spring and to which all things return. Position it in the middle of the ritual space, and place inside it a large handful of holly to represent the Holly King, the shadow aspect of the male deity that rises to power just as the Summer Solstice tips the world into increasing darkness. Put on the altar a glass vial filled with water, a flower, a piece of oak wood, and a candle.

Your tools in place, it's time to clear the space and cast the circle. Choose a small branch or twig from a pine tree, selecting a piece that has plenty of needles intact. Pine is a magickal plant associated with many gods and goddesses, and its purifying, protective energies are a perfect complement to the holy day of Midsummer, a time when the sun reaches its apex of power, charging the world with a final dose of strength and light. Dip the needles in the water and then walk around the ritual space clockwise, waving the needles and sprinkling the water as you fill your mind with a peaceful, loving energy and visualize baneful energies being blasted out, forced away by the pure light you are projecting. This action clears the ritual space of any stale or negative energies, and it's one of many ways this feat can be accomplished. Choose a different sort of space cleansing if you prefer; for instance, you could clear the ritual area with a few whisks of your magickal broom.

Once the space is cleared, call the quarters and cast the circle. You can do so in your usual manner, or try something a little different for Midsummer that evokes the particular qualities of the elements you feel are most in tune with this sabbat's energies. For example, since Midsummer is a day of powerful solar forces, when you call on the element of fire, you might focus on fire in the form of sunlight. When summoning the element of water, you might think of evaporation, rainbows, or sunshine twinkling on the surface of a lake. For air, you might imagine how a sun-warmed breeze feels on your skin, or picture the way the air looks distorted when viewing it through heat. For earth, you could think of the warm ground, or fiery lava spewing up from underground.

Once the circle is cast, invoke the Goddess. If you are practicing with a group, the **High Priestess** should take this role, calling the Goddess into herself so that she not only attunes with this energy, but also *becomes* this energy. If a **High Priest** is present, he should now invoke the God to the same ends. The **Priestess/Goddess** then prepares a special potion of plain water infused with solar energies. Simply fill a vial with fresh water, then hold it over a candle flame while chanting:

By the power of fire, by the power of light, by the power of the sun, let love shine bright!

The High Priest then takes the vial and hands it to the person playing the role of the Pan-inspired Puck. If there isn't a High Priest, the High Priestess can do this part. "Puck" then dips a flower bloom into the potion and carefully anoints the eyelids of the covenmates. If practicing alone, simply apply the potion to your own eyelids. The **Priestess** then says:

The Oak King bids us farewell on this night. Let us revel with him once more; let us rejoice and love!

This call signals the start of the revelry. Just as Lysander and Demetrius in *A Midsummer Night's Dream* were overcome with love when Puck charms them with the juice of a magick flower, so too should your covenmates let love fill their hearts and passion guide their bodies, expressing their love of the God through friendly hugs, kisses, and caresses. Let the comfort level of your covenmates guide the parameters of this part of the ritual. It can be as casual as a simple hug passed around the circle, or as intense as a Great Rite performed in the circle by the priestess turned Titania and the covenmate turned Oberon—or Bottom, if you want to stay truer to the story. If you're performing this ritual solitary, summon the Oak

King aspects of the Horned God at this time and invite the deity to enjoy your body as an offering. Let your hands be guided by a higher power as you explore your body as if it were not your own, allowing yourself to be given over as a vessel of pleasure with which to quench the God's thirst.

After reveling in pleasure for a bit, have your merry band of fairies and other participants spiral around the circle, building up the energy. As the energy pulsates and builds, the High Priestess and High Priest join hands over the fire as they call out intentions for the group. These are stated in positive terms, just like any other spell goal. For example, the priestess might call out *"Our group grows in strength, unity, and power,"* as the flames leap higher. When the energy of the circle is at its absolute height, the coven members come to a stop and the **High Priestess** takes up the piece of oak wood from the altar, saying:

As the sun's power wanes, so too must we bid farewell to our Lord.

The wood is passed around the circle, each person sending into the oak their gratitude and well-wishes for the Oak King's solar return. The High Priestess then casts the wood into the fire. As it burns, the High Priest/fairy king receives a kiss from the fairy queen priestess, who tells him goodbye and bids him to rest. The High Priest then lays down behind the fire. The other covenmates each pick up a handful of soil and begin circling again, sprinkling small amounts of dirt on the body of the priest. This symbolizes the imminent "death" of the Oak King, the positive, active aspects of the masculine deity.

Next, the High Priestess pulls the holly out of the cauldron, passing it around the circle so that everyone present has some. As she does this, the High Priest shakes the dirt from his body and re-emerges from behind the fire. The **High Priestess** kisses the High Priest in greeting, saying:

We welcome back our Holly King, ruler of the underworld and king of the dark year.

The **coven members** hold their holly skyward and answer:

Welcome, Holly King. All hail the Dark Lord!

The **priestess** then states:

The Oak King will rise once more; until then, we dream as the earth slumbers, we slumber as the earth dreams.

Everyone then lies down in the circle quietly, open to any messages or visions that might come at this time. Any coven members dressed as fairies might sneak around to different members of the group at this time, bestowing kisses and blessings to the dreaming Witches. You might even see a few real fairies flying about the edge of the ritual space, appearing as tiny lights or weird glimmers that simply don't look quite real.

The ritual complete, the circle is cut, and the deities dismissed. Follow with fireside food, music, and partying, getting as wild as you dare in celebration of this most magickal night of the year. Whether you have a group or you're on your own, your Midsummer ritual can really be something special, leaving you with a magickal memory steeped in night, with which to dream away the time until the Sun grows stronger once again.

Notes

Lammas

Lammas:
Food for Thought

Natalie Zaman

THERE IS A PASSAGE IN Marion Zimmer Bradley's *The Mists of Avalon* where Morgaine, many years removed from her life as a priestess, goes through the painstaking process of relearning her craft. An essential element of her reclamation is the reestablishing of her connection to the earth. Day by day, she watches the changing face of the moon, readapting herself to its monthly cycle. She wanders the fields and forests looking for "the little people," calling out to them and leaving offerings with no guarantee of an answer. All she knows is her need to reconnect, her yearning to rejoin the cosmic dance.

I realize that Morgaine's journey is a fictional one, but its underlying theme is real enough. I find it difficult to be in tune with seasons when I'm not working with them day to day. Thanks to a hectic lifestyle, I often find myself in a state of disconnect, especially when winter turns into summer. As the world around me changes, I feel those first prickings of longing, my disconnect sharper for the life swelling and budding everywhere I look. I want to be a part of it.

Working in the garden has been my means of reconnecting to earth and spirit. While the sabbats present us with opportunities for mystical observation, the agrarian calendar is at their core. My practices have become increasingly focused on exploring the connection between the divine and the very physical turning of the Wheel of the Year; those actual changes in light and air and temperature that are the seasons. Like Morgaine, I'm on a quest to retune myself to the rhythms of the earth.

Among other discoveries, the process has made me very aware of how far removed I am from where my food comes from—a mundane concern; but once, spirituality and survival were closely linked. It's become very important to me to be reacquainted with this very necessary aspect of life—and like in so many other mundane parts, I've found an underlying connectivity to the magical, the spiritual.

Some food for thought: Nowadays it's a novelty for most folks to grow or go out and gather their own food. Special time is set aside apple or pumpkin or berry picking—and these outings become opportunities to reconnect with nature and spend time with family and friends. This, I feel, is the heart of ritual—the spirit that gives events and the motions that go with them, meaning. And so year after year, I look forward to my time in the garden and the results of my labors—Lammas, the first harvest.

꙳

The latter end of the goddess season brings—along with the humidity and the critters without which no summer on the East Coast would be complete—a brief period where abundance swells on the vine. The change is gradual. After a usually cold, wet winter (and part of spring) warmth becomes most welcome. At mid- to late June, the growing heat takes root, literally, in the form of plants, trees, and flowers. The Summer Solstice celebrates what's been building since Yule; life that was asleep during winter, stirred and budded in spring, and is wide awake and ready to work in summer. In the garden, stalks thicken, flowers burst and drop their blossoms, and fruits and vegetables—only tiny seedlings a few short months ago—ripen, grow, and beg to be picked.

The secular world associates "harvest" with the autumnal months, but summer's height and subsequent waning days see a glut of produce flood farm stands and backyard gardens. On the

Wheel of the Year, this first harvest—called Lammas and Lughnasadh—is celebrated at the beginning of August (usually the 2nd),
about six weeks before the Autumnal Equinox.

In addition to marking the fruit harvest, this turning point observes the start of the ripening of the grain, which will be gathered
later in the year. One ritual performed at this time was the baking
of a loaf from the as yet underripe grain. It was not—and is not,
should you attempt to reprise this tradition—a savory treat. But the
purpose of this ritual was not to feed the body so much as the spirit.
Eating this bread was an act of faith—in the gods, in the earth, and
in one's own ability and labor that the grains would ripen, that
there'd be plenty for all, and that once again, the family, and the
community would survive the coming winter.

While this was a time for serious reflection and planning, there
was also fun—in the form of open-air festivals featuring games and
tests of strength (the god Lugh for whom Lughnasadh is named was
a sportsman), markets for sharing and trading those first fruits, and
communal interaction. We still see the remnants of this today. Summer's long days and (hopefully!) fair weather make a perfect setting
for Renaissance festivals, county fairs, and carnivals—all modern
pastimes with, sometimes unbeknownst to revelers, ancient roots.

❦

Over the past several years, we've attempted to turn our postage
stamp of a suburban backyard into what is essentially a mini-farm.
We took on this project for practical reasons. With the state of the
economy, we wanted to take a stab at becoming more self-sufficient.
We also wanted to consume food that wasn't processed or treated
with chemicals. So in addition to shopping locally and organically,
we grow and/or raise what we can. And of course, a spiritual bent
emerged.

An important aspect of self-sufficiency is living with the seasons—knowing your environment, what you can grow, when you
can grow it. Before we started our project, I felt like I was merely
marking my calendar with specific days to stop and regroup, eking

out an hour or two for rituals that sometimes had meaning for me, sometimes not. By inserting myself literally into the Wheel of the Year, I hoped to reestablish and strengthen my fragile connection to the earth and its divinity, incorporate it into my practice, and make that practice more meaningful. It would just be a matter of getting my hands dirty.

Simple, no?

Things started out well enough. I grew herb plants that flourished, and eventually potted and then plotted tomatoes, peppers, and courgettes (zucchinis)—admittedly crops that in my neck of the woods, one would have to make an effort to kill. A couple of years of success boosted my confidence, and we added chickens and potatoes to the mix—again, things that were relatively "easy"—according to my research.

Then came the "Summer of enlightenment," which could just as accurately be dubbed the "Winter of discontent." My potatoes fell victim to a moldy blight that spread to even my indestructible tomatoes. No combination of spells or science seemed to work to revive the garden. I watched helplessly as plant after plant festered and died, bringing with it flies to chase the rot. Then a fox got one of our chickens—despite our well-built coop, despite our natural repellent efforts, despite what I thought were ardent prayers. Sometimes things just go wrong.

The disaster brought on one of those Helen-Keller-Miracle-Worker-Aha-Moments. You know, the one where she has her hand under the gushing spigot, and suddenly she digs deep into the past and pulls out understanding; this "thing" is water. Thankfully, my life isn't dependent on my crops. If I fail, I won't starve. But the idea that I could do nothing, that the success or failure of our work was beyond my control, was unnerving. With my discomfort came a concrete understanding of the connection between spirituality and survival. Once upon a time, the consequences of failure were dire. All you could do was lay your head in the lap of the universe and trust that all would work out. It gave a whole new meaning to the phrase "in perfect love and perfect trust."

I try to maintain the sacred in the every day and the every day in the sacred. Summer is daily walks through the garden; pruning, picking, observing, protecting. Nestling crystals in the soil at the base of my plants' stems, weaving the leavings from hairbrushes through the wires of the coop to keep foxes away, bringing in mail-ordered clutches of ladybugs and praying mantises to keep scavenger bugs at bay. Remembering to do my daily rounds in a clockwise (invoking/growing) direction. Remembering that everything I do—even seemingly mundane tasks—can be meaningful, and even hallowed with attention and care.

Resources for Reconnecting:

Visit the Backyard Gardener to see which plants will do well in your area (http://www.backyardgardener.com/).

Plants are affected by the gravitational pull of the moon much the same way that the ocean is. Our Garden Gang has moon planting charts and moon phase calendars to plot out your planting (http://ourgardengang.tripod.com/moonplanting.htm).

Find locally grown produce and earth-friendly events at Local Harvest (http://www.localharvest.org/).

Easy preserving recipes can be found at Pick Your Own (http://www.pickyourown.org/). The site is also a resource for farms to visit where you can pick your own fruit.

The Practical Herbalist (http://www.thepracticalherbalist.com/) and the Plants, Fruits and Vegetables: The Powerful Healing blog (http://fruitvegihealing.blogspot.com/) are two of many places on the web to discover the healing properties of the fruits you're harvesting.

Cosmic Sway

Daniel Pharr

LUGHNASADH, ALSO KNOWN AS Lammas, marks the first harvest and is therefore Thanksgiving to Druids and Pagans around the world. This is the first of three harvest times in the cycle of the year, the second is Mabon, and last harvest is on the Full Moon around Samhain. The Druids understood the power of the moon and planned all their community events on new and Full Moons. The last day of the Samhain harvest always occurred on the Full Moon, primarily for light as the sun sets early that time of the year. Lughnassadh and Mabon were set to occur on whichever lunar aspect was closest. This year, Lughnassadh is calculated to occur at 4:21 am EST, August 7, and the New Moon occurs at 5:51 pm, August 6. So for Druidic purposes, the high holiday of Lughnasadh begins this year on August 6 after sundown and the holiday games and hand-fastings would be the next day.

The traditional dates for Lughnasadh are August 1 and 2. The Full Moon would have come nine days earlier, too early for the holiday of "First Fruit," and the next Full Moon is not until late August. The waning Gemini Moon will be shining, weather allowing, on the evening of August 1 for the beginning of the traditional Lughnasadh, although the traditionalists would probably refer to this high holiday as Lammas. Lughnasadh is a Celtic word and refers to the Fire god Lugh who created this holiday to honor his mother who died clearing the island of Ireland for agriculture. Lammas, put in place by the Church to co-opt Lughnasdh and convert Pagans, comes from the Christian tradition of bringing a loaf of bread (Loaf-Mass) made from the first harvest of wheat, to the church.

The Gemini Moon–August 1

The Gemini Moon, on this traditional holiday date, will keep conversations lively, and the Moon in the Sixth House will bring attention to the household pets and their heartwarming antics and cuddles. The Moon rules the Seventh House, which is about energy of partnerships, both business and personal, and will bring activity to all relationships. However, given the other factors, the heart relationships will be more activated, especially around communication. Mercury in Cancer and in the Seventh House both place importance on familial communication and heartfelt interactions, but the Gemini Moon is about talking, not communicating, and the Moon square Venus will place more barriers to sharing the deep feelings that have been buried for some time. These feelings, having been previously hidden, want to come out, and until they are lovingly shared, unease could exist in the love relationship. The Moon square Chiron brings the Wounded Healer into the mix, trying to rise above the pain and hoping to teach others to do the same. Venus and Mars add more heat to this pressure cooker. Venus in Virgo will influence relationships with the expectation of precision, punctuality, and practicality—in short, perfection. Although some joy may be found in detailed conversations analyzing every aspect, Venus in the Eighth House will add further intensity. Mars in the Seventh House provides the fuel for intimate relationships right now, seeking out one-on-one intimacy in the midst of this possible turmoil. Sagittarius is rising right now and with it comes relaxed warmth and an enthusiasm for the lessons learned from the adventure.

Leo New Moon–August 6

The New Leo Moon ushers in the Lughnasadh celebration on the calculated dates of August 6 and 7. This will be a good one, with Leo asking for folks to shine and display themselves and their talents, seeking praise and recognition along the way. What could be more fun than a whole community vying for the spotlight and a place at the front of the stage? Prophecy and future-oriented leadership may seem like destiny calling.

The Moon is in the Ninth House and rules the Ninth House. Mercury is also in the Ninth House. Understanding the global aspect of your spiritual path and learning about spiritual philosophy in general are important right now and could lead to travel and interactions with foreign cultures. Travel might also occur on an ethereal level, accessing and understanding the akashic records or searching for the wisdom that overlies all else. Traveling and adventure-seeking with your partner will enhance the journey. With Venus in Virgo, nightlong discussions of the day's events will create much joy. And with Mars in the Eighth House, you may experience strong urges for some alone time in your love relationship. With Scorpio rising, intensity and drama will be rising as well.

As the evening progresses, some of the aspects will change as the astrology moves to the calculated time for Lughnasadh. The celebratory games on Lughnasadh should be geared toward friends and family rather than feats of strength, cunning, and guile. In their heyday, the games of Lughnasadh would have consisted of militaristic events such as throwing stones, tossing poles, and racing horses. The Moon will be in the Fourth House and ruling the Second and Third Houses, making family a priority, and feeling comforted and safe within the bounds of family, while inventorying personal resources. Communication of all forms, including telepathy, will be enhanced. Mercury in the Third House will also work to improve communication and assimilate information, as will Gemini on the Ascendant. Venus in the Fourth House will focus on harmony within the family.

Lughnassadh Rites

As with the Lughnassadh celebrations of old, this year's high holiday could be carried across two days. A balefire in honor of the Fire god Lugh would certainly be appropriate for the evening of August 6. This will never be a solemn celebration. The energy of the fire will turn the gathering into a party, just as Lugh would want it. The three F's—Fire, Food, and Fun—will rule the evening. Eat, tell stories, dance around the fire. Remember, this is a day of thanksgiving, so a moment of solemnity will be appropriate when thanks is giving to the gods and goddesses for the another year of bountiful harvest, both actual and metaphorical. Then there is the meal, like any Thanksgiving meal, complete with all the bounty from the summer growth. Hens might be more appropirate than a turkey. Meats, fowl, or fish from the region (like salmon), or pork, might also be a good choice. Pork was sacred to the Celts, and their gods served unending portions of pork at the hospitality table. Of course, grains, fruits, and vegetables are always staples. Move to the fire for dessert and let the party begin.

The next day, August 7, after rising from the night before, enjoy an afternoon picnic, serving the leftover foods in a natural setting. Lughnasadh is not complete without games, especially those played outdoors. Horseshoes or rings, volleyball, croquet, or bocce ball, badminton, touch football, or disc golf, would all offer loads of family fun.

Lughnasadh was one of two high holidays, the other being Beltaine, that handfastings were common. These unions of marriage, were for a period of a year and a day, and of course could easily be renewed, but could also easily be dissolved after the time elapsed. Imagining how these trial marriages fit into the revelry of the holiday spirit is not difficult. Re-creating the idea of handfasting through mock marriages of commitment to behavior or ideals for a year a day might also be fun, and reminiscent of the New Year's Resolution.

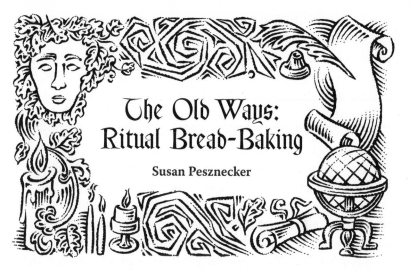

The Old Ways: Ritual Bread-Baking

Susan Pesznecker

MANY PEOPLE REGARD THE making of bread as something akin to alchemy or sleight-of-hand. In truth, bread-baking *is* magick! Because of the "staff of life" associations with all kinds of grain, bread-baking also links us to generations that have come before. The ancient Celts celebrated the harvest grain at Lughnasadh. Corn was stone-ground and used to bake corn bannock—a flat, round, unleavened loaf. The bannock was carried around the place of celebration—or one's home bounds—three times, deosil (sun-wise). After the third circuit, the bearer stopped in front of her home, broke off a piece of bannock, threw it over one shoulder as an offering, and then named something she wished to appease or propitiate in the coming year. The remaining loaf was then shared communally.

Despite many believing that breadmaking is complicated (just look at the number of bread machines sold every year), it's a simple process that anyone can master. Indeed, bread recipes are among the most forgiving in your kitchen. And the tastiest, too!

The Principles

Principle 1. *Yeast is alive!* Yeast is a tiny plant that lives in a sort of suspended animation until it's encouraged to awaken by warm conditions and the presence of food. What does yeast eat? Simple: carbohydrates, in this case sugar and flour. Once activated, yeast divides and multiplies explosively, giving off carbon dioxide as it works. The CO_2 is what makes dough rise, filling it with millions of tiny bubbles.

In order for yeast to activate and rise properly, the immediate environment must be snugly warm—ranges of 90 to 110 degrees F (about the temperature of a hot bath) are about right. If the yeast is dropped into liquid that's too hot, it will die and the dough won't rise. If, on the other hand, conditions are too cold, the yeast will just sit there and won't do much. "Proofing" the yeast means coaxing it to life—with food, warmth, and liquid—before it's added to the bread recipe. This also ensures the baker that she has a viable bit of yeast.

Principle 2. *All breadmaking follows a simple process.* First, the yeast is brought to life in a warm liquid environment. Second, flour and additional ingredients are added, according to the recipe. The raw dough is kneaded, put through one or two risings, punched down, shaped, and baked. Allowing the dough to rise in a warm place gives the bread lightness and develops its texture, while punching down removes the risen gas bubbles and prepares the dough for shaping and rising. Working with bread dough is fun and takes muscle. All of the kneading and punching is, after all, one way our grandmothers got rid of their pent-up frustrations.

Before baking, the dough is shaped. It's then baked in a moderate oven (generally about 350 degrees F) until it's golden brown and smells heavenly. A properly-baked loaf sounds hollow when thumped on the bottom.

The Ingredients

For best results, use the best products you can find. Any general-purpose wheat flour works: whole wheat or refined, bleached or unbleached, organic or non. But special bread flours are higher in gluten and make a gorgeous loaf. When buying yeast, check the expiration date and store in the refrigerator. Again, always proof the yeast before blending it with the other ingredients—this makes sure it's viable.

Water and milk are the typical liquids in bread recipes, though occasionally fruit juices, alcohol, or other liquids are included. Most bread recipes include at least a small amount of sweetener, such as white or brown sugar, honey, molasses, agave nectar, or maple syrup. These provide food for the yeast and yield a higher, lighter loaf than loaves with no sugar. Some loaves don't use any sugar, such as traditional French bread and many rustic loaves. Sugarless dough has its own wonderful nature but will never rise as exuberantly as dough containing sweeteners.

Many recipes include fats, e.g., oils or butter. These add a richness, tenderness, and flavor while creating a softer crust and crumb.

A Note About Bread Machines and the Like

Although bread machines are a wonderful convenience, the machine separates the baker from the process and from the end result. If your intention is to create a loaf that will be part of a ritual or celebration or in which you hope to infuse the bread with magick and intention, you really need to get your hands dirty. Er, doughy.

Working Magick

Now comes the fun part: you'll find that every part of your baking can take on a magickal element.

Preparation: Wash your hands before beginning—this ensures cleanliness as a cook and allows you to purify yourself before beginning. Use your hands to work the dough—you must feel and experience the dough in order to understand it. It also creates a magickal connection between you, the process, and the result.

The utensils: Reserve special tools for breadmaking—at the very least, you might purchase a special wooden spoon. Charm, anoint, engrave, or bless your tools to service. I inherited (and treasure!) my grandmother's rolling pin and a huge ceramic bread bowl that has been in our family for at least six generations.

The bond: As you touch and stir and handle the dough, immerse yourself fully in the experience. Consider your magickal purposes or intentions at the time, and work them into the dough. My grandmother used to tell family stories as she worked with the dough, believing that the family's magicks became part of the result.

Ingredients: Herbs and spices can be used for specific intentions or results. Infused waters will add solar, lunar, stellar, zodiacal, planetary, or herbal influences. Fresh and dried fruits, nuts, and seeds lend unique magickal correspondences (and flavors!) to your baked masterpiece. Any ingredient can be blessed to purpose.

Stirring and kneading: Work deosil (sun-wise) for growing energies, beneficence, and celebration. Work widdershins for gathering energies, binding, and contemplation.

The Moon: Breadmaking will work any time, but the process absolutely works best (i.e., big, wonderful, golden, delicious loaves!) during the Moon's waxing phases. A freshly baked loaf can add wonderfully to a full Moon esbat.

Sigils, Symbols, and Marks: Carve symbols, words, and sigils into the dough as you knead, allowing that magick to become a secret, unseen part of the end result. You can also carve marks onto the surface the shaped dough; these will bake with the dough and become part of the end result. For best results, use a very sharp thin blade. Brush with an egg wash for golden highlights.

Color: A few drops of yellow food coloring in the dough will create a rich yellow bread—perfect for solar rituals or celebrations. Use color as desired for other effects, but work with one or two drops at a time. You might have to work hard to convince people to eat purple bread!

Intention: As you work, feel your own energies poring into the bread-to-be. Concentrate on whatever you wish to manifest, and imagine that as the dough rises and bakes, those manifestations will be realized. Feel the connection with generations past. Don't forget the butter and jam!

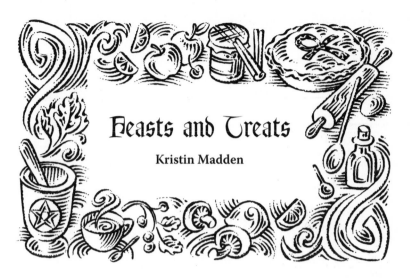

Feasts and Treats

Kristin Madden

ALSO KNOWN AS LUGHNASADH, this late-summer sabbat celebrates the grain harvest and honors the sacrifice of plants and animals so that the human community might survive. Lammas is a time of breaking bread, eating fresh corn and other fruits, playing games, enjoying outdoor activities, and relaxing in the heat of summer. Each of these dishes reflects the energies of Lammas in unique ways.

Parmesan Crusted Catfish

Fishing and summer just go together. Add a delicious breading to your favorite fish, and you have the ideal dish for a Lammas evening.

Prep Time: 5 minutes
Cooking Time: 30 minutes
Serves: 4

½ cup flour
¼ cup grated Parmesan cheese
⅛ cup ground pecans, almonds, or cashews
½ teaspoon (each) garlic powder, salt, and pepper

4 catfish filets
Olive oil cooking spray
2 tablespoons lemon juice

Mix together all ingredients except catfish and lemon juice. Spread evenly on plate.

Rinse catfish filets in water, pat dry with paper towels, then coat entirely with crust mix. Place in baking dish that has been sprayed with oil. Sprinkle with lemon juice. Cover and bake for 30 minutes at 400 degrees F.

Corn Pudding

Fresh corn is a staple in many areas at this time of year. Corn pudding is a great alternative to the typical corn on the cob and is perfect for Lammas/Lughnasadh game festivities.

Prep Time: 5 minutes
Cooking Time: 40 minutes
Serves: 6–8

2 eggs
1 can whole corn
1 can creamed corn
½ cup sour cream
½ cup butter, melted
12-ounce package cornbread mix

Beat eggs until foamy. Combine eggs with all other ingredients. Leave out 1 tablespoon of cornbread mix. Pour into baking dish and top with 1 tablespoon cornbread mix. Bake at 350 degrees F for 40 minutes.

Peach Smoothie

Peaches are in season at this time of year and they offer the idea way to cool off at Lammas celebrations.

Prep Time: Overnight, plus 15 minutes
Serves: 4–6

5 peaches, peeled and pitted
½ cup vanilla yogurt
2 tablespoons honey
1 teaspoon vanilla extract
Optional: ¼ cup berries or chopped bananas

Freeze peaches overnight. Allow to thaw slightly then chop.

Purée yogurt, honey, and vanilla extract. Add peach pieces and optional ingredients. Process until creamy.

Cherry Clafouti

Prep Time: 20 minutes
Cooking Time: 30 minutes
Serves: 6–10

2 tablespoons plus ½ teaspoon butter, softened
2 cups cherries, pitted
¼ cup sugar
1 cup cream
4 large eggs
½ cup flour
¼ teaspoon salt
¼ cup cocoa powder

Butter the inside of a pie plate with ½ teaspoon butter. Fill with cherries. In a separate bowl, blend sugar, cream, eggs, flour, salt, and remaining butter until smooth. Pour mixture over cherries. Bake for 30 minutes at 350 degrees F. Dust with cocoa powder and serve warm.

Crafty Crafts

Linda Raedisch

HERE ON THE EASTERN seaboard of the United States, August marks both the tail end of summer and the beginning of hurricane season. It is also the time to celebrate the Celtic god, Lugh, also known as "Lugh of the Mighty Blows," a god of thunder and lightning as well as the sun.

Thursday's To-Do List: Gather Houseleeks!

Back in the days of thatched-roof houses, lightning was particularly dangerous. One strike could set the whole house on fire. To protect against such calamities, the inhabitants planted houseleeks, known in this country as "hen and chicks," on the roof. Like the plantain, the houseleek is a toughie. The juicy fleshiness of the leaves give it the strength to withstand hail, fire, and general neglect. By incorporating houseleek in the thatch, it was hoped that the plant's sturdy magic would be imparted to the whole structure. Even Charlemagne, who usually didn't hold with native magic and who loved to pass laws about who should grow which herbs where, decreed that everyone in his empire should grow houseleeks on their rooftops, whether tile or thatch. (They were probably already doing it!)

Perhaps unbeknownst to Charlemagne, Witches were said to gather the houseleeks for their brews always on a Thursday, the day sacred to the Germanic thunder god, Thor, because they were most powerful on this day. In Switzerland, houseleeks were placed on a post inside the fireplace to prevent Witches from entering the house that way.

You don't need a thatched roof, fireplace, or even an old boot to grow houseleeks. All you really need is a houseleek. If you're a gardener, you probably have a few broken pieces of flowerpot hanging around. Sprinkle some soil in the curve of a largish potsherd and settle your houseleek upon it. As long as she gets a little water and sunlight, this hen will soon start to hatch chicks.

The Foxes' Wedding: An Invitation to Decline

There's nothing more magical than when water and sunlight come together: the sun breaks through a hole in the black clouds, turning the rain that keeps falling into a golden shower. This phenomenon of rain from a sunny sky is known in Japan as the foxes' wedding. The foxes' wedding is not quite the happy occasion it sounds. The most riveting expression of this long-held folk belief can be seen in Akira Kurosawa's film, *Yume*, or, "Dreams." In one of the film's chapters, a little boy happens upon the eerie stop-and-go procession of upright-walking foxes in their formal kimonos strolling through the rainy woods. Having witnessed this forbidden wonder, the boy can no longer return home. He either has to kill himself or seek the fox at the end of the rainbow and beg his forgiveness.

In Japan, it does not pay to get on the wrong side of foxes. There used to be, and in some remote villages perhaps still are, certain families who were believed to own ghostly foxes which they could send out to do their bidding. Such houses were easily identified, it was said, by the row of foxes sitting out on the roof tiles at dusk, waiting to be dispatched on their errands. Real foxes, sacred to the rice god Inari, are sometimes encouraged to live within the precincts of the god's shrine. Food is put out for them, including the fox's favorite dish of fried tofu.

To me, the most magical thing about foxes is how seldom I see them. When I do catch a glimpse of one, it always comes as a surprise. The russet-coated gentleman with his long black stockings is highly visible against the snow, but he rarely deigns to show himself that way. I have never seen a fox as road kill. The last time I crossed paths with a fox in my neighborhood, he was streaking toward the densely wooded back lot of an Episcopal church. This church's garden also happens to house a Japanese bronze temple bell, a parishioner's gift from the 1960s. Is there a connection? One can never be sure with foxes.

Much as I would love to put out a little dish of fried tofu for our neighborhood *kitsune*, it's usually not wise to feed wild animals. If you too are tempted, go and comb through your library's collection of origami books instead. Many will have instructions on folding paper foxes. I recommend the classic *The World of Origami* by Isao Honda. Here you will find instructions for folding both a seated fox and a fox mask. Make a whole family and install them in the front window. Or, if you don't want your neighbors to know you keep foxes, put them on a high shelf. Offer them a little fried tofu now and then. Once your spirit foxes have had a chance to taste it, you can eat it yourself.

Rainbow Crows

While you've got the origami books out, why not fold some crows or ravens? With their glossy-black rainbowed plumage, these birds, too, embody the stormy summer. In folktales the world over, both the raven and the crow start out as white. Then they fall down the chimney, eat snake eyes, or tee off some god or other who thinks that turning their feathers black is a punishment. Personally, I like the black.

Of the two birds, the raven is by far the more glamorous. For one thing, it's bigger. A raven can fly away with a large slice of pizza while the poor crow can only peck at the remains of a flattened chipmunk. There are certainly more stories about ravens. The earliest Valkyries

were more like ravens with women's faces than shining battle maids. In Cornwall, it was believed that King Arthur, rather than taking his ease at Avalon, had been transformed into a raven. In the crow's favor, my South Indian neighbor tells me that crows seen by the Full Moon are the spirits of dead grandmothers coming back for a visit.

In New Jersey, crows are all we've got, and I like them very much. Our own murder-in-residence does very well for itself among the dumpsters behind our apartment house. These birds do so well for themselves, in fact, that they sometimes look like they're having trouble getting off the ground. In the summer, they get up early, scavenge a good breakfast, then hang around in the gutters and sweet gum trees to TALK. I sometimes worry that our semi-exposed garbage will attract black bears, but if any of them are drawn in by the smell, they'll soon be driven away again by all those raucous cat-calls. Our crows can certainly hold their own against the local preda-tor, a red-tailed hawk, whom they pester mercilessly, poor guy.

With the crows, clouds and sunshine making rainbows *outside* the house, it only remains to bring a few rainbows *inside* the house this Lughnasadh. To do so, try the following craft.

Lightweight Witch Ball

Today, spheres of bubbly, swirling glass known as "witch balls" are made and sold for decoration, but in 1920s rural England they were still hung in windows for their original purpose of warding off Witches. In colonial New Jersey, cobalt blue witch balls were placed over the mouths of pitchers to prevent witches from spoiling the

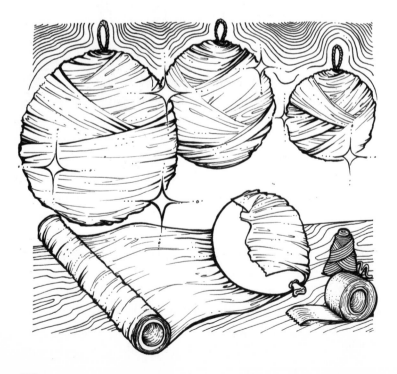

milk. I'm not sure what it was about these beautiful, blown-glass baubles that was supposed to so unnerve the Witches, but today we can all enjoy them.

This craft is the poor Witch's answer to the genuine article, which can be quite pricey. The method is similar to that used to make the body of a piñata, but instead of covering your balloon with papier-mâché, you will use plastic wrap and packing tape. The result is a cheap, lightweight accent to hang in your window. When the sun shines through it, the wrinkles in the plastic wrap create tiny rainbows.

Tools and Materials
1 round party balloon, blown up to about 4½ inches diameter (or
    about twice the size of a large Christmas ball)
Plastic wrap
Clear packing tape
Needle, pin or other sharp object
Scissors
String

Cover the balloon completely in plastic wrap. Let there be wrinkles! Now cover the wrapped balloon in one-inch strips of packing tape, overlapping edges and smoothing them down as you go. It will take a little while, but it's important to have complete coverage. That said, leave a half-inch-square space around the knot in the balloon so you'll be able to extricate the deflated balloon when you've finished the taping. Ready? Stick the pin in the balloon. Pop! Use your scissors to snip away any plastic wrap in the way of the half-inch space.

When you've wrangled your dead balloon out of your translucent sphere, use a final strip of tape to attach a string loop and close up the hole at the same time.

All One Family

Sandra Kynes

LAMMAS PARTNERS WITH IMBOLC on the Wheel of the Year, and like its opposite, the change in the length of the day becomes noticeable. Although this is not one of the solar sabbats, for me, the sky is the predominant aspect of this time of year. The bright sun and hazy days are offset by dazzling thunderstorms that charge the night sky with enormous energy. When I was a child, my family's house had an enclosed sun porch on the second floor, which gave us a good vantage point for watching thunderstorms. We could see for miles and follow the progress of the brilliant, sometimes multicolored, claws of lightning bolts reaching down to earth. It was mesmerizing, but with safety in mind my parents ushered us off the porch before the strikes came too close.

Respect for thunderstorms is important as they are very dangerous, but we can enjoy them and employ their power for magic and ritual safely from within our homes. Spellwork during a storm can give our intentions an incredible boost. While they may not occur when we want, we can channel their energy for ritual. In the lead-up to Lammas my family and I start preparing our altar early in hopes of a thunderstorm within a night or two of our celebration. If your child is afraid of storms, this may help him or her overcome it.

If we are lucky and a storm occurs, we light two candles and stand in front of our altar holding hands. The person on each end places their free hand on the altar, creating a circle. As the lightning adds illumination to the room and the thunder crashes overhead, we begin. I usually lead with verbal instructions to focus attention on our feet and visualize the storm's energy moving through the earth below our house. Mother Earth tames this energy and makes it safe for us to imagine that we are drawing it up as soft white light through the basement, through the floor, and into our feet. As the storm continues, we proceed to pull energy up through our bodies and arms to the altar, charging it with white light and energy. We continue for a few minutes and then release our hands. While this charges the altar, it also energizes us, especially small children. I have found it useful to lead a grounding exercise, give everyone a little bit of chocolate or use my special blend of patchouli, cypress, and vetivert essential oils stabilize our individual energy.

Thunderstorms are not the only sky show this time of year; meteor showers also present a fascinating display and for several days around July 29 the Delta Aquarids can be seen. While this meteor shower is best viewed from the Southern Hemisphere they can be seen in the northern temperate latitudes, or roughly from south of Florida to the Arctic Circle. From here, the meteors appear to radiate from the southern part of the sky. To locate Delta Aquarii, which is the third brightest star in the constellation Aquarius, look south just before dawn to find the great square of the Pegasus constellation. If you were to draw a line down from the two stars on the right of this square you'll find it. The best time to view the meteors is from midnight to dawn. Without school to worry about, staying up extra late or getting up really early can be a special treat for kids.

Depending on where you live, artificial and ambient lighting may be an issue when stargazing, so you may need to find a place other than your backyard for viewing. An alternative is to visit a planetarium. While it doesn't have the connection to the natural world in the same way as being outdoors, it may fit your schedule and accommodate small children more easily.

The most famous meteor shower is the Perseid, which occurs after Lammas from approximately August 5 to 13. Unlike the Delta Aquarids, the Perseid build to a peak and the meteors occur in all parts of the sky, so you don't have to pinpoint Perseus. In case you want to, look toward the northeast and you will find him just below Cassiopeia. While spotting meteors is easier and more dramatic on a moonless night, seeing a brilliant "shooting star" in moonlight is still exciting. However, watching for meteors can require patience and to keep young minds focused I found that talking about the Greek mythology behind the constellation names helps to hold interest. Perseus was the hero who killed the dreaded Gorgon Medusa, who had snakes for hair. Cassiopeia was a beautiful but arrogant queen who declared that she was more beautiful than all the sea nymphs, which angered Poseidon who then exacted retribution. In addition to mythology, introducing children to the night sky adds another dimension to their appreciation of the natural world.

Coming back to Earth, another way we like to mark Lammas is to spend time in the garden and have a special meal. After all, this is the festival of first fruits and a celebration of the earth's bounty. It's easy to forget how important a successful harvest was to our ancestors. A good harvest meant a comfortable survival in winter, but a poor one meant difficulty. That's why this is a good time to pause and give thought to where our food originates as well as reverence for the cycles that produce it. I love the idea of having a vegetable garden, but space is at a premium in my backyard and flowers usually win. I think that's because my first garden had only flowers. I was about nine years old when my parents dug out a plot for me to do with whatever I wanted. The only thing that grew were zinnias, but they were absolutely magical to me.

I also have wonderful memories of playing in my grandmother's gardens. Her vegetable garden produced a lot of food that she "put up" for the winter. She grew everything you can think of for salads including onions, which were plentiful and did double-duty as pest control. Her rhubarb patch was simply out of this world. Not that I'm a big fan of eating it, but it was a fabulous spot when we played hide-and-seek. I was small enough to conceal myself under those huge green leaves where I enjoyed the smell of the tall red stalks.

Although the gardens I have had are modest compared to my grandmother's, I'm an avid gardener, as is my son. Even when he was small we had brainstorming sessions about what to plant each year. Sometimes we kept seeds from the autumn to have continuity from one year to the next. One of my son's favorite things to grow is sunflowers. Although the seeds are not ready to harvest at Lammas, their tall majesty and huge flower heads symbolize the abundance of summer. As far as edible plants go, I usually end up with just tomatoes and herbs, but they taste all the sweeter for having been nurtured by my own hands. While it's not enough for a complete meal on Lammas what we grow is something we pay special attention to and savor.

In addition to keeping our ways, I believe that it's important for children to get their hands in the soil; to slow down to watch plants grow. Life is too rushed, but a garden gets them (and us) to get in touch with the important things in life. In addition, caring for a garden helps children learn about nurturing and responsibility. Whether we grow plants that provide food, flavoring, or simply sweeten the air, tending them keeps us all in touch with the Goddess and her bounty.

Ritual: Lammas Jam-Boree

Natalie Zaman

DO YOU EVER FIND yourself deep in February wishing for a hint of the sun? That the days could be just a little warmer? A little longer? It's happening, of course, but winter—especially those last few weeks—has a way of testing both spirit and patience. What we do earlier in the year to prepare for the darker days makes all the difference.

It's difficult to think of winter in August, but Lammas asks us to consider the past and ponder the future. If summer has been kind (because let's face it, sometimes it isn't—I offer summer of 2011's hurricane Irene as a case in point), I'm knee-deep in fruit, be it from my own berry bushes, or a visit to my local farm stand. There's plenty to eat and plenty to share, but there won't be so much as a pit come winter if I don't do something *now*.

I know, it's easy enough to buy summer produce out of season at just about any supermarket—but a hothouse-grown, transported raspberry isn't the same as one plucked off the bush, warm and sweet on my tongue. You can have your summer produce when the Wheel turns to winter by preserving, capturing the essence of the season in a (recycled!) jar.

What follows is a crafting ritual that my family and I attempt each Lammastide. Like most things we do, it blends the sacred and the everyday, and provides an opportunity to reestablish our connection with the seasons, the earth, and our ancestors. It and its preparation was written with family practice in mind, but can be performed by solitary practitioners and larger groups (more hands make for lighter work!).

Items Needed

4 crystals, to represent the 4 quarters

2 crystals, to represent the God and Goddess

Compass to determine placement of Quarter crystals (Placement is determined by your tradition. We place air in the east, fire in the south, water in the west, and earth in the north)

Recipe for jam using seasonal, local fruit of your choice. Note: Jam can be substituted for other fruit preserves such as jellies and cordials. You'll just have to adjust your ingredients and storage accordingly.

Seasonal, locally grown fruit of your choice

Baskets, bowls and/or containers to hold and separate fruit

Sugar

Pectin. There are many recipes for jams, jellies, and fruit butters, but the basic ingredients are fruit, sugar, and pectin. There are pectin-infused sugars, but if you can't find sugar with pectin in it, pectin can be bought separately. The amount of fruit you have to work with (usually done by the pound) determines the amount of sugar and pectin you will use.

Recycled glass jars (heat resistant) with lids or mason jars

Means to sterilize jars. Jars can be sterilized without the use of special equipment. See resources listed on page 264 for tips on preserving and the jar sterilization process.

Labels for jars

Green pen or marker

Water with sea salt

Cinnamon oil. This oil, together with the water and sea salt mixture will be used to bless your storage jars with the elements. The water and sea salt represent water and the earth. The cinnamon oil represents air (via the olfactory senses) and fire—cinnamon is a "hot" herb!

Squares of green cloth cut to a size so that they will cover the lids of your jars. An appropriate color for Lammas, green symbolizes life and abundance (remember that horrible green loaf?)

Green ribbon

An intention. Part of this ritual will be to "infuse" the preserves you are making with a wish or hope for the future. For us, this is the magical element of the process, and aids in teaching the connection between intent, action, and visualization. For practical purposes, we use one simple intention for the whole batch, but have each participant have their own as well. The intention can be something directly related to Lammas, such as a wish for bounty in the coming winter, but you may also want to consider relating the intention to the fruit you've harvested. All fruits and vegetables have healing and metaphysical properties. Again, check the resources on page 264.

Ice cream and/or plain pound cake for sharing

Before we begin, a word on…

Timing. One thing I've come to learn over the course of a few years in doing this particular ritual is that nature works on her own calendar. Do not feel like you have to wait "for the day." August 2 may fall midweek when you can't take a day off from work, it could rain, or your farm stand may be closed. What's more, the environment can and will be naughty—one year when I waited for Lammas day to begin harvesting, I got up in the morning to find that my bushes had been decimated by the local deer population. I understand the need to share (the lovelies left me enough to make a crumble or two), but I really missed my jam that year.

Work area. This is a crafting ritual done completely in the kitchen. I've found that things go smoother and that it's easier to maneuver if as much as possible is done beforehand—including cleaning and creating sacred space. In fact, I try to keep the kitchen in a perpetual state of sacred space—this is the place where food is prepared and where we gather and share as a family. It's difficult to think of a more important place that is in need of blessing and protection. (But, of course, you can do this during the ritual if that's what you're comfortable with).

I also try to keep kitchen altars small, minimized to representations of God, Goddess, and elements to "supervise" the proceedings. I use stones because with lots of hands—many of them little ones—there are fewer chances of accidents. Crystals are fine (and safe!) representatives for quarters and deities, but if you work best with light-bearing symbols, consider using battery-operated candles. They can be tucked into corners and in shelves without any fear of a fire hazard.

Have all of your ingredients measured and laid out and your equipment in place prior to starting. With mundane details attended to, you'll be able to focus on the magic you'll be cooking up.

Words. Words are powerful. Language—what we say and how we say it, carries great weight in our day-to-day lives, and perhaps more so in ritual. It's been my experience that what's important in prayer is that your words are heartfelt, honest, and most importantly, your own. Don't be afraid to put your intentions and words of welcome into your own voice. I know I've felt awkward and embarrassed when speaking invocations, but your words aren't as awkward as you might think—remember, you are loved, and what comes from the heart is the most powerful of all. If you still feel uncomfortable, write down what you're going to say beforehand on index cards and keep them handy. (The universe doesn't mind cue cards!) This will not only give you a chance to hone your words but will also remove the fear of having to memorize and gives a means of saving what you've done for future use.

I believe that spirituality should challenge the soul, but it should also be comfortable and familiar—and so we tend to use simple wording and casual language to state intentions. My family's approach to ritual is very informal and laid back, which is not for everyone. Do what resonates for you and for your group; feel free to incorporate your traditional invocations in the appropriate places, and use the invocations as presented here as inspiration.

Planning. Part of this ritual requires that you go out and gather the fruit you'll be using. If you grow your own, you won't have far to travel, but if you don't, you'll need to do some research on places you can pick your own produce. (Check the resources on page 264 for a list of websites that will help you locate a farm near you.) It's also a good idea to read over your recipe so that you become familiar with the ingredients and procedures to avoid any surprises. I'm a big believer in test runs, especially when it comes to cooking that I'm going to be sharing with others. (Anyone who's eaten a loaf baked by me knows it really is an act of faith. Breads are not my forte.) Some people are fine with winging it. Me? I like to practice.

The Ritual

Gather

On the chosen morning of the ritual, rise with the Sun, and do whatever you usually do to prepare for the day. Visit your sacred-space-kitchen and visualize having a productive day in the field. Ask for blessings and abundance for the day:

> *Earth, air, water, and fire,*
> *Ground, breathe, swell and inspire.*
> *Father God and Mother Goddess*
> *Bestow blessings on this first harvest.*

Speak your request aloud or say it silently in your heart, whatever you feel comfortable with. And then—get out and gather your fruit!

Some food for thought: The point of this exercise is to be outside, in nature and to connect to past, present and future. Immerse yourself in the process. Enjoy it and take your time. Listen to the sights and sounds around you. In your mind, travel back in time. Think about your ancestors doing similar work. How do you think they felt about it? Embrace this touchstone.

Homecoming

When you return to your kitchen, fruit in hand, take a moment to ground before you begin. What we usually do is put all the fruit on the table and gather around it. Once everyone is settled, take a moment to invoke the elements and the God and Goddess:

> *Be welcome, air! Thank you for your presence and for your part in bringing this first harvest home.*
>
> *Be welcome, fire! Thank you for your presence and for your part in bringing this first harvest home.*
>
> *Be welcome, water! Thank you for your presence and for your part in bringing this first harvest home.*
>
> *Be welcome, earth! Thank you for your presence and for your part in bringing this first harvest home.*
>
> *Be welcome, Mother Harvest! Thank you for your presence and for your part in bringing this first harvest home.*
>
> *Be welcome, Father Sun! Thank you for your presence and for your part in bringing this first harvest home.*

Pick Over

Distribute the fruit evenly between each participant. Place two bowls in the center of your table. If you have someone leading the ritual, have them explain that one bowl is designated for the fruit you will be preserving and sharing when the work is done. The other is for that which is inedible—pieces that are under- or over-ripe, damaged, or blighted. The discarded produce will not go to waste; when the pick over is done, the contents of the second bowl will be left out for birds and other animals who are equally dependent on the produce of the earth to live. During the pick over, participants should repeat the intention either silently or aloud, visualizing the wish being infused into the fruit, seeing it come to pass in their mind's eye.

Vessel Blessing

Before making the jam, the jars you'll be storing it in must be sterilized and blessed—they have an important job to do! Line the jars up
in front of your altar and bless each one. Run your finger from the
bottom up (to represent filling) and then clockwise around the body
of the jar. When the water and sea salt mixture combine, say:

> *From a seed in the ground,*
> *And fed by water*

And then the cinnamon oil:

> *Kissed by air,*
> *And warmed by the sun,*
> *Now preserved for a day of need.*
> **End the blessing with the intention.*

We avoid anointing jars at the rim. Even though the jars will be
sterilized, any residuals could interfere with the sealing process.
Once all the jars have been blessed, begin the sterilization process.

Transformation

While the jars are being sterilized, prepare your jam per your recipe—don't forget to set aside some of the fruit for sharing first!

Every recipe usually involves the following steps: washing,
crushing, pouring (sugar/pectin), stirring, watching. Have each participant take at least one turn in each step of the process, speaking or thinking the intention with each turn. Watch the fruit as it
changes from solid, to pulp, to liquid. Visualize the intention meld-
ing with the fruit as it breaks down and transforms. Important: Remember to stir in a clockwise/invoking direction!

Bottling

When the jam is ready, fill the jars. Speak or think the intention as
each is filled, and then as each as capped and sealed. Place the jars
in front of the altar as they are finished; they will seal as they cool.

Sharing

While you're waiting for the jam to cool, share the fruits of the harvest (this would be the "cakes and ale" of a traditional circle). Have one of the participants put out the discarded fruit to be enjoyed by wildlife. Depending on where you live and/or where you do this ritual, this may have to wait for a later time.

Serve the berries reserved from the jam pot with cake and/or ice cream with the blessing:

Enjoy today,
But save for tomorrow.
God and Goddess bless.

A Final Blessing

Cap each jar with a square of the green cloth, fastening it down with ribbon. Tie the ribbon in three knots (in honor of the three faces of the God and Goddess) thanking them for aiding in this work:

Thank you, Mother and Father, God and Goddess, for helping us to preserve the sun. Stay at our side through the dark days of winter. The sun will return.

Thank you, air, for your aid in preserving the sun. May we feel your warm breezes in the dark days of Winter, and remember the sun will return.

Thank you, fire, for aid in preserving the sun. My your warmth inspire us to brave the dark days of Winter and remember that the sun will return.

Thank you, water, for your aid in preserving the sun. May we be like you in the dark days of Winter, fluid and adaptable, remembering that the sun will return.

Thank you, earth, for your aid in preserving the sun. May we be steadfast as you are through the dark days of Winter and remember that the sun will return.

Place a label on each jar, speaking the intention one last time. If the jam is going to be shared with people outside the circle, write their names on the labels, picturing the intention coming to light for them. Handle the jars with care as they may still be hot.

Troubleshooting

Sometimes, things will go wrong, even with folks who are experienced in making preserves. But no effort is ever wasted, it's just a matter of using what you've made in a different way. Here are solutions for two common problems:

Your jars don't seal. You can tell if a jar has sealed by pressing down on the lid—if it snaps or pops back up, there is no seal to preserve the fruit. If this happens, your jam can be kept in the refrigerator, but its shelf life won't be as long (two to three weeks). Write the date on the label and use as soon as possible.

Your jam doesn't "gel." If you find that your jam has a very runny consistency, don't worry—it's still usable! Runny jams can be used as syrups over ice creams and cake (or try incorporate it into a bread pudding recipe!).

Good Lammas!

For Further Reading:

Beth, Rae. *Hedgewitch: A Guide to Solitary Witchcraft.* London: Robert Hale Limited, 1990.

Campanelli, Pauline and Dan. *The Wheel of the Year.* St. Paul, Minnesota: Llewellyn Publications, 1993.

Corbin, Pam. *Preserves, River Cottage Handbook No. 2.* London: Bloomsbury, 2008.

Fearnley-Whittingstall, Hugh. *The River Cottage Year.* London: Hodder and Stoughton, 2003.

Hamilton, Andy and Dave. *The Self Sufficientish Bible: An Eco Guide For Living in the 21st Century.* London: Hodder and Stoughton, 2010.

Pavord, Anna. *The New Kitchen Garden.* New York: DK Publishing, Inc., 1999.

Sawyer, Pat Kirven. *Ancient Wisdom, The Master Grimoire.* Arlington, Texas: Seventh House Publishing. The Woodlands, 2005.

Zimmer-Bradley, Marion. *The Mists of Avalon.* New York: The Random House Publishing Group, 2000.

Notes

Mabon

Autumn Resurgence

Janina Renée

WHEN THOSE OF US who live in temperate climates think of fall Equinox, images that may come to mind are harvest feasts, autumn leaves, and the onset of colder weather as the daylight begins to wane; so autumn rituals focus on harvest, ingathering, and preparing for winter. However, in thinking along conventional lines, we may sometimes forget other possibilities for ritual exploration. An example of this is the association of this sabbat with Mabon, whose mythology revolves around a divine son of a divine mother, part of a mother-son pair from a medieval Welsh story, which seems to have nothing to do with autumn. As a character in the tale of "Culhwch and Olwen,"[1] Mabon vab Modron became one of King Arthur's men after being rescued from an ages-long imprisonment that began after being abducted from his mother as an infant. However, this Mabon is thought to be the survival of a Celtic god. Neopagan use of Mabon for Autumn Equinox is of recent coinage,[2] which is why many older Wiccans and Pagans are initially confused when we hear this term, having never used it in our own traditions.

My own exploration of Mabon/Equinox has come from paying attention to what is going on in nature where I live and associating with Pagans whose rituals are based on other cultures. For Mabon, this has resulted in my discovery of a second spring in autumn, which has also led me in a roundabout way to the story of a divine son of a divine mother.

My experience with planning seasonals started in the 1970s, when I was active in several festival communities. Because we lived in Southern California, it was a challenge to design rituals that were relevant to our geographical region, as so many of our Pagan-Wiccan traditions came from northern Europe.[3] However, we got a larger sense of the possibilities from other local groups. We enjoyed exquisitely staged rituals put on by The Order of the Temple of Astarte, whose seasonal cycle is based on pre-biblical Canaanitic religion. The OTA celebrate Autumn Equinox as the "Festival of Seven Gates" in which Astarte descends to the underworld, performs the dance of the seven veils, slays Mot the god of death (who represents the scorching heat of the sun), and then revives her lover, Baal (the Green Man) who had been slain at Midsummer. We were also privileged to associate with Feraferia, a group whose name means "wilderness celebration," and who dedicate the Autumn Equinox to Artemis and Dionysius as deities of wilderness and wildness.

As California has a Mediterranean climate, I looked more deeply into the mythology of that part of the world, and made a discovery that altered my understanding of the story of the goddess Persephone (who is also known as Kore, "the maiden"). As the legend of Persephone is commonly explained, Persephone was abducted and forced into marriage with Hades, the Lord of the Dead, so she must spend part of the year with him in the underworld. While Persephone is with Hades, her mother, the Earth goddess Demeter, grieves by withdrawing her life-giving energy, so the vegetation dies and the world descends into barren winter. When Persephone emerges from below to rejoin her mother, spring returns as the green world is revitalized. However, scholars have identified a different stratum of this legend where Persephone doesn't return in the spring, she returns in the fall.[4] She doesn't spend the winter in the underworld, she spends the summer there, because summer is the fallow season in the Mediterranean, and fall is like a second spring to them.

Essentially, Persephone/Kore is a spirit of vegetation, especially of the seed or grain. In Europe, she is referred to as "the corn maiden," corn being a generic term for grain—primarily wheat, but in more ancient times, barley. During the summer, the Greeks stored their seed grain in underground silos (hence the idea of the maiden goddess taken into the underworld), and because their underground food store comprised their wealth, it was in the realm of Hades/Plouton, god of the wealth of the earth. However, in the autumn, after the summer drought was past, the seed grain was brought out and planted, (in this, the maiden rejoins her mother, the nourishing earth). When it germinated, the fields were green again. The greater Eleusinian Mysteries and Thesmophoria, which involve a ritual cycle with Demeter and Kore, coincided with these events in the agricultural cycle.

This alternative interpretation of the Persephone legend makes her story meaningful for people who live in other climatic zones. Because the symbolism of descent and re-emergence resonates on many levels, you can just as well celebrate the return of Persephone in spring or in fall.

I now live in Michigan, where the worst heat of August keeps me indoors, so I experience my own re-emergence in autumn, similar to my emergence in spring, when kinder weather allows me to resume my rambles in nature. Another way that I became aware of a sort of second spring in this four-season climate was when, on my walks along the tree margins that separate farmers' fields, I noticed that fresh patches of the herb motherwort were spreading in places where the thinning tree canopy or cleared crops allowed more sunlight. There are a number of plants that come out in early spring to get their share of sunlight before the trees leaf, so it isn't surprising that some plants take advantage of these openings of light.

Recognizing new growth in autumn holds a philosophical message about second chances and offers reassurance to individuals who fear they have missed out on certain things in life. The regrowth of motherwort has its own Kore-like qualities and combines the symbolism of Maiden and Mother, reminding us that Persephone and Demeter are viewed as different faces of one goddess. It is interesting to note that in addition to serving as an herbal calmative for nervous conditions, motherwort is also recommended for female complaints, including those involving seasonal and life-cycle issues such as menstruation, PMS, and menopause. With motherwort, as with all plants, you can benefit from their medicinal qualities on an ethereal level when you extend your mind to them in greeting. Extending greetings to the different features of the natural world also helps put us in good relationship with nature.

As we put our minds and bodies in sync with the seasonal tides, our experience is also affected by larger climatic trends such as global warming. I have long looked forward to the Autumn Equinox as the end of the ragweed season, but now they say that warming trends are resulting in added weeks of misery for allergy sufferers. To mitigate ragweed sensitivity, I use herbal, magical, and over-the-counter remedies. As the magical protection, I carry a small packet of ragweed for a homeopathic effect. I also mentally reach out to greet the ragweed plants that proliferate around me and gratefully acknowledgethat ragweed is an important foodstuff for many birds and other animals. Ironically for suffering humans, ragweed's genus name is *Ambrosia*. Also, the species name of the common ragweed is *artemisifolia*, which indirectly invokes the Goddess of the Wild.

Coincidentally, the start of ragweed season in this area is around the ides of August, about the same time as the big festival of Diana/ Artemis at the ancient sanctuary of Diana Nemorensis (Diana of the Wood) in Aricia. To replace this worship, the Christian Church designated August 13 as the Assumption of the Blessed Virgin, and it later became known as "Our Lady in Harvest." This somewhat coincides with the date of Lammas, specifically "old Lammas," before calendar adjustments resulted in offsets of about 10 to 11 days. Knowing that Artemisifolia has its own seasonal festival spread that runs from Lammas to Autumn Equinox gives us additional respect for ragweed.

Another plant that may benefit from global change is poison ivy, which I notice is gaining more ground each year. Poison ivy berries are a favorite food of yellow-rumped warblers, which are locally abundant in autumn. Perhaps because they are somewhat larger-bodied than other warblers, they have a more leisurely migration than smaller birds that have to go farther south, some of them to the ever-diminishing rain forests. I don't know whether the yellow-rumps' ability to stick it out longer is giving them a survival edge over other birds, but I have a theory that they are hanging around and eating more poison ivy berries, and then spreading the seeds through their droppings. Despite being so noxious to humans, poison ivy turns bright red in autumn, so at least it contributes to our show of fall colors.

Because poison ivy is a form of ivy, it is sacred to Dionysius/Bacchus, whose story parallels Kore's in significant respects, and who was in fact closely affliated with Demeter and Kore. Because of its clinging habit, ivy is a symbol of devotion, which is why the heart symbol originally took its shape from the ivy leaf. To show their ardent devotion, the followers of Dionysius wore garlands of ivy and carried a staff called a thyrsus—a long slender pole with a ball of ivy fixed to its pine cone tip. They also put garlands on their drinking cups, offering bowls, etc. When you see renderings of Greeks and Romans with wreaths in their hair, it is important to remember that those decorations weren't mere window dressing—wearing the sacred plants was believed to put people in direct psychic alignment with whatever gods they were invoking. If you decide to honor the god of the vine, however, please don't use any poison ivy.

Although I try not to judge by appearances, I get the creeps at the sight of poison ivy because its irregular outlines make it seem misshapen, and the leaves are sometimes dotted with angry blisters, adding to its sinister mien. Yet, in its irregularity, it does suggest the unruly, shapeshifting nature of Dionysius/Bacchus. He is one of those gods that you can't judge from appearances, because the images of this deity that most Americans have been exposed to are cartoon grotesques. However, Dionysius has many different forms and titles, with many different permutations and variations of his mythos. Before he became the god of wine, he was identified with the life force of nature, especially as the life-giving principle of moisture and the greening force in nature (i.e., "The Green Man).

The cult of Dionysius may have originated in the area of Phrygia and Thrace (comprising modern Turkey and the Balkans), and a significant part of its focus was on a mother-son relationship, similar to the mother-daughter relationship of Demeter and Kore. Just as Persephone/Kore is often depicted in Greek art as a maiden rising out of the earth, Dionysius is depicted as a young man (a Kouros) rising out of the earth. Sometimes Dionysius and his mother Semele are pictured rising out of the earth together, face to face, on equal terms. Semele actually is the earth itself (her Thracian name Zemela, for earth, is linguistically associated with the Lithuanian Zemyna and the Slavic Mati Syra Zemlya, invoked as the "Moist Mother Earth"). Semele is sometimes portrayed as a giant head looking out of the earth. The part of her myth that says she was a king's daughter who was killed when Zeus appeared to her in the form of lightning, actually hearkens to the belief that lightning was needed to fertilize the earth. Essentially, Demeter and Semele are one. On top of that, Dionysius has been identified as the son of Demeter or Persephone. In one Roman tradition as Liber, he is the husband of Persephone/Libera. Dionysius was honored in the Eleusinian festival at Autumn Equinox, where his statue was carried in procession.

Among his other manifestations, Dionysius was worshipped as a newborn infant in a cradle. In another phase of his mythos, he was dismembered (sometimes in the form of a bull), and then reborn. This recalls the "John Barleycorn" legend which tells how the grain has to be cut down to be reborn, and also similar to Kore's descent and return from the world of the dead. Dionysius also goes down to Hades to rescue his mother, on whom he bestows immortality and installs as one of his maenad priestesses.

As for his role as the god of wine, in the lands where he is believed to have originated, the intoxicating brew was not made of wine grapes, but of fermented grain (particularly barley), which brings us back to the spirit of the corn. The emperor Julian pointed this out in a poem, where he asks, "Who and whence art thou, Dionyse? ... for lack of grapes from ears of grain your countryman the Celt made you ..."[5]

Returning to Mabon, the information we have on him is limited, so much of what is written about the character and his divine affiliations is not known but inferred. However, Mabon has Kouros qualities, as his name emphasizes his youth—*Mabon vap Modron* means "young man/son, son of mother." This parallels Dionysius, whose name is thought to mean "young man—son of God/Zeus."[6] Like Kore and Dionysius, his relationship with a great mother goddess is emphasized, Madron being identified with Matrona, and his abduction and imprisonment also echoes the stories of Kore and Dionysius, being interpreted as a stay in the underworld.

In the actual story, King Arthur's men rescue Mabon from a dungeon, though it isn't mentioned who imprisoned him and for what reason. They were searching for Mabon because they were on a quest which involved hunting a monster boar, and they had been told that Mabon was the only person who could ride a certain horse and handle a certain hound needed to fulfill the quest. To find Mabon's place of imprisonment, they first had to question a number of very ancient animals. Apparently Mabon was ages old, though he must have been in the form of a fit young man to participate in the dangerous hunt. It isn't explained how someone who had been imprisoned since he was three days old acquired such great riding and animal-handling skills, but that's fairy-tale logic.

The hero Mabon is considered to be a survival of a Celtic god Mabon/Maponus, who is concerned with "the skills of poetry and music,"[7] and may also be something of a solar deity, as his name is paired with Apollo in dedicatory inscriptions. Although Mabon is repeatedly called the son of Modron in some sections of the "Tale of Culhwch and Olwen," elsewhere the story mentions a Mabon son of Mellt, and the context suggests this is the same Mabon. The patronymic Mellt may derive from "Meldos," making Mabon the son of lightning. Although we don't know whether Mabon has any historical association with Dionysius, the idea of being a son of lightning recalls the story of Zeus and Semele.

As for honoring Mabon at Fall Equinox, a lot of people are trying to make sense of that, as his legend has no autumnal associations. However, people who live in regions with cold winters could view Mabon as the principle of sunlight, with the equinox sun's descent into darkness as his abduction into the underworld. On the other hand, others might prefer to focus on the idea of resurgent life, even in autumn.

Notes and Sources:

1. "Culhwch and Olwen" is part of a collection known as "The Mabinogion," which is said to mean something akin to "Tales of Youth." It is not a collection of tales focused on Mabon, who is only mentioned in the one story. However, a character who figures in more of the stories is Pryderi, who, like Mabon, was kidnapped as an infant; this leads some to believe that Pryderi is Mabon's counterpart. My translations of the Mabinogian are by Gwyn Jones and Thomas Jones, (1949, rev. ed: London: Dent, 1974), and T.P. Ellis and John Lloyd, (Oxford UP: 1929).

2. The naming of this sabbat is attributed to Aidan Kelly.

3. My partner in ritual was my then-husband Ed Fitch, "The Johnny Appleseed of the Craft." Ed, who is twenty years older than me, had prior years of experience because he had been among the Bucklands' first Gardnerian initiates in this country. During the Sixties, he assisted as their secretary, corresponding with people who had questions about the Craft. Due to a dearth of training materials, Ed designed and disseminated *Pagan Way Rituals* and the *Outer Court Book of Shadows*, which he released as public domain in order to promote their spread. He also used Air Force standby flights to jet around the country on weekends to help training groups get started.

4. This is well explained in Martin P. Nilsson's *Greek Folk Religion.* (1904. rpt. New York: Harper-Torch, 1961, p. 52.)

5. Harrison, Jane Ellen Harrison. *Prolegomena to the Study of Greek Religion.* (Cambridge UP, 1903), p. 416. Julian thought Dionysius of Celtic origin, because Celtic tribal expansion penetrated Thrace.

6. Ibid 412, citing Kretschmer.

7. Ross, Anne. *Pagan Celtic Britain: Studies in Iconography and tradition.* New York: Columbia, 1967, p. 369. Bare feet slip into socks, wooly sweaters wrap close. We draw into ourselves, and inside our homes. No longer gardening and swimming, we curl up with books, stoke the fire, and take stock before winter. Mabon feasts draw us nearer to family and friends.

Cosmic Sway

Daniel Pharr

MABON, THE MIDPOINT OF AUTUMN, marks the time of the second harvest and another time of thanksgiving. Winter is on the way, arriving in just six short weeks. Autumn is the transition from the outward expanding energy of summer to the inward contracting energy of winter. The natural forces that work on the weather systems also work on every living creature, including, and most importantly, the human body and psyche. Plants recede, animals store food and fat, and we also make adjustments in body and mind. Over the twelve weeks of autumn, we adjust our thinking from outdoors to indoors, and we adjust our bodies to become reacquainted with cold and darkness. Instead of action, we turn to thoughts, ideas, emotions, and relationships.

The Full Moon precedes Mabon by three days, arriving just after midnight on September 19. Mabon is traditionally September 21, but this year is calculated to be September 22 at 4:44 pm EDT. The middle harvest would likely take place under this Full Moon, with the celebration occurring afterward. The Full Aries Moon will provide energy for action, and will motivate movement. Days are waning and the Moon begins waning, too. The Aries Moon will shine its light upon relationships of all arrangements. In every action involving another is a hidden, overlooked, or nocturnal relationship guiding the processes and these relationships will not be ignored. Intuition is strong, as is the need for action and communication brought on by the Moon in the Third House. Intuition is key to understanding the needs of folks that are in supporting roles. They don't say much or ask for anything, but the Moon rules the Eighth House, and that is all about the people that support your efforts. Understanding their needs and meeting them will go a long way to maintaining and improving those relationships. Beware of drama right now. The Moon square Pluto makes emotional situations much more intense. You could find yourself drawn in to an emotional drama with no quick escape. Mercury in Libra is a double-edged sword, providing the demeanor to broker peace in an embattled relationship, but also drawing you—the diplomat—into the conflict, which will likely upset personal harmony. Mercury in the Tenth House amplifies communication skills and supports your efforts. Venus in Scorpio intensifies the desire for relationships, but oddly, will cause a leaning toward secrecy while demanding full disclosure from the other person. Venus in the Eleventh House will also support you in the role as peacemaker. However, Mars in Leo will enhance self-confidence, affecting behavior and impacting everyone. Don't get carried away. Mars in Leo will also increase the need for creativity and self-expression through creative means. Sagittarius rising will bring enthusiasm into the mix and Mars in the Eighth House will have you seeking out friendly relationships in the form of joint ventures. This is all favorable for planning and managing the Mabon celebration.

Mabon Ritual and Feast

Mabon sits on the cusp of the action of summer and the contemplation of winter. Try as we do, plans are more easily made than carried out. All plans seem important when laid, but nature suggests that action follows focus. The plans completed are the ones that were focused upon, and the ones remaining are, therefore, the least important. Instead of dragging these undone plans around through the winter like sled with a broken runner, release yourself from the self-imposed responsibility of having not found project fruition.

Gather the clan. Build a fire. Honor the many accomplishments of the year by bringing the finished product of a completed task, or a representation, or even a note describing the accomplishment. Call the deities and cast the circle as is your custom. Make the circle big enough to move freely. En masse, carry the accomplishments around the circle, showing each other and the gods and goddesses with pride. After showing, telling, and congratulating for the work completed, move on to the unfinished projects. Individually, bring a branch with notes stuck or threaded on to it. The notes describe the task left undone, what activity or distraction was more important than that task, and the reason the task was deemed less important. These are not excuses to explain away a difficult situation; rather they are simply choices and reasons. The truth is of prime importance. Sometimes folks feel self-conscious about inactivity when they have chosen to watch a movie, play video games, or sleep, rather than doing that one thing needing to be done. Bringing the truth into the open releases the guilt. Step up to the fire with the Branch of the Undone, and read each note allowed, or describe aloud what is written on the note. Start with "I burn the..." An example might be:

I burn the need for cleaning out the garage, which was important because the cars do not weather well in the winter and remains undone because I did not want to do it and decided instead to find joy in video games.

After reading the undone notes, place the branch in the fire.

I release myself from these commitments.

Each person in the circle takes their turn burning the branch of the undone and releasing their commitments. As Mabon is the second harvest festival, the second thanksgiving if you will, this is also a time to give back. Another person's burning of the undone may strike a chord. Should you be moved in some way, give back a little, say thank you with your actions, and offer to help. Make a plan right then to go over and help complete the task. Make it a group effort. A half-dozen people showing up to clean a garage will complete the task in an hour or two, and everybody feels better. After the ritual is closed, feast upon the bounty of the season. Potatoes are particularly appropriate, as are other tubers. A complete thanksgiving meal is not necessary but is certainly most welcome.

For the traditionalist, the Moon will be in Taurus on September 21, bringing a need for stability and tradition. The planets with the strongest celestial influences remain in the same signs. However, Aquarius is now rising, which will bring intellectualism and extroverted expression to the forefront. The lunar and major astrological aspects for the calculated date of Mabon, September 22, will not have progressed much. There will be plenty of energy for the festivities and be sure to make it a group event.

Mabon Morning

Mabon morning would be the morning after the equinox, September 23. Wake up early, rise with the sun, and go outside. Find a place to sit and listen and feel. Hear the bird song, feel the ground and the air, breathe in nature. Experience the natural world awakening and coming alive. Now that the cycle of the year has crossed the halfway point between the end of summer and beginning of winter, the race to darkness will speed up. Take a moment to create a sacred space, if only in your mind. Bid the birds, animals, fish, insects, and plants a fond farewell. Wish them a safe winter and a revitalized emergence in the spring. Turn to the south and say goodbye to the days of summer. Turn to the north and welcome the nights of winter, still weeks away but on the horizon.

The Old Ways: Wintering-In

Susan Pesznecker

IT'S SUMMER'S END, AND the Autumn Equinox approaches. The world begins to prepare for the long winter sleep, and there's a chill to the air coaxing us to put extra blankets on the bed and turn on the furnace. During the cold nights and the shorter days, we feel the coming dark months and are pushed to get ready: to put away food and bring in firewood, to get out our wool sweaters and flannel sheets, to start a stack of books to be read on those long winter afternoons while a pot of soup simmers on the stove. It's time for wintering-in.

A home is one's sanctuary, and homes in autumn and winter must feel safe and snug, ready to keep us warm and protected during the cold months to come. Feeling spiritually whole and having an internal and external sense of peace and order is important to emotional health and security during a time of year we instinctively associate with darkness and peril. The orderly surroundings provides a sense of well-being during the dark months and inspires one's magicks, too.

Making Plans

Begin by considering the summer months that have just passed. What have you grown and harvested in the past months, literally and figuratively? Make a list of your successes and a second list of those aspects that could have gone better. Now think about what you'd like to accomplish during the winter—it a perfect time for projects. Start a stack of books to be read. Plan next year's garden. Make a new magickal tool or practice your divination skills.

Preparing a Stash

A traditional part of wintering-in is the laying in of supplies and food for the long winter. Sociologists call this "gathering." For many of us, this is an instinctive urge that goes back to times when people didn't have grocery stores and literally had to survive on what they could store during the summer months. Of course, it goes back even further, to Neolithic "hunter-gatherers," who hunted, gathered, and stored food during the warm months, hoping to amass enough to stay alive through the season of ice and snow. It's knowledge that seems to be built into animals. Look, for example, at the squirrel's stash of nuts and seeds, or the acorns buried by jays for winter munching. Likewise, fill your pantry or freezer with foods that will nourish your winter months.

Warming the Homescape

It's time to put away summer clothes and summer house-linens. Make sure the clothes are clean and dry when they're boxed. Caring for seasonal goods provides a sense of order, which supports a peaceful environment. Having half of your wardrobe in storage leaves more space in your closets and drawers, contributing to a sense of order and calm.

Take stock of your winter clothing and outerwear, inspecting woolens carefully for moth damage and hanging them outdoors on a dry day to freshen. For a simple but effective moth sachet, combine equal parts of dried lavender flowers and dried cedar shavings (use pet litter from pet store). Fill mesh bags (or clean nylon stockings); hang them in closets or tuck in drawers among your woolens. Replace every three to four months for best results.

Dress your home for winter with slipcovers, flannel sheets, warm blankets, and fluffy comforters. Toss "throws" over chairs and couches, ready for cuddling. Decorate your home for the season and make liberal use of candles. Consider, too, the magick of colors: red, orange, and chocolate browns help create a feeling of warming.

A Healthy Home

Levels of pollutants in indoor air can be from two times to more than a hundred times higher than outdoors, largely due to volatile organic compounds that evaporate or "off gas" from various home materials and cleaning products. Open your windows when you can—even if just for ten minutes—to let the good air in and the bad air out.

Brighten a space with fresh flowers. Many houseplants—particularly the peace lily and rubber plant—are powerful indoor air purifiers, cleaning the air for several cubic feet around them. During the fall and winter, water houseplants sparingly and don't feed them—like you, they're feeling the season's reduced rhythms.

A Healthy You!

With autumn and winter come cooler temperatures and ebbing daylight. Our bodies respond with decreased energy levels and reduced resistance and stamina. Given that most of the fall and winter are spent indoors, it's no surprise that we often develop illnesses during these months. To stay healthy, follow a varied diet, sleep well, and get regular exercise. Meditating for even five to ten minutes a day supports the immune system and promotes a sense of calm.

Make use of incense, smudges, herbs, and essential oils to boost your wellness.

Garlic: kills bacteria and viruses; warms and stimulates.

Ginger: dries and clears congestion, improves digestion; enhances circulation.

Juniper: deeply purifies, cleanses, and protects; clears the mind.

Nutmeg: warms and stimulates; supports circulation.

Sage: antiseptic; fights respiratory infections; opens airways.

Thyme: antiseptic; stimulant; effective against respiratory illnesses.

Try this "Winter Immuni-Tea" to boost your resistance. To 1½ cup freshly boiled water, add ½ tablespoon freshly grated ginger, 1 teaspoon freshly grated lemon zest, 1 teaspoon freshly grated orange zest, 1 to 2 cardamom seeds, 1 to 2 drops vanilla extract, a grating of fresh nutmeg, and a cinnamon stick (or a dash of powdered cinnamon). Steep for 5 minutes; sweeten with honey as desired.

Winter Magick

Creating a seasonal altar helps you "sync" with the season and feel its beauty. For Mabon, work with harvest golds, oranges, and browns. Add dried ornamental corn, acorns, small pumpkins, chestnuts, etc. Cauldrons, black feathers, and dried twigs and leaves would also be appropriate decorations. Don't forget candles!

Bring the elements into your space. Earth grounds us and provides a center. Use natural stoneware on your table. Set stones, rocks, and crystals around your home, and use sea salt in your kitchen. Air is energizing and improves clarity of mind. Burn incense or diffuse essential oils. Hang mobiles inside your home.

The fire element is energy in pure form. To bring in fire, burn candles and smudges. If you have a fireplace, burn wood or special fire logs. Cook with fiery spices and peppers. Water calms, soothes, and heals. Try a small tabletop fountain, or set out a bowl or cauldron of water.

Give your home a psychic cleansing. Smudge the entryways and corners using sage or sweetgrass or asperge with salt water, moving deosil form one room to the next. Clap hands to disperse old, stagnant energy, then use a bell or rattle to welcome fresh, sacred energy. Bring protective elements in or hang protective talismans over doors and windows. Repeat: "May the winds inspire you, earth protect you, water heal you, and fire always warm the hearth."

As you winter-in, envision yourself well prepared for the season and ready to gather energy for the coming spring, when life renews once again. Say hello to autumn!

Feasts and Treats

Kristin Madden

MUCH LIKE OSTARA, THE time of Autumn Equinox is about balance, though we move into the dark half of the year at Mabon. We feast on the remaining corn and grains as we delight in the final fruit harvest. Apples, pomegranates, corn, and fall spices are symbols of the season that bring great pleasure. The recipes for this sabbat bring in the traditional with spicy new elements for a truly comforting exploration of light and shadow that often comes during the waning year.

Pomegranate Chicken

Whether you honor Persephone's return or celebrate Rosh Hashanah at this time of year, pomegranate is a powerful symbol of the season. This dish should offer a delicious and mystical dinner for your Mabon feast.

Prep Time: 50 minutes
Cooking time: 40 minutes
Serves: 4

2–4 boneless chicken breasts
Juice and seeds of 2 pomegranates
4 tablespoons flour
½ teaspoon salt
¼ teaspoon pepper
1 onion, chopped
2 tablespoons butter
2 cups chicken broth
Optional: grapes

Soak chicken in pomegranate juice for 45 minutes. Remove from juice, pat dry, and coat the chicken with flour, salt, and pepper. Save juice on the side.

Sauté onion in butter until transparent. Add chicken and sauté until browned.

Add pomegranate juice and chicken broth. Simmer 25 minutes. Add pomegranate seeds and grapes just before serving.

Cheddar Cornbread with Roasted Garlic Butter

Cornbread is a customary offering at this time of year. This season, spice things up with cheddar and garlic for a unique depth of flavor.

Prep Time: 15 minutes
Cooking Time: 55 minutes
Serves: 4–8

Roasted Garlic Butter
4 cloves garlic, unpeeled
Olive oil spray
8 tablespoons butter, softened

Cornbread
1 cup flour
1 cup cornmeal
1 tablespoon brown sugar
1 tablespoon baking powder
½ teaspoon salt

½ cup cheddar cheese, shredded (divided)
1 cup buttermilk
2 egg whites
¼ cup applesauce

Cut the end off of each garlic clove. Place in a small ovenproof dish and spray with oil. Bake at 250 degrees F for 30 minutes. Press cloves out of paper and then mash. Mix well into butter and refrigerate until needed.

Combine flour, cornmeal, sugar, baking powder, salt, and 2 tablespoons cheese. In a separate bowl, combine buttermilk, egg whites, and applesauce.

Stir applesauce mixture into flour mixture. Pour into a greased square baking pan. Bake for 20 minutes at 400 degrees F.

Remove and sprinkle with remaining cheese. Bake for 5 more minutes. Serve warm with room-temperature garlic butter.

Autumn Spice Cordial

As we move into the dark half of the year, toast your shadows and the light within each of us by raising a glass of this warm, spicy cordial.

Prep Time: 5 minutes
Cooking Time: 18 minutes
Serves: 4

1 cinnamon stick
5 whole cloves
1 teaspoon (each) nutmeg and mace
16 ounces apple juice
16 ounces pomegranate juice
4 cups grape juice

Cook cinnamon stick, cloves, and other spices on medium for 3 minutes. Stir in juices and bring to boil. Simmer 15 minutes.

Discard cloves and serve warm.

Apple-Berry Fritters

Served with vanilla ice cream, these are a simply fabulous celebration of the fruits of the season.

Prep Time: 5 minutes
Cooking Time: 15 minutes
Serves: 4

⅓ cup flour
2½ teaspoons brown sugar
1 teaspoon baking powder
2 teaspoons vanilla extract
1 tablespoon (each) ground cinnamon and nutmeg
¼ teaspoon salt
3 eggs
4 tablespoons cream
1½ cups oil
3 large apples, peeled, cored, and chopped
2 tablespoons confectioners' sugar
½ cup fresh berries

Mix flour, brown sugar, baking powder, vanilla, spices, and salt. In a separate bowl, beat together eggs and cream. Combine both mixtures until smooth.

Heat oil to 375 degrees F in a deep pan. Coat the chopped apple pieces in batter. Drop by large spoonfuls into oil and fry until golden. Drain on paper towels and dust with confectioners' sugar.

Serve with ice cream and berries.

Crafty Crafts

Linda Raedisch

WHAT BETTER WAY TO greet Mabon than to go out on a good gather? Start by looking for some nice, big, shallow acorn caps. I prefer red or white oak. Bring your caps inside for a few days to dry out. Pin oak caps have a habit of going square as they dry, which is not so aesthetically pleasing. Use a fine brush to paint the insides of your acorn caps with metallic gold paint. Leave the outsides *au naturel*. Arrange them on a saucer—preferably a fancy, antique one, but any saucer will do—with a tealight in the middle. The caps will look like a scattering of fairy coins.

If painting acorn caps seems like too much work, consider filling your saucer with rose hips: fat red *Rugosa*s or a black variety for a more Gothic look. The glossy skins of Italian chestnuts also look good in the candle flames, as do the last of summer's cherry and plum tomatoes, rescued from the frost, in various stages of ripeness.

Scarlet, a bold, bright red all by itself, is a good color to celebrate at this time of year. Depending on how far north you live, you're either seeing the first touches of scarlet on the maples, or you are walking in a lazy flurry of scarlet leaves. Red is a protective color, the brighter the better. In the Middle Ages, bed chambers were adorned with scarlet draperies to guard against the Plague. In China and Japan, red beans were eaten for the same purpose. By all means, you should go and get your flu shot, but bring some scarlet in to the house for added protection.

Leafy Lantern

This lantern is so easy and cheap to make (The leaves are actually free!) that you'll want to fill the house with them. When plugged in, the fall leaves look they're encased in ice. Yes, the leaves will gradually lose their color, but they'll continue to look good for a week or more.

Tools and Materials
Fistful of autumn leaves

Large glass jar: I like the huge wide-mouthed kimchi and pork sung jars I get at the Asian grocery store, but if you don't happen to eat those things, a large applesauce jar will do.

Wax paper

Clear tape

Clear Christmas lights (or, as they call them in England, "fairy lights," which I much prefer.)

Go outside and gather the most beautiful fall leaves you can find. Oak? Forget about it! Go for the maples and sweet gums. I'm also fond of sassafras leaves which look like little ghosts with their arms upraised. Press the leaves in a heavy book overnight, or gather your leaves early in the morning, then assemble your lantern as darkness falls.

Tear off a length of wax paper long enough to wrap around your jar. Lay your paper on your work surface and fold it in half lengthwise. Arrange your leaves artfully inside the folded paper. If you're very particular about the arrangement, you can use a few dabs of glue to hold them in place. Wrap the paper around the jar and secure with a strip or two of tape. Fill your jar with the fairy lights and plug in.

You can easily fill a large jar with a string of thirty-five lights, or you can line up five or six lanterns side by side, letting just a handful of lights fall into each.

Wee Spirit Doll

Other than the odd poppet stuffed up a chimney, the European tradition has nothing akin to the magical dolls of Japan. In ancient times, dolls cut from plain white paper were rubbed all over the body, then cast into moving water as a way of dispersing evil. Dolls of white stuffed cloth were given to newborn babies to protect them from illness and danger. When made of red cloth, such a doll could scare away the smallpox demon.

The simple doll that follows is made of two star-shaped pieces of felt, stuffed and whip-stitched together, with a hole for the little wooden face to peek out. The tips of the limbs are joined together in the manner of the *kukuri-zaru* or "bundled monkey" doll. I have also drawn inspiration from some small stuffed figures sewn to the back of a nineteenth-century Altaic shaman's dress. With their pointed hoods, they look just like Christmas gnomes, but they are actually the daughters of the sky god Ulgen. Their purpose is to help the shaman in his flight through the worlds.

Tools and Materials

Paper and pencil
Scissors
Red felt
½-inch diameter wooden bead or ball
Glue
Cotton balls pulled apart (no more than five)
Needle and thread

If you have the technology to draw a perfect pentagram, go ahead and do so on a plain piece of paper. If not, fold your paper in half and sketch one half of a five-point star, making each arm of the star about 1½ inches long. Cut out, unfold, and you should have a tidy star about 4½ inches wide. Use this as a template to cut two identical stars out of the red felt.

In one of the felt stars, cut a small circle (a little less than ½ inch diameter) about an inch below the tip of the uppermost point of the star. This is the hole for the face to peek through. Glue your wooden bead or ball in the same position on the other felt star. When the glue is dry, you may proceed to whip-stitch the two stars together (with the bead on the inside!), stuffing as you go. Be careful not to overstuff. Your doll needs to be flexible for the next step.

When sewing is complete, join the tips of the arms together with a stitch or two. To these, join the tips of the toes. Your doll will now sit comfortably in the palm of your hand. Please resist the temptation to draw a face on your doll! Japanese magical dolls do not have facial features. In fact, adding a face may very well reduce their efficacy.

All One Family

Sandra Kynes

SUMMER IS DRAWING TO an end. Nights are chilly and sometimes tinged with frost, yet many September afternoons are warm and fair as we begin that slow slide into autumn. In northern New England, this turning of the Wheel of the Year brings dramatic changes with foliage blazing into an array of brilliant colors and summer birds gathering in huge flocks preparing for their journey south. If we're lucky, we'll catch a glimpse of monarch butterflies like choirs of orange angels heading out on their epic flight. We marvel at their ability to find the path of their ancestors, traveling a route they have never taken to a preordained destination they have never been.

One of the things we like to do to celebrate Mabon is to hike through a local marsh. Granted, most people would be thinking of fields and harvests at this time of year, but here on the coast of Maine salt marshes carry a strong sense of seasonal shift and feel like the right place to bid farewell to summer. We occasionally kayak through this marsh, but just before or on Mabon we like to make a special trip to walk the paths and view things from a different perspective. We often see muskrats or otters, and we keep a keen watch for herons or the exotic glossy ibises.

This season brings a strong reminder of cycles as we collect long strands of fading grasses such as salt-meadow, black rush, and sedge to make autumn wreaths for the front and side doors of our house. We dress the wreaths with sprigs of orange and red bittersweet held in place with looping cords of ivy or other vines. While they may look like simple autumn decorations to our neighbors, for us they hold a great deal of meaning. As a circle, the wreath itself symbolizes cycles, movement, and change. The bittersweet represents the balance of this sabbat and how we may be sad that summer is at an end, but we have the brightness of Yule ahead. In the Celtic tree calendar, this is the time of vine (September 2 to 29), which is followed by ivy (September 30 to October 27). On our wreaths, the ivy and vine represent the twists and turns of the last twelve months.

Involving children in making things for the sabbats or related decorations helps them feel involved and that they are contributing their efforts. Even small children sense that these projects are different from other craft-oriented activities. Once everything is spread out on the kitchen table and we get started with the wreaths, I like to initiate chanting. These begin with whatever I can think of to relate to the season, but they soon give way to improvised chants and songs. Engaging children's creativity this way helps them internalize the sabbats and begin a personal and important commitment. I've seen my son gaze at things he's created for sabbats with a satisfaction that seems to go beyond the pride of making something nice. By involving them in fun projects, children learn the significance of our traditions on a fundamental level. I think they also learn the importance of pitching in and doing things for family and community. Overall, time spent like this around the kitchen table draws us closer to each other as well as our Pagan traditions.

On our outing to the marsh, the children also collect cattails, which we dry and stand in a tall vase beside our family altar. In the marsh, cattails indicate the boundary where fresh water meets salty seawater. We go to the marshes because they are an in-between sort of place; neither completely solid earth or just water. The Celts believed that places like this—the water's edge or a forest boundary—were places of mystery, spirit, and strong magic. Likewise, Mabon is an in-between part of the year when we can feel a shift in energy as the natural world discloses some of her mysteries.

Autumnal mists and fogs also create a sense of being in between places or at some kind of threshold. If it's a foggy day on our trek to the marshes, we spend a little time trying to discern shapes in the mist—like seeing images in clouds. Small children are delighted with this game and once we were all amazed to watch as the fog seemed to melt away revealing a snowy egret standing at the water's edge. It was one of those moments when the soul gasps because it feels as though the Goddess has shared a secret.

On Mabon or the day before, my family and I incorporate a backyard cleanup into our sabbat activities. As mornings deepen, there are fewer crickets to serenade us in the garden, but the crows remain plentiful. Sometimes we stop and watch as they loudly caw and flit from tree to tree or chase seagulls from their territory. Crows seem particularly symbolic for this time of year. Their midnight feathers shine as the afternoon sun slants through the trees and their sudden takeoffs send flurries of leaves to the ground.

There are usually enough leaves on the ground, mostly from the giant maple tree next door, to warrant a good raking. A few particularly colorful leaves will be kept, pressed, and then used to decorate our Samhain altar next month. We all pitch in to wrestle the piles of leaves into bags for collection. While we are not permitted to burn leaves in our town, we do a limited and symbolic burning using a fire pit outside. We start a small flame with a few leaves, then add a piece of each besom broom that we made in the spring. As we commit each piece of besom to the fire we chant in unison:

Now that autumn has begun; besom broom your work is done.
Besom burn in fire bright; bless us on this Mabon night.

Just as Mabon and Ostara are days of balance, we connect these days and balance the year with the acts of creating and then destroying ritual besom brooms.

Another small and symbolic thing we do at this harvest time is gather in the last of the herbs from our garden. While it's a rather modest harvest, it's an activity in which children can help after the herbs are cut. Whatever lavender is left—flowers and leaf branches—gets tied up with ribbons into small bundles that will hang in the kitchen. Throughout the winter, warmth from the oven will disperse its sweet herbaceous fragrance throughout the house, reminding us of summer. We also cut and tie up little bundles of sage to use throughout the year for purification before rituals. Until needed, these also hang in the kitchen adding a richness to the potpourri of warm scents.

Now that the Sun is setting earlier, we return to candlelit dinners for special occasions. Children are in charge of decorating the table with fruits and vegetables of the season as well as other appropriate objects. The main course for our dinner on Mabon is roasted root vegetables from our local farmers' market. Carrots, parsnips, potatoes, and beets along with a few onions fill the house with a rich aroma while the oven chases away the evening chill. Toward the end of the baking, I add shredded apple (symbolic of Mabon) and a drizzle of maple syrup (symbolic of Maine). During the meal we take turns talking about the things for which we are thankful. However, before taking our seats we stand at our places around the table and say:

Mother of us all, we are grateful for your beauty and bounty. May we serve you and all on this earth through your wisdom, guidance, and love. Blessed be.

Mabon: Harvest Feast of the Gods

Janina Renée

THIS FEAST CELEBRATES THE spiritual forces associated with food. It is partially inspired by the Jewish Passover seder, where items of food are taken up in turn while the head of household explains their historic and religious significance. This ritual is also partially inspired by an element of Chinese Earth Opera, a ritual entertainment enacting mythical and historical legends. Earth Opera is usually performed by ordinary villagers in open fields, and it infuses lucky, protective energies into a community. The entertainment opens with actors dressed as the gods coming out to greet the gods before starting the performance. Thinking about this idea of "the gods greeting the gods" led me to think, "Why not the gods feeding the gods? Why not the gods feasting the gods?"

The idea of gods offering food to other gods has a basis in tradition, because in Taoist lore, Xi Wang Mu—the Queen Mother of the West—renews the gods every 3,000 years by giving them the peaches of immortality at her birthday banquet, and the Norse goddess Idunn restores the other gods with her golden apples. In the *Iliad*, we see the gods showing hospitality, as when Hera comforts Thetis by placing "a fair golden cup in her hand." The gods even make offerings to themselves, as in classical art scenes, where gods are portrayed pouring libations or gesturing with offering bowls. The ancients understood that the gods could not be fully comprehended, because they were connected to an other-dimensional reality that was beyond even their own comprehension, so images of gods making offerings may denote their honoring their own transcendent Mysteries.

So this ritual calls for persons playing the roles of different gods, goddesses, and nature spirits to first greet the deities they represent, then the collective company of personified deities, and then serve them symbolic dishes. How you stage this ritual depends on how many participants you have. For a small group, you might want to shorten the list of presenters/dishes. For a larger group, it is not necessary for everyone to make a presentation. If individuals come up with costumes suggestive of the beings they represent, this will enhance the visual drama of the ritual, but it is not strictly necessary.

As for the different beings and foodstuffs, there is much room here for customization. There are major classes of food, and their associated deities and world regions I have not been able to include, and lack of space also prevents me from giving the presenters more to say about the legends and lore of their symbolic dishes. I focus more on foods coming to harvest around Autumn Equinox in the American Midwest because that's what I know. However, readers who live in different climatic zones or chooose to take advantage of the wide range of foods available via rapid transport may simply adapt the ritual accordingly. Likewise, the deities listed here are beings directly associated with my chosen foodstuffs in their myths or have others symbolic correspondences with certain foods.

Many foods have multiple mythic associations, as in the case of corn (maize), which the Aztecs identified with several different gods and goddesses, and which North American Indians personified as different sets of corn maidens or youths, or corn mothers or fathers, or kachinas, but I had to settle on just one. Also, in having to choose one mythical personage over another, I went with the ones on whom I had the most usable information. However, persons with access to different information could rewrite this ritual for a different set of characters and dishes. Some of my phrasing may seem a bit quaint or obscure, as I draw from Homeric, Orphic, and other traditional sources. Naturally, you can alter the wording however you like. Because the relationship between foods and deities is so vast, one could construct different feasts, with different foods and deities for every season or occasion.

An issue I encountered in creating this ritual is the fact that different beings may have taboos regarding different foodstuffs. For example, when the queen of Eleusis offered wine to Demeter, the goddess said she couldn't have it, and instead asked for water mixed with barley meal and mint (a drink that was later served to initiates in the Mysteries). Because polytheistic religions can vary widely, even within their own cultic practices, different communities of worshippers may have made different offerings to different aspects of their deity, sometimes with foodstuffs that would have been less acceptable in other phases of the cult practice. Generally, foods in their most natural state were preferred because they go back to a more ancient stratum of society. So, milk and porridge were preferred over wine and bread, because the latter are more refined and processed products of later civilization. Thus, there are whole classes of deities who are supposed to be served wineless offerings ("nephalia"), including Eos, Helios, Selene, and Aphrodite Ourania. For this reason, this ritual has Dionysius offering grape juice—as he was not just the god of wine, but god of vegetation and nourishing moisture. If you prefer to use wine in this ritual, do it at your own discretion. Sometimes worshippers worked around food proscriptions, as when women offered wine to the Bona Dea, but referred to it as "milk." Because we can't be aware of every little food taboo, I have included some wording at the beginning of the ritual to excuse any inadvertent transgressions.

So, to perform the ritual, the company is assembled around the table and the food waits on a nearby sideboard. Those who have food presentations may be costumed, but those who do not have roles to play may also choose to be costumed as gods, nature spirits, or other entities. As some Neopagans focus on the divine youth,

Mabon, at Autumn Equinox, you may wish to have persons representing Mabon, his mother Modron, and his father Mellt, seated at the head of the table as guests of honor. If you wish to incorporate this into a larger seasonal circle ritual, draw your circle around the banquet space, then do your opening sequences, call the quarters, etc., in your preferred manner. When ready to begin the feast itself, two persons acting as host/hostesss or priest/priestess announce:

Priestess:
In celebration of Mabon's harvest,
we welcome the gods and goddesses,
spirits of nature, spirits of our ancestors,
and all our other friends in Spirit,
to partake of this autumnal feast.

Priest:
With deep respect, our participants, here,
take on the roles of gods and spirits
so that we may offer spiritual nutrition
to the world of gods and spirits.

Priestess:
In offering an array of foodstuffs,
we may present some unsuitable
to some assembled here,
so for this, we beg your kind indulgence.

Priest:
If some dishes are not agreeable to all,
let it be understood
that although our human actors consume them
the entities they portray
may temporarily withdraw,
yet return their good wishes—
knowing these offerings
are made in good faith and sincerity.

Priestess:
So, let our first presenter now arise,
as we begin the performance of this feast.

The first to come forward personates **Dionysius**. If he wishes to costume, Dionysius is typically portrayed with a crown of ivy or grape leaves, and he may wear other Dionysian emblems, such as the leopard, bull, dolphin, or pine cone. He carries a pitcher of grape juice to pour for all present. (The powers of the grape are all the more awesome, now that we know about the age-reversing qualities of resveratrol.) **Dionysius** speaks:

I give my greetings to lightning-born Dionysius,
*   asking that you be propitious to us,*
*   for seasons to come, and for years to come.*
I also greet this festive company in the name of Dionysius,
*   the son of the Moist Mother Earth.*
As the force that nourishes green life and growth,
*   and the spirit of ecstasy and inspiration,*
I offer you this refreshing juice,
*   to restore you with healing moisture.*
So may the life of your spirits be ever refreshed!

Dionysius then returns to his seat at the table, and the next presenters come forward. While all of the other dishes have single presenters, these come as a trio: **Demeter** and **Kore**, walking together, as they are so often portrayed together in art, and—a few steps behind them—**Fornax**, Roman goddess of the oven. Kore could dress to suggest greening life, and Demeter a golden harvest. Fornax could have symbols of the kitchen—she could dress as a kitchen Witch, as those old cast iron stoves used to be known as "kitchen witches." **Kore** presents a salad with wheat or barley sprouts to denote tender, re-emergent life; **Demeter** presents a whole grain cereal or porridge dish to represent the mature harvest; and Fornax offers a loaf of bread, which denotes the transformation of the raw into the baked. First, **Kore/Persephone** presents her dish, saying:

I greet you, Kore, known of old
as the Beautiful One of the Earth,
and I greet this fair-born company
in the name of Kore Kalligeneia,
as I present this dish that represents
the newest growth of greening life.
May you all know the delight of wandering
through fields of green grass.
May you ever enjoy rich increase
and smiling, precious peace.

Then **Demeter** offers her cereal dish while saying,

I greet you, Demeter, of the Golden Blade,
Bestower of Splendid Gifts,
and I greet this glorious company
in the name of the Universal Mother.
As you enjoy this cereal dish,
product of summer's golden grain,
I wish you health and concord,
and all the seasons' wealth.

Demeter and **Kore** return to their place at the table while **Fornax**, who has been standing behind them, now steps forward. She says:

I greet you, Fornax, goddess of the oven,
and I greet you in the name of Fornax, the Fire Mother.
Enjoy this bread, the product of Fire and Air,
and Earth and Water combined,
in the oven that transforms the raw stuff of life.
Know that we all have the Creative Force within us
to incubate our own transformation,
to generate our self-re-creation.

An individual representing **the Sun** presents some sunflower seeds, (or a sunflower seed dish). Because many people regard the sun as male, (Helios-Apollo, Surya, Meso-American sun gods), we'll portray him as such here (though cultures including the Germanic, Slavic, and Japanese perceived the sun as female, so this is an option for a group with more women). He could be wearing gold jewelry, sun symbols, and other solar emblems (such as the lion, ram, horse, or hawk). **The Sun says**:

> *I greet the shining solar deity,*
> *Lord of the Seasons, who drives all life and growth,*
> *as I greet this noble company*
> > *in the name of the Daystar.*
> *I bid you enjoy these sunflower seeds,*
> > *harvested from the golden flowers*
> > *that stand sentinels of the solar season.*
> *The sunflower, which is often the first crop*
> > *to be planted in the spring*
> > *and the last to be harvested in autumn,*
> > *is rich in concentrated solar force.*

A person representing **The Corn Maiden**, the Native American spirit of the form of corn known as maize, makes her presentation. Throughout the Americas, this spirit was variously known as a god or goddess, or even as a group of spirit maidens or mothers representing different colored varieties of corn, but for today's ritual enactment, we'll picture a more generic sort of corn maiden or mother, offering roasted ears of the sweet corn that most Americans are familiar with (with the cobs chopped up into two- or three-inch pieces for ease in serving). Persons who are familiar with Native American corn varieties and preparations (such as corn tortillas, cakes, or atole), as well as tribal personifications such as kachinas may prefer to use one of these and reword the ritual accordingly. The corn spirit may be dressed in green and yellow, or with costume suggestive of Native American traditions. As she offers the corn, **the Corn Maiden** says:

> *I greet the Spirit of Maize, as I greet you all.*
> *As the Corn Maiden,*
>> *I offer you these sweet ears of corn.*
> *In many legends, corn maidens sacrifice themselves,*
>> *descending into the earth*
>> *to arise again, strong and shining.*
> *As you enjoy this corn, may your powers be renewed,*
>> *forever strong and shining.*

Another New World foodstuff harvested in August and September is wild rice, the gift of the Woodlands' culture hero/trickster, variously known as **Wenabozhoo**, Manabozho, Nanabush, etc. An individual representing Wenabozhoo presents a wild rice dish. He might be dressed in woodland garb, and/or wear rabbit symbolism, as this figure is often represented as a rabbit. **Wenabozhoo** says:

> *I greet you, Wenabozhoo, hero of many wild adventures,*
> *and I greet you all in the name of Wenabozhoo,*
>> *as I bring you this dish of wild rice.*
> *Known as manoomin and ripe in Manoominke-giizis,*
>> *The Moon of Wild Rice,*
> *this graceful, feathery grass,*
>> *is harvested with canoe and paddle,*
>> *as it whispers its name*
>> *over the spreading marshlands.*
> *Let this wild rice dish nourish the wild soul within you.*

The Norse goddess **Idunn**, who tends the apples that renew the lives of the gods offers apples or an apple dish. (She may have the apples cut to show the inner star.) **Idunn** says:

> *I greet you, Idunn, goddess of youth,*
> *And I greet this storied company in the name of Idunn.*
>> *As you enjoy this storied fruit,*
> *sacred also to the legends of the Isle of Avalon,*
>> *and the Garden the Hesperides.*

May these apples bring you shining health,
just as the apple conceals within
the ovarian seed-star of the healing goddess.

Next is a dish of nuts brought by **Sylvanus Callirius**, spirit of the hazel tree. He is a Romano-Celtic emanation of Sylvanus, who was guardian of all trees, as well as the forest. He may be dressed in brown, green, or forest camouflauge, with costume pieces suggesting a spirit of the forest, and especially of hazel trees. As he steps forward to make his presentation, **Sylvanus Callirius** says:

I give greeting today, to Sylvanus Callirius
and I greet you all in the name of Sylvanus Callirius
the spirit of the hazel tree.
I bid you partake of the hazel nuts,
fruit of wisdom, fruit of poetry,
symbol of abundance and fertility.
As you enjoy this token of the wild harvest,
may your wisdom be strengthened,
may your poetry shine in beauty,
and may you take pleasure
in the plenitude of life.

As the final dessert offering, **Oshun**, the Orisha of love, passion, fertility, pleasure, luxury, and spellcraft makes her presentation. Because both pumpkin and honey are among her special emblems/offerings (she uses them to heal). She might present honey roasted pumpkin seeds or honey pumpkin bread. In the Afro-Caribbean tradition, **Oshun** is distinguished by her honeyed laughter, and she loves beautiful ornaments of brass and gold, elegant fans, mirrors, bells, and shells (often in the number Five), and her colors are yellow and gold. **Oshun** says:

I greet you, Oshun, Iyalode, Ori Yeye O!
And I greet you all in the name of Oshun,
the Mother of Secrets, overflowing with beauty.

As the pumpkin's golden orb glows as
*   an image of completion and abundance,*
and the honey reminds us of the sweetness of love and life,
*   so may you always know love and fulfillment,*
*   so may your lives be truly sweet!*

As Oshun returns to her place, the **priestess** says:

Now that the gods and spirits
*   have tasted each dish,*
We thank them for their presence,
*   and bid them remain for the rest of the feast,*
*   or depart if they wish.*

Priest:
Meanwhile, our human company
*   are free to finish the feast.*

When the feast is over, you can move on to other seasonal activities, or close the circle in your normal manner.

Notes

The Swell Seasons

In *Seasons of Witchery*, the newest release in Ellen Dugan's best-selling series, she offers readers a wealth of magickal ways to celebrate the Wheel of the Year. With her trademark warmth and practicality, Ellen shares a bit of history and lore on each sabbat as well as simple yet meaningful ideas for honoring each season. There are colorful decorating suggestions, fun craft projects, tasty recipes, insightful journal notes about her enchanted garden through the year, and natural magick aligned with each holiday. This charming and friendly book will inspire readers with new ideas, fresh spells, and seasonal rituals to make their own sabbat celebrations more personal and powerful.

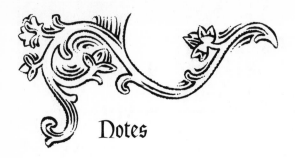

Notes

Notes